Vera Axyonova

The European Union's Democratization Policy for Central Asia

Failed in Success or Succeeded in Failure?

**AN INTERDISCIPLINARY SERIES
OF THE CENTRE FOR INTERCULTURAL AND EUROPEAN STUDIES**

**INTERDISZIPLINÄRE SCHRIFTENREIHE
DES CENTRUMS FÜR INTERKULTURELLE UND EUROPÄISCHE STUDIEN**

CINTEUS ▪ Fulda University of Applied Sciences ▪ Hochschule Fulda

ISSN 1865-2255

7   *Barbara Lewandowska-Tomaszczyk / Hanna Pułaczewska (Eds. / Hrsg.)*
    Intercultural Europe
    Arenas of Difference, Communication and Mediation
    ISBN 978-3-8382-0198-6

8   *Janina Henning*
    In Dubio Pro Europa?
    An Analysis of the European External Action Structures
    after the Treaty of Lisbon
    ISBN 978-3-8382-0298-1

9   *Claas Oehlmann*
    Europa auf dem Weg zur Recycling-Gesellschaft?
    Die EU-Rohstoffinitiative im Kontext der Strategie Europa 2020
    ISBN 978-3-8382-0401-7

10 *Volker Hinnenkamp / Hans-Wolfgang Platzer (Eds. / Hrsg.)*
    Interkulturalität und Europäische Integration
    ISBN 978-3-8382-0573-1

11 *Vera Axyonova*
    The European Union's Democratization Policy for Central Asia
    Failed in Success or Succeeded in Failure?
    ISBN 978-3-8382-0614-1

Series Editors

Gudrun Hentges
Volker Hinnenkamp
Anne Honer †
Hans-Wolfgang Platzer

Fachbereich Sozial- und Kulturwissenschaften
Hochschule Fulda University of Applied Sciences
Marquardstraße 35
D-36039 Fulda
cinteus@sk.hs-fulda.de
www.cinteus.eu

Vera Axyonova

THE EUROPEAN UNION'S DEMOCRATIZATION POLICY FOR CENTRAL ASIA

Failed in Success or Succeeded in Failure?

ibidem-Verlag
Stuttgart

Bibliografische Information der Deutschen Nationalbibliothek
Die Deutsche Nationalbibliothek verzeichnet diese Publikation in der Deutschen Nationalbibliografie; detaillierte bibliografische Daten sind im Internet über http://dnb.d-nb.de abrufbar.

Bibliographic information published by the Deutsche Nationalbibliothek
Die Deutsche Nationalbibliothek lists this publication in the Deutsche Nationalbibliografie; detailed bibliographic data are available in the Internet at http://dnb.d-nb.de.

Zugl. Dissertation an der Bremen International Graduate School of Social Sciences.
Datum der Verteidigung: 17. Dezember 2013

∞
Gedruckt auf alterungsbeständigem, säurefreien Papier
Printed on acid-free paper

ISSN: 1865-2255

ISBN-13: 978-3-8382-0614-1

© *ibidem*-Verlag
Stuttgart 2014

Alle Rechte vorbehalten

Das Werk einschließlich aller seiner Teile ist urheberrechtlich geschützt. Jede Verwertung außerhalb der engen Grenzen des Urheberrechtsgesetzes ist ohne Zustimmung des Verlages unzulässig und strafbar. Dies gilt insbesondere für Vervielfältigungen, Übersetzungen, Mikroverfilmungen und elektronische Speicherformen sowie die Einspeicherung und Verarbeitung in elektronischen Systemen.

All rights reserved. No part of this publication may be reproduced, stored in or introduced into a retrieval system, or transmitted, in any form, or by any means (electronic, mechanical, photocopying, recording or otherwise) without the prior written permission of the publisher. Any person who does any unauthorized act in relation to this publication may be liable to criminal prosecution and civil claims for damages.

Printed in Germany

For Ludmila, Viktor and Björn

Editorial

This series is intended as a publication panel of the Centre of Intercultural and European Studies (CINTEUS) at Fulda University of Applied Sciences. The series aims at making research results, anthologies, conference readers, study books and selected qualification theses accessible to the general public. It comprises of scientific and interdisciplinary works on inter- and transculturality; the European Union from an interior and a global perspective; and problems of social welfare and social law in Europe. Each of these are fields of research and teaching in the Social- and Cultural Studies Faculty at Fulda University of Applied Sciences and its Centre for Intercultural and European Studies. We also invite contributions from outside the faculty that share and enrich our research.

Gudrun Hentges, Volker Hinnenkamp, Anne Honer & Hans-Wolfgang Platzer

Editorial

Die Buchreihe versteht sich als Publikationsforum des Centrums für interkulturelle und europäische Studien (CINTEUS) der Hochschule Fulda. Ziel der CINTEUS-Reihe ist es, Forschungsergebnisse, Anthologien, Kongressreader, Studienbücher und ausgewählte Qualifikationsarbeiten einer interessierten Öffentlichkeit zugänglich zu machen. Die Reihe umfasst fachwissenschaftliche und interdisziplinäre Arbeiten aus den Bereichen Inter- und Transkulturalität, Europäische Union aus Binnen- und globaler Perspektive sowie wohlfahrtsstaatliche und sozialrechtliche Probleme Europas. All dies sind Fachgebiete, die im Fachbereich Sozial- und Kulturwissenschaften der Hochschule Fulda University of Applied Sciences und dem angegliederten Centrum für interkulturelle und Europastudien gelehrt und erforscht werden. Ausdrücklich eingeladen an der Publikationsreihe mitzuwirken sind auch solche Studien, die nicht 'im Hause' entstanden sind, aber CINTEUS-Schwerpunkte berühren und bereichern.

Gudrun Hentges, Volker Hinnenkamp, Anne Honer & Hans-Wolfgang Platzer

Foreword

Over the last decade, the role of the European Union as an external democracy promoter has attracted an increased scholarly attention. The major part of the literature has so far centred on democratization effects of the EU enlargement processes and the EU's political engagement in the European neighbourhood. Fewer authors have looked at the EU's democracy and human rights promotion in regions beyond its immediate sphere of influence. Vera Axyonova's study of the European Union's democratization policy for Central Asia is a rare example of a systematic and very detailed investigation of the EU's attempts to advance its normative agenda in this post-soviet region.

This book, based on Axyonova's PhD dissertation, presents the results of a thorough years-long research. Being aware of external and domestic constraints for the EU's democratization policy in Central Asia, the author focuses on scrutinizing micro-level effects of the EU engagement and explaining conditions and reasons for varying outcomes of the EU efforts. To this end, she provides an in-depth analysis of specific EU democratization instruments in two Central Asian countries featuring different degrees of autocratization. Axyonova particularly traces the application of EU sanctions against Uzbekistan, examines the EU's bilateral human rights dialogues with Kyrgyzstan and Uzbekistan, and analyses the implementation of European civil society support programmes in the two countries.

The author uncovers crucial information through her recurrent field research and multiple expert interviews conducted in Europe and Central Asia. A reader is puzzled by peculiar facts about the role of Germany in the process of sanctions enforcement, low expectations of EU officials concerning the human rights dialogues, and negotiations about financial support between the European Commission and the Uzbek government. These insights, diligent investigation, and well-structured argumentation linking the study of EU democratization instruments and their effects to the research of the substance of external democracy promotion constitute the main added value of Axyonova's study.

Prof. Dr. Hans-Wolfgang Platzer

Acknowledgements

First of all, I would like to use this opportunity to thank my PhD supervisors Prof. Dr. Matthijs Bogaards, Prof. em. Dr. Dr. h. c. Beate Kohler and Prof. Dr. Marlene Laruelle for their advice, encouragement and patience. Their guidance throughout the whole process was essential to the successful completion of this research. I am also very grateful to the Bremen International Graduate School of Social Sciences for providing an excellent academic environment and financial support for pursuing my PhD research. It was equally a privilege and a challenge to be part of the programme with such a high density of outstanding young scholars.

Further, I wish to express my gratitude to the Centre for European Policy Studies, and specifically to Dr. Michael Emerson, whose comments and advice have been an incredible source of inspiration. My research stay at CEPS was an extremely enriching experience and an exceptional opportunity to conduct field work in Brussels.

A special note of thanks is devoted to the Centre for Intercultural and European Studies at Fulda University of Applied Sciences, and particularly to Prof. Dr. Hans-Wolfgang Platzer for his support and making this publication possible.

I also would like to express my great appreciation to everyone who provided valuable feedback on various aspects and at different stages of my research. To Prof. Dr. Ulrike Liebert, PD Dr. Heiko Pleines, Dr. Janna Wolff, Dr. Arndt Wonka, Dr. Herwig Reiter, Prof. Dr. Rainer Baumann, Dr. Nate Breznau, special thanks to my colleagues from Europe-Central Asia Monitoring programme Jos Boonstra and Tika Tsertsvadze, and all those, whom I cannot mention here by name for space reasons. I am equally grateful to all my interview partners from various organizations and institutions in Europe and Central Asia. Without their insights and expertise this research would not have been possible.

Finally, I would like to thank my family for their unconditional support and encouragement. As a sign of my appreciation, this book is dedicated to my parents Ludmila and Viktor and my husband Björn.

Vera Axyonova
January 2014

Contents

Foreword IX

1. Introduction 1
2. European Union as an External Democracy Promoter:
   Theoretical and Conceptual Foundations 11
   2.1 Conceptualizing the EU as a Normative Actor 11
      2.1.1 EU-Level Normative Commitments 11
      2.1.2 The EU Conception of External Democracy Promotion 13
   2.2 In Search for an Appropriate Theoretical Framework: Explaining
       External Factors of Democratization 19
   2.3 Towards a Comprehensive Typology of EU Democracy
       Promotion Tools 25
      2.3.1 Categorizing Democratization Tools: An Overview of
            Existing Typologies 25
      2.3.2 Building-up a Distinct Typology 28
3. Evaluation of EU Democracy Promotion: A Framework for
   Analysis 31
   3.1 Evaluating Successes and Failures of
       External Democracy Promotion 32
      3.1.1 Existing Approaches 32
      3.1.2 Methodological Challenges in the Context of the Current Study 36
      3.1.3 Opting for a Distinct Research Strategy 38
   3.2 Explaining Successes and Failures of
       External Democracy Promotion 42
      3.2.1 What Factors Matter? 42
      3.2.2 The EU Engagement in Central Asia: Main Assumptions 45
   3.3 Further Methodological Considerations 58
4. The EU Sanctions Against Uzbekistan 63
   4.1 Tracing Implementation of the Sanctions 63
      4.1.1 The EU Sanctions and Conditions for Their Withdrawal 65
      4.1.2 The EU Sanctions at Work 66
      4.1.3 Summary of the Results 74

4.2 Explaining the Outcomes of EU Sanctions ... 75
4.2.1 Lack of Credibility as an Explanation for Failure ... 76
4.2.2 Substance of the EU Demands and Their Implications as Explanatory Factors ... 80
4.2.3 Possible Interfering Effects ... 87
4.3 Concluding Remarks ... 88

5. Structured Human Rights Dialogues ... 91
5.1 Tracing Implementation of the Dialogues ... 92
5.1.1 The Issues in Focus of the HRDs ... 93
5.1.2 Evaluating the Results: What Has (Not) Been Achieved ... 96
5.2 Explaining the Outcomes: Multiple Causes of Failure ... 101
5.2.1 Process-related Factors ... 102
5.2.2 Substance of the Promoted Norms ... 105
5.3 Concluding Remarks ... 108

6. The Institution Building and Partnership Programme and the European Instrument for Democracy and Human Rights ... 111
6.1 Tracing Implementation of the Programmes ... 111
6.1.1 The IBPP at Work ... 112
6.1.2 The EIDHR at Work ... 117
6.1.3 Summary of the Results ... 122
6.2 Explaining the Outcomes of the IBPP and EIDHR Application ... 123
6.2.1 Assistance Transparency and Ownership ... 124
6.2.2 Substance of the Promoted Norms ... 125
6.3 Concluding Remarks ... 130

7. Conclusion ... 133

References ... 141

Annex I: List of Expert Interviews ... 169

Annex II: IBPP Projects implemented in Kyrgyzstan in 2002–2009 ... 172

Annex III: IBPP Projects implemented in Uzbekistan in 2003–2010 ... 175

Annex IV: EIDHR Regional Projects implemented in Central Asia in 2003-2010 ... 179

Annex V: EIDHR Macro- and Micro-Projects (CBSS) implemented in Kyrgyzstan in 2004-2010 ... 181

Abbreviations

AAP	Annual Action Programme
AF	Action Fiche
AIDCO	EuropeAid Co-operation Office
CBSS	Country-Based Support Schemes
CIDA	Canadian International Development Agency
CIS	Commonwealth of Independent States
CSO	Civil society organization
DANIDA	Danish International Development Agency
DCI	Development Cooperation Instrument
DG DEVCO	Directorate-General Development and Cooperation—EuropeAid
DG RELEX	Directorate-General for External Relations
EC	European Community
EEAS	European External Action Service
EIDHR	European Instrument for Democracy and Human Rights
ENP	European Neighbourhood Policy
EU	European Union
EUSR	European Union Special Representative
GIZ	Deutsche Gesellschaft für Internationale Zusammenarbeit
GONGO	Government-organized non-governmental organization
HR	Human rights
HRD	Human rights dialogue
IBPP	Institution Building and Partnership Programme
ICRC	International Committee of the Red Cross
IP	Indicative Programme
ISAF	International Security Assistance Force
LFA	Logical Framework Analysis
MEDA	Mésures d'Accompagnement Financières et Techniques
NATO	North Atlantic Treaty Organization
NGO	Non-governmental organization
NSA/LA	Non-State Actors and Local Authorities in Development
ODIHR	Office for Democratic Institutions and Human Rights
OSCE	Organization for Security and Co-operation in Europe
PCA	Partnership and Cooperation Agreement
PHARE	Poland and Hungary: Assistance for Restructuring their Economies

RoLI	Rule of Law Initiative
SIDA	Swedish International Development Cooperation Agency
TACIS	Technical Aid to the Commonwealth of Independent States
UN	United Nations
UNCTAD	United Nations Conference on Trade and Development
UNDP	United Nations Development Programme
UNHCR	Office of the United Nations High Commissioner for Refugees
UNICEF	United Nations Children's Fund
USAID	United States Agency for International Development

1. Introduction

Over the last decades, the European Union (EU) established itself as an actor in external democracy and human rights promotion. Historically, the EU's democratization policy[1] mainly focused on states in its immediate neighbourhood, especially those with the prospects of integration into the Union. The commitment to democracy has become an indispensable part of EU accession criteria. It also guides the European Neighbourhood Policy (ENP) towards adjoining states without EU membership perspective. With the Maastricht Treaty, the Union declared consolidation of democracy, the rule of law, good governance and respect for human rights to its foreign policy objective, also vis-à-vis more distant regions (cf. European Union 1992: Art. J.1/2 and Art. G.130u).

To pursue this objective, the EU developed a set of tools, ranging from assistance programmes (such as the European Instrument for Democracy and Human Rights) and dialogue platforms (e.g. human rights dialogues and international civil society forums) to political conditionality tools that involve linking of certain incentives (such as development aid and closer economic and political cooperation) or sanctions (limiting of previously offered benefits) to compliance with human rights and democratic standards by target states (cf. European Council, Political and Security Committee 2006: 4; European Commission 2007e: 9). While the EU intends to use these tools to promote democratic political practices worldwide (cf. European Commission 2001a; Council of the European Union 2009a; Council of the European Union 2012), it is expected to have significantly better prospects for democracy promotion in states that are striving for accession, have established close political and economic ties to the Union, and are already in the process of political liberalization (cf. Pravda 2001; Schimmelfennig and Scholtz 2008; Schimmelfennig 2009a; Freyburg and Richter 2009; Youngs 2010). In this regard, serious doubts remain concerning the effectiveness of using EU tools to foster democratization in authoritarian states that do not have EU membership perspective and are not part of closer political and economic cooperation through the ENP.

---

[1] Here, *'democracy promotion'* and *'democratization policy'* are used interchangeably for the sake of better readability. The working definitions of these terms are further elaborated in chapter 2. The study uses Oxford English Dictionary spelling.

This research deliberately focuses on EU engagement with such states, as they pose a challenging test for the promotion of democracy and human rights by the European Union. The study particularly scrutinizes possibilities and constraints for EU democratization policy in post-soviet Central Asia, a region comprising Kyrgyzstan, Kazakhstan, Uzbekistan, Tajikistan and Turkmenistan. These states are commonly viewed by scholars as a difficult environment for external democracy promotion (e.g. Warkotsch 2006b; Bossuyt and Kubicek 2011; Boonstra 2012), which is confounded by growing authoritarian tendencies across all Central Asian countries between the mid-1990s and 2010 (cf. Freedom House n/a). In these countries the European Union cannot apply its strongest instrument to foster democratization in offering the potential for membership, nor does it extend closer cooperation links under the European Neighbourhood Policy. The EU is thus confronted with extremely unfavourable domestic and external conditions for democracy promotion in Central Asia.

Nevertheless, the European Union pursues a democratization agenda in the region. It has included a 'democracy and human rights clause' into the bilateral Partnership and Cooperation Agreements signed with each of the Central Asian states (e.g. European Communities, their Member States and Republic of Uzbekistan 1999: Art. 2). Moreover, the Union's political strategy for the region—'*The EU and Central Asia: Strategy for a New Partnership*'—adopted in 2007 states that the promotion of human rights, good governance, the rule of law and democratization is one of the EU's key priorities in the region (Council of the European Union 2007c).

In this context, the question arises whether EU democracy promotion efforts have been at least partly successful so far and, if so, to what extent. While trying to answer this question, the present study does not intend to evaluate success of EU democracy promotion at the polity level. In view of the unfavourable domestic and external conditions, the EU can hardly be expected to quickly liberalize Central Asian regimes (cf. Warkotsch 2009). Instead, this study looks at the effects of EU democratization policy at a micro-level, tracing concrete norms and changes that could (or could not) be successfully endorsed through the application of EU instruments in Central Asia. The evaluation of successes and failures poses another question that needs to be answered, namely what factors make EU democracy promotion more (or less) successful in a challenging for democratization environment, i.e. what accounts for the variation in the outcomes of EU democracy promotion efforts. This is the second question that guides the present research.

With these questions in mind, the current work stands at the intersection of three major clusters of scholarship—EU studies, Central Asian studies and democratization research. Over the last decade, the latter cluster of literature has been increasingly engaging with the European Union as an external promoter of democratic norms and human rights standards (Schimmelfennig et al. 2002; Fierro 2003; Kubicek 2003; Börzel and Risse 2004; Vachudova 2005; Jünemann and Knodt 2007; Freyburg et. al. 2009, to name just a few). Yet, scholars have largely focussed on EU democracy promotion in the accession candidates or the immediate EU neighbourhood (e.g. Schimmelfennig 2005; Vachudova 2005; Kelley 2006; Wichmann 2007; Freyburg et al. 2009; Freyburg and Richter 2009;).

The EU political engagement in Central Asia, including democracy and human rights promotion, has attracted attention of scholars only recently. The research has largely focused on the supply side of external democratization, including the motives behind EU actions, EU strategies and instruments applied.

Thus, Urdze (2010) elaborates a new approach towards analysing EU democratization policy and instruments based on a content analysis of EU documents. She further investigates the EU's interests that determine the choice of specific tools applied in the example of the Central Asian states. The conclusions drawn by Urdze suggest that EU policy is often guided by European economic interests and security related motives of Member States.

Similar conclusions (although based on different methodological approaches) are made separately by Crawford (2008) and Cooley (2008). Comparing the EU's stated democratization objectives with the practice of EU engagements on the ground, Crawford reveals a gap between the lofty European rhetoric and the actual policy implementations in Central Asia. He explains this gap through the trade-offs between the EU's value-driven agenda and the realist aims to maintain security, energy supplies and political stability (Crawford 2008: 186-188). Cooley (2008), who investigates the EU and U.S. military cooperation with the Central Asian states and the European energy related interests, also sees them in contradiction with the transatlantic normative commitments. Both authors thus provide interest-based explanations for the limited scope of the EU democratization efforts.

Bossuyt and Kubicek (2011) go beyond the above research agenda by focussing on the substance of EU democratization policies in Central Asia. The authors argue that the variance in the substance of what is promoted in different Central Asian states is explained not only by EU self-interest but also by intentional adaptations to the respective target states. Where target states are more politically open and are expected to resonate better with normative substance, the EU is more active, and in states more closed it is narrower in its policies. In explaining the limits of EU engagement, Bossuyt and Kubicek thus account for the domestic context in the Central Asian countries.

Hoffmann (2010) examines obstacles and prospects for good governance promotion in Central Asia with a specific focus on recent developments following the 2007 *'EU and Central Asia: Strategy for a New Partnership'*. Among the main obstacles, she identifies the EU's prioritization of interest-based policy objectives over the advancement of European values and the nature of political regimes in Central Asia. Hoffmann thus takes account of both external and domestic factors that limit the EU's prospects for successful good governance promotion in the region.

Finally, in his numerous studies on the subject, Warkotsch (2006b; 2007; 2008b; 2009; 2011) also concentrates on the prospects for and impediments to the EU democracy and human rights promotion in Central Asia. He reviews various democratization tools available to the Union and discusses their aptness for the region. Drawing on the rationalist-constructivist theoretical debate on which mechanisms lie behind external democratization efforts, Warkotsch distinguishes between tools that try to manipulate a target government's *'strategic calculation'* of costs and benefits of norm compliance, guided by the logic of consequence, and *'normative suasion'* tools relying on the power of normative argument, guided by the logic of appropriateness (Warkotsch 2008b and 2009). In view of local realities and inconsistencies in EU policies, the author concludes similarly to Hoffmann that the European Union has only limited prospects for successful democracy and human rights promotion in Central Asia. At the same time, Warkotsch does not exclude the possibility of minor improvements in the long run, so long as the EU is able to adapt its policy to the situation in each country and time-period (Warkotsch 2008b).

The scholarship of EU political engagement in Central Asia has thus mainly focussed on the EU's motives behind the narrow scope of activities and insufficient efforts affected by the prevalence of realist interests over normative commitments and domestic constraints in the target countries. While the authors generally maintain that the EU has done little to foster a transition to democracy in the Central Asian states, there has been no systematic evaluation of the effectiveness or impact of EU engagement in the region. This study seeks to fill this gap by assessing successes and failures of EU democratization policy for Central Asia with the focus on micro-level changes that could or could not be achieved as the result of the application of EU democratization instruments. It is thus assumed here that the EU is severely constrained in exerting a direct liberalizing influence on political regimes in Central Asia but nonetheless may have succeeded in endorsing certain norms and changes that could be associated with the broader democratization process.

In explaining the outcomes of EU efforts, this study takes account of the previous findings concerning the unfavourable domestic and external conditions for democratization in Central Asia. At the same time, the analysis goes one step further. Drawing on a proposition by Warkotsch that the EU might have better prospects for promoting *'certain human rights dimensions'* rather than *'democracy in the narrower sense'* (Warkotsch 2008b: 69),[2] this study suggests that the substance of what is promoted matters for the success of EU efforts in difficult environments. This assumption together with the differentiation between *'politically sensitive'* and *'politically neutral'* reforms proposed by Golovko (2010) provides a foundation for the key hypothesis to be tested in the current study. Namely, that in an environment challenging for democratization the EU is more likely to be successful, if its instruments promote less politically sensitive norms and changes (see discussion in chapter 3).

Using the works of the above scholars as a point of departure, the research also draws on broader secondary and primary sources. After specifying the EU's conceptualization of democracy promotion based on scrutiny of EU documents, chapter 2 reviews various theoretical approaches in explaining external factors of democratization (e.g. Whitehead 2001; Schimmelfennig and Sedelmeier 2005; Levitsky and Way 2010), in order to identify an appropriate theoretical framework for the current analysis. An approach combining rationalist and constructivist insights from the studies of international

---

[2] While Warkotsch (2008b and 2009) suggested this as a policy recommendation, he has never formulated a testable hypothesis concerning possible effects of the substance on the outcomes of the EU democratization efforts.

socialization (cf. Kelley 2004; Checkel 2005; Warkotsch 2009) is assumed to be most appropriate for the purposes of this research. The chapter then examines the tools available to the European Union for democracy promotion and the existing typologies used to characterize these tools proposed by other scholars (e.g. Carothers 1999; Diamond 1999; Youngs 2001; Börzel and Risse 2004; Jünemann and Knodt 2007; Burnell 2008; Reiber 2009). The existing approaches differentiate various categories of tools, but most commonly these are based on contents (e.g. democratic assistance vs. political conditionality) or character (e.g. positive vs. negative tools).

This work offers a different approach towards categorizing the available EU instruments based on their underlying logic of functioning (mechanisms behind) and the (micro-level) changes that the tools are expected to trigger. Three main groups of EU instruments are identified: (1) conditionality-based (drawing on strategic calculation of costs and benefits, i.e. functioning through incentives and sanctions that are expected to trigger the targets' compliance with externally promoted norms), (2) dialogue-based (relying on normative suasion by the logic of appropriateness that would lead to the internalization of promoted values by the targets in the long run), and (3) democratic empowerment (assistance programmes aiming at increasing democratic capacities of the targets). In comparison to the other typologies, this approach allows a clearer empirical differentiation between various types of tools and can be used for the evaluation of successes and failures of these tools at the micro-level.

Chapter 3 provides the analytical framework for the current study. It first reviews existing methodologies for evaluating effectiveness and impacts deriving from theoretically oriented and empirically grounded research (cf. Underdal 1992; European Commission 1999; Helm and Sprinz 2000; Hegemann, Heller and Kahl 2013). Taking account of the strengths and limits of these approaches, the chapter develops a research strategy that allows a systematic evaluation of EU democracy promotion efforts in such regions as Central Asia. The approach suggests assessing successes and failures of the EU with reference to the above instrument typology, based on the achievement of micro-level changes that its democratization tools are expected to trigger. Finally, the chapter incorporates literature engaging the factors that potentially affect the outcomes of external democratization (e.g. Smith 1997; Kubicek 2003; Schimmelfennig 2003; Checkel 2005; Reiber 2009; Warkotsch 2009), and elaborates a list of favourable factors (or scope conditions) for successful democracy and human rights promotion.

The chapter arrives at the overall assumptions and the key hypothesis guiding this study.

The subsequent empirical part comprising chapters 4 to 6 presents three case studies of the EU's usage of democratization instruments in Central Asia that are exemplary for the three aforementioned types of tools: sanctions imposed on Uzbekistan between 2005 and 2009, bilateral Human Rights Dialogues established by the 2007 'Strategy for a New Partnership', and the EU's civil society support programmes—the European Instrument for Democracy and Human Rights (EIDHR) and the Institution Building and Partnership Programme (IBPP). The chapters trace and evaluate the application of these tools and discuss possible explanations of the outcomes of the EU engagement in accordance with the assumptions stated in chapter 3. The study employs process-tracing combined with elements of the congruence method (George and Bennett 2005), spanning the years 1991-2010 (i.e. starting with the independence of the states concerned) with a particular focus on the 2000s when the relevant EU democratization tools were introduced.

While all five Central Asian republics share crucial similarities in terms of their soviet legacies, socio-cultural idiosyncrasies and political traditions of authoritarian rule (Eschment 2000: 2; Warkotsch 2006a: 7-8), their transition processes after the break-up of the Soviet Union differed to a certain extent. This resulted in varying degrees of political liberalization (or autocratization). Thus, observers conventionally divide the region into a more democracy oriented *'semi-authoritarian north-eastern tier'*, including Kazakhstan, Kyrgyzstan and Tajikistan, and *'an authoritarian or even dictatorial governed south-western tier'*, consisting of Uzbekistan and Turkmenistan (Warkotsch 2008b: 62; cf. Zhovtis 2008: 26). In the course of the 1990s, particularly Kyrgyzstan was regarded as a Central Asian *'island of democracy'* (Gumppenberg and Steinbach 2004: 156), as the only state in the region, where free elections, functional opposition, relatively independent press, and active state-independent civil society organizations existed. Although later political developments demonstrated that the initial democratic course of the country was not stable (International Crisis Group 2001), after an uprising in April 2010 and a subsequent referendum in June 2010 Kyrgyzstan has become the first republic in the region with a parliamentary system of government.[3] On the opposite side of the regime spectrum among the Central Asian states are Turkmenistan and Uzbekistan, with totalitarian features in the former and strong consolidated authoritarian rule in the latter (cf. Zhovtis 2008: 26; Warkotsch 2009: 249-250). The differences in the countries' political development and functioning suggest that the outcomes of EU democratization efforts in the two tiers should also differ to a certain extent.

The current analysis focuses on two countries—Kyrgyzstan and Uzbekistan—representing the two groups of states in the region. Testing the hypothesis on the entire range of the Central Asian states is economized because the selected country-cases maximize variation on the possible outcomes of EU democratization efforts—with Kyrgyzstan being a state where European engagement is most likely to be successful and Uzbekistan entertaining the opposite expectations.

While among Central Asian republics Kyrgyzstan clearly presents the most-likely case for success, the choice of Uzbekistan over Turkmenistan for failure is less obvious. Turkmenistan is commonly regarded as one of the most authoritarian and closed regimes in the world (Freedom House n/a) and hence would seemingly provide a 'more suitable' least-likely case for the present study. However, EU engagement with this country has been minimal, mainly because the Partnership and Cooperation Agreement (PCA) with Turkmenistan still needs to be ratified by the European Parliament and thus has not yet entered into force. Hence, the EU could not use some of its democratization tools in the country (e.g. conditionality linked to the 'democracy clause' in the PCA, certain forms of political dialogue, and civil society support programmes) that are generally available for other parts of Central Asia. An analysis of the Turkmenistan case could thus provide only very limited insights with regard to the research questions of this study. In addition, Uzbekistan is preferred here because it has been the only Central Asian state to experience EU democratization and human rights related sanctions, which makes it crucial for an investigation of successes and failures of EU conditionality. The empirical chapters (4 to 6) thus evaluate and

---

[3] One could argue that contemporary Kyrgyzstan presents a case of a hybrid regime with some features of electoral democracy, while other Central Asian states could be regarded as authoritarian with varying degrees of power concentration. On different approaches towards defining hybrid regimes see e.g. Bogaards (2009) and Diamond (2002).

explain the outcomes of EU democratization policy in Central Asia with the examples of Kyrgyzstan and Uzbekistan.

Finally, the conclusion of the study summarizes the evaluation results, highlighting few successes of the EU, and emphasizes the relevance of the substance of the promoted norms and changes for the outcomes of EU efforts. It further discusses implications of the key findings for external democracy and human rights promotion in the broader region.

This work complements existing scholarship of EU political engagement in Central Asia and advances the democratization research agenda by linking the study of substance to the study of instruments and their effects. It thus responds to the reflections by Frank Schimmelfennig (2011) on the academic merits of examining the substance of EU democratization policy.

2. European Union as an External Democracy Promoter: Theoretical and Conceptual Foundations

This chapter provides the concepts and theoretical framework for the current research. First, it refers to normative commitments in EC/EU documents in order to conceptualize the European Union as an external democratizer. As the analysis of democracy promotion activities requires clarification of their substance (i.e. specification of what is actually promoted), the chapter examines the EU understanding of democracy promotion and its components and elaborates working definitions used in the present study. Second, the chapter considers the existing theoretical approaches to the international norm transfer and their explanatory power for the case of EU democratization policy in such regions as Central Asia to identify an appropriate approach for the current research. Finally, the chapter reviews external democracy promotion tools available to the European Union. Taking account of the existing typologies of democratization instruments, it elaborates a distinct approach towards categorizing the EU tools based on their underlying logic (mechanisms of international norm transfer) and the changes that are expected to occur as the result of the tools' application.

2.1 Conceptualizing the EU as a Normative Actor

2.1.1 EU-Level Normative Commitments

It is commonly stated that the European Union is a community of values based on the principles of democracy, liberty, respect for human rights and fundamental freedoms, and the rule of law (e.g. European Commission 1995; Manners 2002; European Union 2006: Art. 6). Although normative orientation was not a focus of the Treaty of Paris or the Treaties of Rome, even the early European Community (EC) defined itself as a value-based entity (Jünemann and Knodt 2007: 13). Thus, the democratic conception of the EC is evident in official pronouncements, such as the final declaration of the Paris Summit of October 1972 and the document on 'The European Identity' adopted by the EC Foreign Ministers in Copenhagen in December 1973. The former declaration expressed the will of the Member States *"to base their Community's development on democracy, freedom of opinion, free movement of men and ideas and participation by the people through their freely elected representatives"* (European Communities 1972). While the latter document confirmed determination of the Community members *"to defend the principles of representative democracy, of the rule of law, of social justice [...] and of respect for human rights"* (European Communities 1973: Par. I.1).

The legal basis for the EC/EU's joint commitment to the democratic principles was later established with the Single European Act of 1986 (European Communities 1987: Preamble, Par. 3 and 5) and most importantly with the Maastricht Treaty (Preamble), as amended by the Treaties of Amsterdam and Nice (European Union 2006: Art. 6). After the Lisbon Treaty entered into force in December 2009, the Charter of Fundamental Rights of the EU has also become legally binding. While mainly focusing on human rights protection, the Charter includes several provisions on elements of democracy, emphasizing that: *"[...] the Union is founded on the indivisible, universal values of human dignity, freedom, equality and solidarity; it is based on the principles of democracy and the rule of law"* (European Union 2000: Preamble).

Historically, these values and principles have developed as a reference of both EU internal and external policies (cf. Jünemann and Knodt 2007: 12; Council of the European Union 2012: 1). Thus, the Member States expressed their will to represent the Community's values and principles in international relations as early as the Paris Summit of October 1972. The connection between the democratic self-image of the EC and its normative orientation in external affairs (or aspiration to export its model to third countries) was further articulated in the above mentioned document on 'The European Identity' of 1973. Later, promotion of democracy and human rights became a stated priority of the EU foreign and development policies. The European Council Resolution of November 1991 on 'Human Rights, Democracy and Development' was the first EC document that established external democracy promotion as both an objective and a condition of the European Community's cooperation with developing countries (Council of the European Communities 1991). Furthermore, the resolution introduced the concept of *'good governance'* to EU development policy.

The 1992 Maastricht Treaty incorporated provisions of the 1991 Council resolution and stated the consolidation of *"democracy and the rule of law, and respect for human rights and fundamental freedoms"* as an objective of the EU common foreign and security policy and development cooperation (European Union 1992: Art. J.1/2 and Art. G.130u), as amended by the

1997 Amsterdam Treaty and the 2000 Nice Treaty (European Union 2006: Art. 11/1, Art. 177/2 and Art. 181/1). The Maastricht Treaty has thus become a cornerstone in the institutionalization of EU democratization policy and can be considered a starting point of democracy and human rights mainstreaming, i.e. *"integrating human rights and democratization issues into all aspects of EU policy decision-making and implementation, including trade and external assistance"* (European Commission 2008: 1).

The commitments to promote European values in international affairs have been repeatedly re-affirmed in EU documents, including the European Commission's Communication of May 2001 on 'The EU's Role in Promoting Human Rights and Democratization in Third Countries' (European Commission 2001a) and 'The European Consensus on Development' adopted by the Council, the European Parliament and the Commission in November 2005 (Council of the European Union 2005c). Finally, the Lisbon Treaty also states that the *"Union's action on the international scene shall be guided by the principles which have inspired its own creation, development and enlargement, and which it seeks to advance in the wider world: democracy, the rule of law, the universality and indivisibility of human rights and fundamental freedoms, respect for human dignity, the principles of equality and solidarity, and respect for the principles of the United Nations Charter and international law"* (European Union 2010: Art. 21). Most recently, these aspirations have been re-stated in the Joint Communication of the European Commission and the EU's High Representative for Foreign Affairs and Security Policy of December 2011 'Human Rights and Democracy at the Heart of EU External Action—Towards a More Effective Approach' and the 'EU Strategic Framework and Action Plan on Human Rights and Democracy' adopted by the Council in June 2012 (cf. European Commission and High Representative of the European Union for Foreign Affairs and Security Policy 2011; Council of the European Union 2012).

If promotion of democracy, human rights, good governance, and the rule of law are assumed to be among the central concepts in the European Union's external relations, the next section clarifies how these terms are defined by the EU and how they are conceptually linked to each other.

2.1.2 The EU Conception of External Democracy Promotion

Although *'democracy promotion'* is an often used term in the EU documents related to its foreign affairs, it is difficult to find a precise explanation of this concept. A discussion paper of the Political and Security Committee of the

European Council on 'The EU Approach to Democracy Promotion in External Relations' states that *"despite an underlying convergence of objectives within the EU, there has been little consistency in public discourse and terminology, neither within and between Member states and within EU institutions, nor generally in the international community"* (European Council, Political and Security Committee 2006: 3). Instead of providing a clear-cut definition, the same document describes *'democracy promotion'* as a *'general concept'* that *"encompasses all measures designed to facilitate democratic development"* (European Council, Political and Security Committee 2006: 3). This vague interpretation is complemented with a description of the scope of democracy promotion: *"It may be targeted towards regimes with very limited freedoms and little political pluralism; it may be combined with peace building in post conflict situations; it may support new institutions and democratic practice in emerging democracies; it may be well integrated in development cooperation, strengthening participation and accountability within sector programmes for achieving MDGs; it may also be offered to more established democracies to assist in dealing with new threats, such as terrorism"* (European Council, Political and Security Committee 2006: 3-4).

With regard to the conceptualization of *democracy*, a more precise definition can be found in later EU documents. However, a survey of earlier documents shows that the EC/EU approach towards defining democracy has changed over time. It gradually developed from a minimalist understanding with a focus on formal governmental procedures, elections, pluralism, and fundamental freedoms in the 1960-1970s to a substantive approach towards democracy at a later stage during the 1990-2000s[4] (cf. Kneuer 2007: 97). Thus, an updated version of the European Commission's 'Programming Guide for Strategy Papers: Democracy and Human Rights' of 2008 states that *"[d]eveloping and consolidating democracy reaches much further than just electoral processes or establishing or reinforcing democratic (governmental or semi-governmental) institutions. [...] It is a question of the degree to which citizens exercise control over political decision-making and are treated as equals"* (European Commission 2008: Annex B).

The same document also gives a more precise definition of democracy to be used in the context of EU foreign affairs, particularly *"[f]or the purposes of mainstreaming 'democracy' into the Community's development coopera-*

---

[4] For differentiation between various approaches to defining democracy see e.g. Tilly 2007: 7-11.

tion and external assistance, the understanding of democracy should be that of a system of political governance whose decision-making power is subject to the controlling influence of citizens who are considered political equals. A democratic political system is inclusive, participatory, representative, accountable, transparent and responsive to citizens' aspirations and expectations" (European Commission 2008: Annex B).

The EU's substantive approach is also exemplified through an emphasis on the interrelation of the concept of democracy with the respect for human rights, fundamental freedoms and the rule of law: *"Democracy and the protection of human rights are inextricably linked: the fundamental freedoms of expression and association are the preconditions for political pluralism and democratic process, whereas democratic control and separation of powers are essential to sustain an independent judiciary and the rule of law which in turn are required for effective protection of human rights"* (European Commission 2006a: 4). The aforementioned Joint Communication of the European Commission and the EU's High Representative for Foreign Affairs and Security Policy of December 2011 also re-affirms that *"[h]uman rights and democracy go hand in hand with the empowering freedoms— freedom of expression, association and assembly—which underpin democracy"* (European Commission and High Representative of the European Union for Foreign Affairs and Security Policy 2011: 7).

Emphasizing interdependence of these concepts, the EU documents are somewhat ambiguous regarding the nature of democracy. On the one hand, democracy, including the rule of law and the protection of human rights, is seen as *"a universal value [...] and is thus a right for all and a goal in itself"* (European Council, Political and Security Committee 2006: 1). On the other, it is admitted that *"democracy is a contested concept"* (European Commission 2008: Annex B) and if *"[h]uman rights may be considered in the light of universally accepted international norms, [...] democracy has to be seen as a process, developing from within"* (European Commission 2006a: 4) with "*no universal model"* for its development (European Commission 2008: Annex B; cf. Council of the European Union 2012: 1).

The EU is generally rather cautious in applying the term of democracy on its own in the documents related to foreign affairs. The above mentioned discussion paper of the Political and Security Committee (2006) explains it in the following way: *"'Democracy' is not frequently used as an umbrella term within the EU. Though few contest that democracy lies at the nexus of peace and security, human rights and development objectives, the term has sometimes been considered too ambiguous and political to be used in isolation"* (European Council, Political and Security Committee 2006: 3). In view of this ambiguity and politicization of the concept, an alternative term of *'democratic governance'* sometimes is preferred by the EU particularly in the development cooperation sphere, which regards democracy, *"along with rule of law, human rights, civil society development, public administration etc as a component of 'governance'"* (European Council, Political and Security Committee 2006: 3).

In contrast to the admitted ambiguity of the concept of democracy, the universal nature of *human rights* (HR) is repeatedly emphasized in EU documents (e.g. Council of the European Communities 1991; European Commission 1998; European Commission 2001a; European Commission 2006a; European Council, Political and Security Committee 2006; European Commission 2008; Council of the European Union 2012, etc.). Numerous international charters and conventions are identified as sources of this universality.[5]

The European Commission's 'Programming Guide for Strategy Papers: Democracy and Human Rights' of 2008 elucidates the concept of HR as follows: *"Human rights are universal legal guarantees protecting individuals and groups against actions and omissions that interfere with fundamental freedoms, entitlements and human dignity"* (European Commission 2008: Annex B). The document further provides a list of rights *"guaranteed to all human beings"*, which includes *inter alia* political rights, e.g. the right to vote and take part in the conduct of public affairs, and fundamental freedoms, e.g. freedom of thought, conscience and religion, freedom of association,

---

[5] The Commissions Communication of 1998 e.g. refers to the United Nations Charter, the Universal Declaration of Human Rights, the 1969 American Convention on Human Rights, and the 1981 African Charter on Human and Peoples' Rights (European Commission 1998: 4). The Political and Security Committee's discussion paper provides a more extensive list of HR-related international documents, e.g. the Universal Declaration of Human Rights, the International Covenant on Civil and Political Rights, the International Conventions on the Elimination of All Forms of Racial Discrimination and the Elimination of All Forms of Discrimination against Women, UN Basic Principles on the Independence of the Judiciary, UN Guidelines on the Role of Prosecutors, the IPU 1997 Universal Declaration on Democracy, Inter-American Democratic Charter 2001, Council of Europe Parliamentary Assembly Resolution 800 (1983) on the principles of democracy, and Conclusions of the CSCE Copenhagen Meeting 1990 (European Council, Political and Security Committee 2006: 1).

expression, assembly and movement (European Commission 2008: Annex B).[6]

As in the case of democracy mainstreaming, the EU links protection of HR to the sphere of development cooperation (e.g. European Commission and High Representative of the European Union for Foreign Affairs and Security Policy 2011: 11), stating its human rights-based approach to development: *"This approach is a conceptual framework for the process of human development that is normatively based on international human rights standards and operationally directed to promoting and protecting human rights. It seeks to analyse inequalities which lie at the heart of development problems and redress discriminatory practices and unjust distributions of power that impede development progress"* (European Commission 2008: Annex B).

The concept of the *rule of law* is explained in the European Commission's Communication of 1998 as follows: *"The primacy of the law is a fundamental principle of any democratic system seeking to foster and promote rights, whether civil and political or economic, social and cultural. This entails means of recourse enabling individual citizens to defend their rights"* (European Commission 1998: 4). According to the document, the rule of law implies *"a legislature respecting and giving full effect to human rights and fundamental freedoms, an independent judiciary, effective and accessible means of legal recourse, a legal system guaranteeing equality before the law, a prison system respecting the human person, a police force at the service of the law,* [and finally] *an effective executive enforcing the law and capable of establishing the social and economic conditions necessary for life in society"* (European Commission 1998: 4-5).

The Communication of 1998 also provides an explanation of the concept of *good governance*, which *"implies managing public affairs in a transparent, accountable, participative and equitable manner showing due regard for human rights and the rule of law"* (European Commission 1998: 7). The document further distinguishes two dimensions of good governance—a political one that refers to strictly political action by the government, and an institutional dimension that encompasses economic and social management of a country's resources (e.g. human, natural, economic and financial re-

---

[6] A list of the most important human rights promoted by the EU in its external affairs is also provided in the earlier documents, e.g. Council Regulations No 975/1999 and No 976/1999 of 1999.

sources, including external development aid) by competent and effective institutions, respecting the listed principles (European Commission 1998: 7-8). This Communication re-affirms the linkage between good governance and a country's development, which was established earlier in the European Council Resolution of November 1991 on 'Human Rights, Democracy and Development'. As it has been mentioned above, this was the first EC document that introduced the concept of *good governance* in the context of the EU development policy. The resolution did not provide a definition of the concept, but specified general principles, on which good governance in the field of development should be based: *"sensible economic and social policies, democratic decision-making, adequate governmental transparency and financial accountability, creation of a market-friendly environment for development, measures to combat corruption, as well as respect for the rule of law, human rights, and freedom of the press and expression"* (Council of the European Communities 1991: Point 5). The later Commission's White Paper on 'European Governance' of 2001 re-stated the principles underpinning good governance as *"openness, participation, accountability, effectiveness and coherence"* and emphasized the importance of each of them *"for establishing more democratic governance"* (European Commission 2001b: 10).

To summarize the above, the EU's documents do not provide clear differentiations between the concepts of democracy, human rights, good governance and the rule of law. On the contrary, interdependence of these concepts with regard to their substance is repeatedly emphasized. Also, the documents are generally vague on the definition and implications of external democracy promotion (cf. Wetzel and Orbie 2012). As the EU does not draw a clear line between democracy, human rights, good governance, and the rule of law, but is interested in spreading these ideals, a very comprehensive interpretation of *democracy promotion* (or *external democratization policy*) is used here, which encompasses these concepts as its elements.

Accordingly, external democracy promotion is conceptualised in this study as conscious and deliberate actions by the European Union to introduce new mentalities, institutions and patterns of behaviour in third countries to support the process of creation of a polyarchic order based on the rule of law, respect for human rights and liberal individual freedoms, including assembly, religion, press, and standing for public office etc. (cf. Grugel 2002: 5).

2.2 In Search for an Appropriate Theoretical Framework: Explaining External Factors of Democratization

This section refers to existing theoretical explanations of external factors of democratization with the aim of testing their applicability for analysing EU democracy promotion in Central Asia.

A substantial literature that has developed around international dimensions of democratization provides various explanations of how external actors can exert influence on domestic processes of political change. Thus, Whitehead (2001) distinguishes three broad categories of these explanatory mechanisms and labels them as *contagion*, *control*, and *consent*.

The notion of *democratization by contagion* presumes that transformation processes and establishment of democratic norms in one country (or group of countries) spill-over and 'infect' other states, and thus, spread across borders through *'neutral transmission mechanisms'* (Whitehead 2001: 6), to the extent that these processes and norms serve as a source of inspiration for domestic actors.[7] In these terms, geographic proximity to democracies (or democratizing states) is often seen as a decisive factor, as it increases the likelihood of democratic 'infection' (e.g. Kopstein and Reilly 2000). Although the contagion argument seems to accommodate certain cases (e.g. Whitehead 2001: 5-8), it is admitted that its explanatory power is very limited (cf. Kubicek 2003: 5; Wichmann 2007: 24-25). Identifying various geographic accumulations and temporal sequences of democratization processes, the approach provides for certain correlations. Yet, as the contagion-based explanations do not rely on an in-depth analysis of the transmission channels, the actors involved or their intentions and preferences, they overlook the interplay of external influence with local conditions and fail to specify causal mechanisms. This results in an inability of the contagion approach to explain deviations in democratic development of various states within the same region. Moreover, focusing on democratization through neutral and unintended mechanisms, the approach does not account for active engagement of external actors in promotion of political change in third countries. It does not provide actor-oriented explanations, but rather background variables, and therefore, is ill-adapted for an analysis of democratization efforts of such actors as the European Union. Finally, assuming geographic proximity to democratic states as an important factor for democrati-

---

[7] Alternative terms that are used in the literature to describe similar processes are *'diffusion'* (e.g. Lauth and Pickel 2009) or *'lesson drawing'* (e.g. Knill and Becker 2003).

zation, the contagion approach is hardly applicable to the case of the Central Asian region, which is located between Russia, China, Iran, and Afghanistan—the states with authoritarian or hybrid regimes overtly lacking in democratic institutions and practices.

The second category identified by Whitehead (2001) *democratization by control* provides for a very distinct explanation of external influence on domestic political processes through targeted, intentional actions of external actors, which directly take control over political institutions of a state with the aim of making them more democratic. This approach implies physical presence of an external democratizer in the country of transition, which results from an intervention per war, occupation or incorporation of the non-democratic state into the democratic one.[8] Although it is argued that democratization by control is not germane to EU actions even in its relations with the accession-states, as the Union does not have a direct control mechanism, by which it could impose democracy on a state (Kubicek 2003: 4-5), one could assume partial applicability of this approach to the neighbouring countries, where the EU is directly involved and responsible for institution-building processes (e.g. Kosovo). Yet, democratization by control is obviously irrelevant in the context of Central Asian countries, where the EU is neither physically present as a dominant actor, nor directly involved into the processes of institution-building.

Unlike the notions of contagion and control, the third approach of *democratization by consent* accounts for *"the actions and intentions of relevant domestic groupings, and interactions between internal and international processes"* (Whitehead 2001: 15). Here, a substantial understanding of democracy as the result of a process of transformation prevails. The key role in the process is attached to the participation of a wide range of domestic social and political actors. External factors seem to play only a subordinate role. Yet, Whitehead (2001) identifies several aspects of international contributions to generation of consent in new democracies, which appear to be relevant to the analysis of EU external democratization policy. First, personalized support for rising opposition forces, which often comprise a *'substantial external component'* (Whitehead 2001: 20), e.g. opposition members originating from the diaspora, local staff employed by international or-

---

[8] The most common examples in the literature are the post-1945 democratization of West Germany through the presence of Allied forces (e.g. Whitehead 2001; Wichmann 2007) or the later incorporation of the German Democratic Republic into united Germany in 1990 (e.g. Kubicek 2003).

ganizations, or representatives of civil society organizations (including NGOs), who receive international donor assistance. Second, international demonstration effects that *"affect the underlying distribution of popular preferences and expectations"* (Whitehead 2001: 21). In this sense, the consent results from the attractiveness of *"a way of life associated with the liberal capitalist democracies"* and *"an almost universal wish to imitate"* it (Whitehead 2001: 21). Third, the role of regional associations of democratic states, which offer support, convergence with, or incorporation for their democratizing neighbours (Whitehead 2001: 18). These offers provide a strong pull-factor for domestic actors in emerging democracies to turn from pursuing purely national agendas to considering possible external effects of their actions (Wichmann 2007: 27). If the first two aspects (personalized support for rising opposition and international demonstration effects) possess certain explanatory power in the context of the EU democracy promotion in such regions as Central Asia, the impact of the regional blocks is applicable here only in terms of providing support, but is obviously irrelevant with regard to the convergence or incorporation. Apart from that, the notion of democratization by consent suggests a rather passive role of regional associations (assuming their almost automatic attractiveness) and a more active pursuit of democracy by the countries in transition, which obviously does not correspond to the reality in *'reluctant democracies'* (Kubicek 2003: 3), such as Central Asian republics. Therefore, further analytical categories are needed to account for specific democracy promotion activities of external democratizers, which are able to overcome the reluctance of domestic actors.

Many studies examining democratization processes and political change in the potential EU members use the concept of *Europeanization* to explain the impact of the European structures and policies on the domestic change (e.g. Schimmelfennig and Sedelmeier 2005; Grabbe 2006; Wichmann 2007). These studies point to particular mechanisms of EU influence on domestic political processes: through (1) direct policy or norm prescription and conditionality (e.g. adoption of the European *Aquis Communautaire*); (2) indirect change of opportunity or constraint structures for domestic actors; and (3) alteration of collective understandings and beliefs of domestic actors which in turn increases the legitimacy of domestic change (Wichmann 2007: 32; cf. Knill and Lehmkuhl 1999). The concept of Europeanization, although not free of ambiguity, carries substantial explanatory power in terms of influence of European integration on the processes of domestic adaptation in accession countries. Yet, the concept is only partially applicable to the ENP states, which do not have a membership perspective, and even less so beyond the European neighbourhood, where direct policy prescription is not possible and effects may be expected only in terms of the change of opportunity structures for domestic actors and/or the alteration of their collective understandings. Furthermore, as Europeanization is a very EU-centred concept, it ignores the impact of other non-European institutions and actors. Therefore, the concept loses its explanatory power in the context of states and regions where the EU is neither the only nor the strongest external actor, as in the case of Central Asia.

In an attempt to explain the variation in regime trajectories after the Cold War, i.e. why certain political regimes democratized while the others remained authoritarian or developed competitive authoritarian features, Levitsky and Way employ the concepts of Western *leverage*, or states' vulnerability to Western democratizing pressure, and *linkage* to the West, i.e. the density of political, economic, diplomatic, organizational and social ties (Levitsky and Way 2005: 21-24; Levitsky and Way 2010: 23-24). The authors particularly assume that states are more likely to follow a democratization path where both Western leverage and linkage are high because they increase the cost of authoritarianism. Leverage can be exercised through mechanisms such as diplomatic pressure, political conditionality (including punitive measures), and military intervention. In turn, linkage to the West is expected to contribute to democratization by (1) heightening *"the international reverberation caused by authoritarian abuse"*; (2) creating *"domestic constituencies for democratic norm-abiding behaviour"*; and (3) reshaping *"the domestic distribution of power and resources"* in favour of pro-democratic forces (Levitsky and Way 2010: 44). As an example, the EU is seen by the authors as the main source of both linkage and leverage in democratizing Eastern European states that sought to join the Union (Levitsky and Way 2010: 88-90).

Notably, the mechanisms of both leverage and linkage are materialist by nature and are assumed to impact actors' rationalist considerations (Levitsky and Way 2010: 45). The approach used by Levitsky and Way thus meets assumptions of a range of studies deriving from the broader discipline of International Relations that explain the cross-border transfer of democratic norms through the process of socialization. *Socialization* is commonly defined as a process of inducting actors into the norms, rules and ways of behaviour *"that are preferred in a society"* (Barnes, Skidmore and Tripp 1980: 35; cf. Alderson 2001; Johnston 2001: 494-495; Warkotsch 2009: 250). In the context of external democratization, *preferred behaviour* is usually understood as *compliance* with human rights and democracy standards (e.g. Warkotsch 2008b; cf. Morlino and Magen 2009).

Within the academic debate on international socialization, authors generally distinguish two main mechanisms for projection of liberal democratic norms and human rights principles to third states: *strategic calculation* and *normative suasion*. One group of scholars argue for a materialist approach to rational actions. The adherents of this rationalist approach suggest that states (or political elites governing the states) are driven by pragmatic self-interest and strategic calculations of costs and benefits when considering political change (e.g. Schimmelfennig 2005). According to this logic of argument, if rewards promised by external actors are perceived by targets to be greater than the costs of compliance with externally promoted norms (e.g. economic gains outweighing the potential losses of power resulting from political liberalization), the possibility of their successful socialization increases (Checkel 2005: 809). The same effect can be achieved, if the targets see sanctions and loss of benefits provided by normative actors as more costly or dangerous for themselves than political reforms. The willingness of a state (or its governing elites) to comply with the requirements of external actors can be reinforced through conditionality, i.e. through linking of certain incentives (such as development aid, closer economic and political cooperation, possibility of accession, etc.) to the fulfilment of economic, social and/or political conditions.

In contrast, the constructivist approach emphasizes normative suasion based on persuasion by the *power of the better argument* and *appropriateness of behaviour* as the main mechanism of international norm transfer. While strategic calculation of costs and benefits is often associated with behavioural adaptation of the target actors and short- to medium-term results, socialization through normative suasion is expected to work in the long run (Warkotsch 2008b: 64). It supposes equal engagement of both normative and target actors in a dialogue, in which the latter ones are persuaded by the legitimacy of norms and values promoted by the socializers. According to constructivists, socializees '*internalize new values*', which in the end is expected to generate deep-rooted long-term political change (cf. Checkel 2005: 813; Warkotsch 2008b: 64).

Notably, the normative suasion logic goes beyond the propositions by Levitsky and Way concerning leverage and linkage mechanisms. The latter approach basically excludes the possibility of non-material interests and non-rationalist actions of the targets (cf. Levitsky and Way 2010: 44), which limits its explanatory power. Moreover, while the approach suggested by Levitsky and Way provides valid explanations of the variance in regime outcomes on the global scale and the emergence of competitive authoritarian regimes, it is less apt for explicating the process of deliberate cross-border norm transfer from a specific Western actor to a particular group of states where both Western linkage and leverage are assumed to be rather low.

Theoretical propositions elaborated in the studies of international socialization combining rationalist and constructivist perspectives (e.g. Kelley 2004; Checkel 2005; Warkotsch 2008b; Warkotsch 2009) appear to be more applicable to the current research. First, they follow an actor-centred approach, which takes account of an active engagement of external actors in promotion of political change in third countries. Second, they provide for specific mechanisms explaining international norm transfer, which account for both rational and non-rational actions of the relevant domestic players and interactions between internal and international processes. Third, in contrast to the aforementioned Europeanization studies, the explanatory power of international socialization mechanisms is not limited geographically to the accessing or neighbouring states of the EU, which allows for an analysis of external democratization effects beyond the immediate European neighbourhood. Hence, the combined rationalist-constructivist approach proposed by international socialization scholars (e.g. Kelley 2004; Checkel 2005; Warkotsch 2009) is taken as a theoretical foundation for the current study.

The final point that needs to be addressed is the interrelation of the two socialization mechanisms—strategic calculation and normative suasion. Although the rationalist-constructivist theoretical debate emphasizes distinction (and sometimes even contradiction) between these mechanisms, this differentiation appears to be less empirical and more analytical (cf. Kelley 2004: 428). In practice, strategic calculation and normative suasion often take place simultaneously and are interlinked making it difficult to separate their effects empirically. In addition, some authors argue that external conditionality and strategic calculation often motivate political behaviour of domestic actors, but normative suasion guides it by providing a point of reference (e.g. Kelley 2004). Therefore, these mechanisms need to be regarded not as contradicting, or mutually excluding, but rather as complimentary. A comprehensive analysis of international socialization must consider both of them, and that is the aim of this study.

2.3 Towards a Comprehensive Typology of EU Democracy Promotion Tools

After reviewing the existing explanations of external democratization factors and identifying the apt theoretical approach for the analysis of the EU democracy promotion in Central Asia, it is now necessary to turn to democratization instruments available to the European Union first by looking at their categorizations and then discussing construction of a distinctive typology.

2.3.1 Categorizing Democratization Tools: An Overview of Existing Typologies

Several EU documents specify the tools used for external democracy and human rights promotion. The brochure on 'The European Union: Furthering Human Rights and Democracy across the Globe' issued by the European Commission in 2007 groups together tools used by the EU within its Common Foreign and Security Policy: *'common strategies, common positions and joint actions'*, *'démarches and declarations'*, *'dialogue and consultations with third countries'*, and *'guidelines on EU policy towards third countries on specific human rights schemes'* (European Commission 2007e: 9). The aforementioned discussion paper of the European Council's Political and Security Committee distinguishes several broader categories of democratization instruments: *'financial and technical assistance and grant aid'* (or *'democracy assistance'*), *'political dialogues and other diplomatic instruments'*, *'financial incentives, conditionalities and sanctions'*, *'trade and investment instruments'*, *'mobilization of civilian and military capabilities'*, *'humanitarian assistance'*, *'multilateral initiatives'*, and finally *'public information, advocacy and monitoring'* (European Council, Political and Security Committee 2006: 4). The report on EU action 'Human Rights and Democracy in the World' issued in 2010 provides further insights into application of the EU democracy and HR promotion tools and divides them into the following groups: *'EU guidelines on human rights and international humanitarian law'*, *'human rights dialogues and consultations'*, *'joint actions, common positions and crisis management operations'*, *'démarches and declarations'*, *'human rights clauses in cooperation agreements with non-EU countries'*, *'activities of the Personal Representative of the SG/HR on Human Rights in* the area of CFSP', 'instruments within the European Neighbourhood Policy', and 'activities funded under the European Instrument for Democracy and Human Rights' (European External Action Service 2010: 17-33).

This brief review demonstrates that the European Union lacks a clear and systematic approach towards defining and differentiating its democracy promotion tools. Categorizations provided in different documents do not correspond to each other. The identified groups of instruments appear to be at best incomplete. If particular instruments are listed, it is not specified to which categories they should be assigned. At the same time, categories identified in the documents are often very vaguely formulated (e.g. 'mobilization of civilian and military capabilities' or 'multilateral initiatives'), and therefore the same instruments may be included into different categories. In addition, the categories often intersect with each other (e.g. 'trade and investment' may be used in terms of conditionality policy). Hence, a more comprehensive classification of EU democracy promotion tools is needed for a systematic analysis.

A survey of the literature on democracy promotion by external actors reveals various approaches towards categorizing their democratization tools. Authors differentiate groups of instruments along many lines, e.g. *top-down* (targeting state elites) vs. *bottom-up* (aiming at civil society) tools (cf. Carothers 1999; Diamond 1999; Huber 2008), *direct*, i.e. addressing essential political characteristics of democracy, vs. *indirect*, i.e. seeking to establish conditions for democratization (cf. Burnell 2008: 627-628), *bilateral* vs. *multilateral* (Pevehouse 2005), legally binding vs. legally non-binding (Urdze 2010: 39), instruments relying on *soft* vs. *hard power*[9] (cf. Nye 2004), or *linkage* vs. *leverage* tools (Levitsky and Way 2005). These classifications can be regarded as complimentary. Thus, an EU-Presidency declaration condemning 'unfair' elections in a third state is a soft, bilateral, legally non-binding, and top-down instrument. In addition, democracy promotion instruments are often categorized in terms of their character along the *positive-negative* dimension (e.g. Burnell 2000; Hazelzet 2001; Jünemann and Knodt 2007: 17; Huber 2008). Tools providing benefits or rewards for democratizing states are generally regarded as positive (or *'carrots'*), whereas instruments seeking to punish or exert pressure on third countries for not complying with democracy and human rights standards are regarded as

---

[9] Hard power is associated here primarily with military intervention for democratization and therefore is more applicable to the U.S. foreign policies and democracy promotion than to the EU.

negative (or *'sticks'*). A further classification often applied by authors is based on the distinction of the instruments' contents. Thus, Börzel and Risse differentiate between three types of tools: *'political conditionality'*, *'political dialogue'*, and *'capacity building programmes'* (Börzel and Risse 2004: 26-28). Youngs combines the character-based and the content-oriented approaches to categorization, distinguishing external democratization tools as positive *'democracy assistance'* and *'coercive instruments'*, i.e. conditionality (Youngs 2001: 28-46). Reiber provides a more differentiated content-based typology, with the main categories being *'conditionality'*, *'legitimization'*, *'material support'*, *'knowledge transfer'*, and *'dialogue'* (Reiber 2009: 214-217).[10] Richter's categorization is even more detailed (Richter 2009: 73-77). She distinguishes between two major groups of tools—*'instruments of influence exertion'* and *'instruments of direct implementation'*. Within the first category, Richter identifies further sub-groups: *'incentive-based tools'*, *'suasion'*, *'knowledge and technology transfer'*, *'observation and control'*, and *'mediation'*.[11]

A critical analysis of the existing categorizations reveals that most of them do not differentiate thoroughly between various democratization tools or contain certain inconsistencies. Thus, the typologies using the content-based approach either do not assign specific programmes/instruments to the identified categories in a systematic way (e.g. Youngs 2001) or allow attributing the same programmes to various categories (e.g. Börzel and Risse 2004). In some cases, differentiation between various categories appears to be redundant. For example, Reiber views *'legitimization'*, which involves non-material incentives and punishments, as a separate category, distinct from economic and political *'conditionality'*. At the same time, the author argues that *'legitimization'* is based on the logic of cost-benefit calculation and is linked to the use of *'conditionality'* (Reiber 2009: 215-216). It is difficult to distinguish between these categories empirically, and therefore they could be merged into one group. The same could be argued for *'material support'* and *'knowledge transfer'*, as they are based on the same logic and the existing programmes of democracy assistance commonly involve both of these elements. Apart from that, the classification offered by Reiber focuses primarily on the instruments targeting state elites, ignoring bottom-up tools directly aimed at civil society actors (e.g. it is not clear to which category

---

[10] Reiber uses positive-negative differentiation only with regard to conditionality application (cf. Smith 2005).
[11] Mediation is applied by external actors primarily in conflict-divided societies.

projects supported under the European Instrument for Democracy and Human Rights should be attributed). The same is true for the typology offered by Richter (2009).

Dichotomous differentiation along the positive-negative dimension also proves to be problematic when applied empirically. Thus, it is often neglected that the same instrument can be perceived as both positive and negative, depending on its targets and the way of its application (e.g. in autocratic regimes support to civil society organizations or opposition forces is regarded as positive by their members, but for government elites such support is often viewed in negative terms). In addition, the degree, to which an instrument is seen as positive or negative, may vary (e.g. a common position imposing limited sanctions is more negative than the one partially withdrawing them).

Further inconsistencies in the existing classifications include interchangeable usages of terms. Thus, discussing the impact of the EU external policies beyond European states, Schimmelfennig (2009b) applies the notion of conditionality as an *'instrument'*, a *'mechanism'* and a *'strategy'* in various parts of his article, which adds to the confusion.

2.3.2 Building-up a Distinct Typology

In view of the shortcomings of the existing typologies, it is suggested to elaborate a distinct approach towards the categorization of the EU democracy promotion instruments. As the purpose of the current study is to evaluate and explain successes and failures in the application of external democratization tools, it is assumed that a classification based on the underlying logic of the tools and the changes that these tools are expected to trigger would be most appropriate.

As discussed above, the international socialization literature distinguishes between two main mechanisms for projection of norms to third states: *strategic calculation* of costs and benefits and *normative suasion* (see section 2.2). Pursuant to the strategic calculation logic, external democracy promotion instruments involve providing certain benefits to target actors under the condition of their compliance with particular norms or exerting pressure and imposing sanctions on the targets if they fail to comply. Thus, democratizers may 'reward' or 'punish' target actors, relying on the principle of conditionality. Here, *conditionality* is defined in general terms as the use of incentives and coercive measures *"to bring about a desired change"* (Checkel 2005: 809). The strongest EU incentive-based instrument is commonly associated with membership conditionality. Yet, other instruments providing material benefits, such as financial and technical assistance, trade opportunities, and grant aid can be used in terms of conditionality as well. Moreover, instruments can provide rewards (or impose punishments) of immaterial nature, e.g. recognition of status or rhetorical praising (vs. refusal of recognition or rhetorical shaming). Instruments involving both material and immaterial incentives and punishments are based on the same underlying logic of cost-benefit calculations and aim at norm compliance by target actors. Therefore, for the purposes of the current analysis, they are assigned to one category—*conditionality-based tools*.

Another group of instruments, such as meetings of highly ranked government officials, inter-parliamentary cooperation, structured human rights dialogues, etc., rely on persuading target actors in the legitimacy of certain norms rather than imposing them through incentives and sanctions. These instruments are not only expected to trigger compliance with certain promoted norms, but also in the long run lead to internalization of these norms through the alteration of attitudes and shifts in the belief system of the socializees (cf. Checkel 2005: 813; Warkotsch 2008b: 64). These instruments thus follow the *normative suasion* logic and are assigned to the category of *dialogue-based tools*.

Both logics of strategic calculation and normative suasion imply that target actors are not automatically willing to accept the norms promoted by external democratizers and therefore need to be either attracted by incentives, forced by sanctions, or persuaded by dialogue. A typology of democratization tools built-up along these two mechanisms would thus ignore the instruments of democracy assistance based on financial support to the democratic institution-building and knowledge-transfer, e.g. capacity-building programmes for civil society organizations and other non-governmental actors. These programmes do not function along strategic calculation or normative suasion logics, but rather imply support of target actors in their intention to acquire the norms and standards of socializers. The aim of these instruments is to increase capacities of the targets and thus empower democratic institutionalization. Therefore, these instruments are attributed to a distinct category of *democratic empowerment*.

While the proposed typology appears to be similar to the one developed by Börzel and Risse (2004), it goes one step further in distinguishing among various EU tools. Börzel and Risse rely on an empirical approach in building their typology, comparing programmes and policies employed by the EU for external democracy promotion across the world. In doing so, the scholars however do not look into specific components of these programmes and policies. As a result, their proposed typology allows attributing the same tools to different categories. For example, according to Börzel and Risse, such programmes as PHARE, TACIS and MEDA are among the EU's *capacity building'* instruments. Yet, the programmes also include financial assistance to target governments, which allows the use of political conditionality.

In contrast, the categorization suggested in the present study draws on theoretical assumptions about the different logics behind the use of tools and the kinds of change that these tools are expected to trigger (i.e. short-term behaviour alterations, shifts in the belief system of the targets, and increases in the targets' capacities that are likely to contribute to the democratization process). The EU's tools are attributed to specific categories based on these assumptions. Empirically this requires distinguishing between various components of the bigger EU programmes, such as TACIS, that may incorporate conditionality-based financial assistance, dialogue platforms, and democratic capacity- and institution-building elements. This would allow avoiding uncertainty with the attribution of the same tools to different categories.

3. Evaluation of EU Democracy Promotion: A Framework for Analysis

This chapter provides a framework for evaluation of the EU's democracy promotion instruments in Central Asia. It elicits factors that explain an outcome of the instruments' applications and states the key hypothesis to be tested in the subsequent empirical part of the work.

With respect to the first research question of the study—whether EU democracy promotion efforts have been at least partly successful in the context of Central Asia, and if so, to what extent—one can view 'success' of external intervention in terms of its effectiveness or impact. Therefore, in order to identify an apt strategy for evaluating success of EU tools in the present study, the first section of this chapter reviews the existing approaches to effectiveness and impact assessment deriving from theoretically oriented and empirically grounded research. It then discusses key challenges for the assessment, which become even more apparent when analysing the EU democratization efforts in Central Asia. Drawing on the insights from the existing approaches and considering their limitations, the chapter elaborates a research strategy that allows an evaluation of the EU instruments in the Central Asian context. This strategy refers to the previously built typology of the EU democracy promotion tools and uses the kind of changes that the tools are expected to trigger (according to their underlying logics) as a point of departure for assessing successes and failures of the EU's efforts at the micro-level.

The next section of this chapter turns to the second research question of the study over what factors make EU democracy promotion more or less successful in an environment particularly challenging for democratization. A review of the literature reveals a range of relevant factors that generally affect performance of external democratization tools. An application of these factors to the Central Asian context exposes inherently unfavourable domestic and external conditions for EU democracy promotion in the region. In view of these conditions, an overall hypothesis concerning the factors that potentially enable relative success of the EU efforts in the countries under study is elaborated.

The final section of this chapter specifies how the study will proceed methodologically and explicates the choice of cases of EU instruments to be scrutinized in the empirical part of the work.

3.1 Evaluating Successes and Failures of External Democracy Promotion

3.1.1 Existing Approaches

There are almost as many methodological approaches and designs in assessing success, i.e. effectiveness and impact, of external democracy promotion as there are studies focusing on the issue (cf. Heller 2013). In general, one could distinguish between two major research branches, which appear to be of relevance: academically dominated approaches to effectiveness evaluation employing counterfactuals and/or comparisons against collective optimum, and a more practice oriented sphere of democracy assistance evaluation. In the following an overview of methodological designs and research strategies employed in these two branches is provided.

Evaluating Effectiveness: Academically Dominated Approaches

Scholars evaluating external democratization efforts of international actors argue that a precise definition of *effectiveness* is crucial for its measurement. Richter (2009: 50), for example, suggests that democracy promotion tools can be effective to the extent that they perform a particular function and thus achieve their objectives or solve the problem they were established to address. This definition of effectiveness, in fact, contains two different foci: *goal achievement* and *problem solving.* In these terms, effectiveness is clearly differentiated from the notion of *efficiency,* which rather focuses on the correlation between the sources used (costs incurred) and the achieved results. Moreover, the concept of effectiveness does not account for possible side-effects and thus ignores broader consequences, which distinguishes it from a more comprehensive concept of *impact* (cf. Underdal 2004: 27; Richter 2009: 50; Heller 2013: 200-201).

With regard to the above definition of effectiveness, a specific instrument may well achieve the purposes for which it was officially employed. Yet, the originally set goals might not fully correspond to the actual problem, which thus remains unresolved although the official objectives are met. Hence, effectiveness of democratization tools can be measured based on the extent to which their stated goals are achieved, and/or with regard to the degree to which the tools address and resolve the actual problem that prompted their application (cf. Levy et al. 1995: 291; Underdal 2004: 27-28).

The goal oriented approach implies presence of clearly stated or identifiable purposes, for which the evaluated tool-set is employed. The problem oriented approach requires an extensive background research of the problem and a system of analysis to establish a plausible fit between the tools under study and the process of problem solving.

Methodologically, evaluation of effectiveness of a tool means comparing its performance against a certain point of reference or standard (cf. Underdal 2004: 31; Heller 2013: 202). This standard must be precise and generally applicable, i.e. it must (1) *"define a point or trajectory against which actual performance can (easily) be compared"* and (2) *"provide a common metric of measurement that can be applied across a wide range of cases"* (Underdal 2004: 35).

In search for such a point of reference, academically dominated studies of effectiveness commonly rely on either *counterfactuals*, i.e. a hypothetical state of affairs that would have come about in the absence of the evaluated tool or intervention, or a concept of *collective optimum*, i.e. a normatively agreed upon 'ideal', 'optimal' solution, against which the actual state of affairs is examined (Underdal 1992: 231). Some scholars seek to combine these two approaches to gain a broader or more robust evaluation strategy (e.g. Helm and Sprinz 2000).

Although such research strategies prove to be convincing for effectiveness evaluation, they lack general applicability and have certain limitations. First, they depend on the existence of a *'well-validated theory'*, providing plausible explanatory mechanisms for drawing causal inferences (George and Bennett 2005: 168). Second, analyses based on counterfactuals and on comparisons against collective optimum require availability of reliable data, especially if they are pursued using quantitative methods and are not complimented by qualitative approaches, e.g. process-tracing (cf. Helm and Sprinz 2000: 634). Finally, counterfactual analysis, or thought experiment that attempts to reconstruct the possible state of affairs by changing only one relevant aspect and keeping all the others constant, is useful only for the research of less complex cases with a limited number of variables and only if this research can draw upon the previously elaborated germane theoretical explanations, general principles, laws, regularities and knowledge of historical facts pertinent to the counterfactual scenario (Fearon 1991: 176; George and Bennett 2005: 168-169).

Evaluating Effectiveness and Impact: Practice Oriented Studies

Another sphere of research relevant to the current analysis originates from attempts of various development agencies to assess performance of their democracy and governance assistance programmes in practice. Empirical evaluation studies created within this field aim either at control for success of the accomplished programmes and projects, or at a more extensive assessment of the assistance impact at the national level (Crawford 2003a: 78). The first category of studies conventionally draws on the so called *Logical Framework Analysis* (LFA/Logframe) or related result-oriented approaches (e.g. *Result-Based Management/RBM* or *Managing for Results/MFR*) and evaluates the performance of democratization programmes and projects against their own specific objectives. The country impact studies are broader in nature and attempt to analyse the contribution of the external democracy assistance to the general processes of democratic change in a particular country or region. As the latter evaluations focus on broader consequences and allow for possible side effects, including negative ones, they go beyond an assessment of effectiveness.[12] Both research strategies applied for impact and effectiveness evaluation are considered here, as they can provide valuable reflections for the choice of own methodology and the subsequent analysis.

The Logframe and the other result-oriented approaches have been widely adopted by major development agencies, including USAID, CIDA, GIZ, DANIDA, SIDA, as well as the World Bank and the European Commission.[13] Methodologically, such studies have the following points in common: concentration on the micro-political (project) level, reliance on quantitatively measurable empirical indicators related to specific project objectives, and inference of causal links between *inputs* (project activities), *outputs* (immediate project results), *outcomes* (achievements at a sectoral level), and finally *impacts* (contributions at the national level) (Crawford and Kearton 2001; cf. Crawford 2003a: 79; Richter 2009: 49).

---

[12] As it has been stated above, the concept of effectiveness does not account for the possible side effects and thus ignores broader consequences (Underdal 2004: 27).

[13] A review of the methodologies of these agencies is provided e.g. by Crawford and Kearton 2001.

The LFA and the related approaches have, however, come under severe criticism by academics for their narrow scope of analysis *"insufficiently grounded in the complexities and the nuances of the political context"* (Crawford 2003a: 78), use of *'highly reductionist'* quantitative indicators (Carothers 1999: 291), and failure to provide plausible causal links between specific projects (micro-level) and the overall process of political change (macro-level), with such linkages being assumed rather than proven (cf. Cracknell 2000: 116; Schmitter and Brouwer 1999: Section IV, 3). As Carothers argues, *"informational bits as criteria of success without grounding them in sophisticated, deep-reaching analysis of the political context produces superficial and dangerously misleading pictures"* (Carothers 1999: 291).

Interestingly, some donor organizations, including the European Commission, have recognised the shortcomings of Logframe and result-oriented evaluations that rely on 'hard' data and lack of provision for long-term goals and potential negative side-effects (e.g. European Commission 1999: 15). This has resulted in a search for alternative approaches that would allow an assessment of the overall influence of democracy assistance on political changes at the sectoral (meso-) or country (macro-)level. Such broader impact evaluations have been employed by a number of development agencies (e.g. the European Commission, USAID, and DANIDA) in parallel to their result-oriented assessments. The impact studies attempt to aggregate findings at the micro- and/or meso-level of analysis without limiting investigations to pre-established project objectives and evaluate impacts with regard to the overall process of democratization in the countries under study. Such an approach requires substantial background information about the changing political situation in these countries and relies to a large extent on qualitative political context studies and process-tracing (Crawford 2003a: 86-95).

An example of an impact study particularly relevant for this research is the European Commission's *'Evaluation of PHARE and TACIS Democracy Programme 1992-1997'* (European Commission 1997). The study uses a mixed method design, relying on both qualitative and quantitative data. For the qualitative assessment of the programme's short- and long-term impact, the evaluators employ seven key criteria: relevance of the programme; consistency of individual projects with the guidelines of the programme; efficiency; adequacy of operational procedures; impact of the programme on individuals, groups, networks and politics; visibility of the projects, programme and the EU; replicability and sustainability of the projects. Yet, in an attempt to evaluate the overall political impact of the PHARE and TACIS Democracy Programme, the study draws conclusions solely with regard to the growth of the NGO sector in the target countries (indirect democratization impact). And even here it provides rather limited country background information and only cursorily addresses possible interfering effects of the other international actors. These shortcomings are acknowledged by the authors of the evaluation report themselves (European Commission 1997: 15 and 56) and by other external experts (e.g. Crawford 2002: 919).

Impact evaluations provide an important starting point for the current research. However, they also cannot satisfactorily resolve inherent methodological challenges, particularly the problem of *causality*, again rather assuming than proving linkages between the micro-, meso- and macro-levels, and the problem of *attribution*, i.e. singling out the effects of assistance of one donor from the results of the efforts of the other actors (Schmitter and Brouwer 1999: Section IV, 3; Crawford 2003a: 78, 87-94). As these challenges appear to be common for all effectiveness and impact evaluation studies, including theoretically oriented ones, it is necessary to review them in more detail.

3.1.2 Methodological Challenges in the Context of the Current Study

In the following, the key factors contributing to the major methodological challenges (causality and attribution) for the studies aiming at effectiveness and impact evaluation of external democracy promotion are summarized. In view of these challenges, applicability of existing approaches to the current research is examined.

First, the multiplicity of external actors in the democratization sphere, possible similarity of their democracy promotion agendas, and interrelationships between them make it difficult to distinguish the contribution of each actor in particular (cf. Burnell 2007: 8). Moreover, the efforts of external actors often interact with internal forces, some enabling and other undermining democracy processes, and therefore a plausible assessment of what would have happened in the absence of external involvement is difficult to make and requires a certain *'act of faith'* (Schmitter and Brouwer 1999: Section IV, 3; Crawford 2003a: 87-88; Richter 2009: 47-48).

Second, there is no consensus among scholars regarding the conception of what elements constitute successful democratization, nor is there a *'clear and legally binding understanding about the ideal design of democracy'*

(Heller 2013: 202). This results in the absence of widely accepted measurement criteria for the evaluation of democracy promotion efforts (Burnell 2007: 7; Richter 2009: 47).

Third, democratization is a long-term process. The effects of democracy promotion usually cannot be observed immediately (especially at the macro-political level), and thus might not be measurable at a certain time point. At the same time, the longer the process, the more intervening factors at play, which again contributes to the problem of attribution (Levy et al. 1995: 293; Young 2001: 117; Richter 2009: 47).

Finally, there might be unintended side-effects (both positive and negative), resulting from external democratization efforts. Such effects are deliberately left out of the scope of goal-oriented effectiveness evaluations (Underdal 2004: 27). Yet, they may be very difficult to capture even within the studies accounting for overall political context, as side-effects may result from democracy promotion activities indirectly (Crawford 2003a: 88; Richter 2009: 48).

The identified challenges for effectiveness and impact evaluation become even more apparent, when applying the described methodological approaches to the research of the EU democratization efforts in Central Asia. The European Union is a 'new-comer' here. It is neither the only, nor the main actor pushing for democracy and human rights in the region. The Organization for Security and Co-operation in Europe (OSCE) and the USA pursue similar democratization agendas. Moreover, the activities of the OSCE are interrelated with those of the European Commission in the Central Asian countries.[14] The UN agencies are also actively involved in human rights promotion and monitoring in the region. This makes the problem of attribution of specific democratization effects to the EU engagement difficult to sort out.

Furthermore, as it has been noted above, evaluating effectiveness of certain tools implies presence of clearly stated goals or at least identifiable purposes, for which the tools were introduced. However, democratization related goals and objectives declared by the EU for Central Asia are vague, with almost no specific benchmarks stated. This is especially true with re-

---

[14] The institutions do not only declare the same (or very similar) democracy related priorities, they cooperate closely on the ground and work on common programmes and projects. For example, joint programmes of the European Commission and the OSCE ODIHR were launched in Central Asia in 2005 and in 2007 (see Annex IV; OSCE Office for Democratic Institutions and Human Rights 2006: 84).

spect to the EU dialogue-based instruments.[15] Although more clear-cut objectives are set for democracy assistance (i.e. democratic empowerment tools) at the micro- and meso-levels, an assessment of specific project and programme outputs allows inferences about the overall contribution of the EU to the processes of political change at the national or regional level only if this is supported by a strong theoretically derived assumptive argument.

Concerning the applicability of the above academically dominated methodological approaches, the complexity and heterogeneity of the Central Asian cases, the large number of intervening variables, and the absence of previously elaborated germane theoretical explanations for the processes of democratization in the region make the use of counterfactuals and comparisons against collective optimum rather unpromising for the evaluation of EU democracy promotion tools in Central Asia.

Based on this summary of the methodological and theoretical challenges outlaid in the previous sections, there appears to be no 'easy' solution or 'the right' theoretical approach in existence for investigating external democratization in general, and especially with respect to the EU in Central Asia. Each study aiming at effectiveness or impact assessment is challenged by the problems of causality and attribution and needs to elaborate its own design based on the case complexity, germane variables, existence of previously developed explanatory theoretical approaches relevant to the field, and empirical data availability.

3.1.3 Opting for a Distinct Research Strategy

Taking account of the above discussion, this section attempts to elaborate a research strategy that allows a systematic evaluation of EU democracy promotion efforts in Central Asia. For this purpose, it is suggested to refer to the typology of EU instruments proposed in chapter 2. The typology distinguishes between three categories of tools: conditionality-based (relying on incentives and sanctions), dialogue-based (drawing on normative suasion),

---

[15] Thus, a fact sheet on 'EU Human Rights Dialogues in Central Asia' describes the aims of the dialogues as follows: to *"discuss questions of mutual interest and enhance cooperation on human rights, inter alia in multilateral arena such as the United Nations and the OSCE,"* as well as to *"raise the concerns felt by the EU on human rights in the countries concerned, gather information and launch initiatives to improve the relevant human rights situation"* (Council of the European Union n/a: 1). Apart from these very general aims, no public EU document contains more specific objectives or benchmarks that would enable evaluation of effectiveness of the human rights dialogues.

and democratic empowerment (institution- and capacity-building programmes). This differentiation rests not only on the distinct underlying logics of (or mechanisms behind) these groups of tools. It also assumes that—although all three instrument types are applied with an intention to democratize the targets—their applications aim at different kinds of change. Thus, incentives and sanctions are expected to make the targets alter their behaviour in the short run to comply with certain norms or rules; dialogue seeks to change attitudes and thus the long-term behaviour of the targets by influencing their belief systems; and finally democratic empowerment programmes aim at increasing target actors' capacities that are likely to contribute to the democratization process.

To assess whether EU democracy promotion has been at least partly successful in the context of Central Asia, and if so, to what extent, this study proposes to evaluate success in terms of the achievement of changes expected to occur as the result of EU tools' applications. To use an example of the conditionality-based instruments, the success of the EU coercive measures would imply that, as the consequence of their implementation, the targets' behaviours are changed and adapted to the European demands. Accordingly, the absence of the expected changes in the targets' behaviours following the instruments' applications would signify a failure of the EU's efforts. Another outcome of the EU engagement could be that only some aspects of the expected change occur (e.g. not all demands of the EU are fulfilled). In this case, the EU would only partly succeed in its instrument application.[16]

Talking about a change occurring *as the result* or *consequence of* a certain tool's application, one again needs to be aware of the inherent challenges of causality and effect attribution. The current research strategy cannot fully exclude potential interference of other actors' influences or completely isolate effects of a particular EU instrument from the effects of another. Nevertheless, an attempt is made here to meet the challenges by concentrating on very specific EU demands, propositions and contents of assistance programmes and by tracing the processes of change step by step.

Another challenge this research faces is the identification of changes occurred. For the conditionality-based tools, identifying their success, partial

---

[16] A similar compliance-based approach is commonly used in studies examining effects of membership conditionality (e.g. Schimmelfennig, Engert and Knobel 2006) or international sanctions application (cf. Brzoska 2013: 145).

success or failure can be based on tracing observable short-term changes in the targets' behaviours.[17] For the dialogue-based tools, the expected changes cannot be directly observed, since the instruments aim at internalization of promoted values by the targets and their long-term, *'sustained'* behaviour alterations (cf. Checkel 2005: 804; Warkotsch 2009: 252). Given that the EU is a relative newcomer in Central Asia, the latter process cannot be traced down in the long run.[18] Whereas the former (internalization of values) is regarded as intangible and can hardly be measured. Previous studies examining international norm transfer (e.g. Risse, Ropp and Sikkink 1999) faced a similar challenge in operationalizing effects of normative suasion (Wetzel 2013: 182). One way to deal with this challenge is to trace effects of persuasion based on changes in the targets' observable behaviour while controlling for the possibility of a short-term strategic adaptation (cf. Checkel 2001). Hence, in order to be able to evaluate performance of EU dialogue-based tools in Central Asia, it is suggested to use a launch of relevant long-term initiatives and reforms that are proposed by the targets within the framework of a particular dialogue platform as an indication of the tools' success. What is decisive here is that the initiatives originate from the targets themselves without prior EU demands or conditionality pressures. This allows distinguishing effects of the dialogue from the consequences of the other tools, e.g. EU restrictive measures.

Finally, for the democratic empowerment tools, success also has a different implication, as the tools aim not at a short- or a long-term behaviour alteration but at a change (strengthening) of the targets' democratic capacities. This change also cannot be directly observed (cf. European Commission 1997: 15). Still, one can assess whether the capacities were altered (strengthened or weakened) through indirect indicators if the notion of capacity is defined in operational terms, i.e. as the ability of actors to carry out their work according to certain standards. However, before the democratic capacities of programme beneficiaries can be improved, the assistance needs to be accepted by the target countries' governments. The acceptance of external democracy and human rights related support cannot be taken for granted in authoritarian regimes, as ruling elites would suppos-

---

[17] An example of such observable short-term behavior change could be an adoption of measures upon which provision of aid or withdrawal of sanctions was previously made conditional by the European Union.

[18] Some dialogue formats that are of particular relevance for the current analysis (e.g. the structured Human Rights Dialogues) were launched only after the adoption of the *'EU-Central Asia: Strategy for a New Partnership'* in 2007.

edly reject capacity-building programmes aiming at political liberalization which threatens their powers. In fact, authoritarian elites should work against liberalization seeking to eliminate a direct foreign assistance to civil society organizations and human rights activists critical of the government (Carothers 2009: 10). Hence, merely the acceptance of external democratic empowerment programmes by non-democratic states (or their governments) could be regarded as a sign of opening and a success in itself. Thus, this research examines the delivery process of EU capacity-building programmes and uses the ability to implement these programmes (without experiencing constraints on the part of the target countries' governments) as an indication of success of democratic empowerment tools.

Table 3.1 summarizes the above indicators of success, partial success and failure of EU application of democratization tools. These indicators will be used for evaluation in the empirical part of this study.

Table 3.1: Indicators of Possible Outcomes of the EU Democratization Tools Application

	Success	Partial success	Failure
Conditionality-based tools	EU demands fulfilled by the targets	EU demands only partly fulfilled by the targets	EU demands not fulfilled by the targets
Dialogue-based tools	Long-term initiatives / reforms launched by the targets in the spheres covered by the dialogue process	Relevant long-term initiatives / reforms launched by the targets only in some spheres, while absent in the others	No relevant initiatives launched by the targets
Democratic empowerment tools	Assistance / capacity-building programmes could be fully implemented	Assistance / capacity-building programmes could be implemented only to some extent	Assistance / capacity-building programmes could not be implemented

3.2 Explaining Successes and Failures of External Democracy Promotion

3.2.1 What Factors Matter?

With regard to the second research question of the current study—what makes EU democracy promotion more or less successful in such regions as Central Asia—a review of the literature reveals a range of relevant factors that can generally affect performance of external democratization tools. Following the strategic calculation logic, Smith suggests that policies of conditionality can be quite effective[19] if the targets want the benefits on offer or fear losing them (Smith 2005: 24). Hence, successful implementation of these policies critically depends on the value attached to the potential benefits by the target states (and groups within the states). As target actors are assumed to be power oriented utility maximizers within the rationalist framework, they will conform to norms of external democratizers, only if compliance increases their political utility and if costs of norm adaptation are smaller than external rewards or costs of external sanctions (Warkotsch 2009: 252). In this regard, characteristics of external actors and their perceptions by the targets are crucial. If a democratizer is not seen by a target government as a strong external power able to provide real benefits or impose punishments, the possibility to apply conditionality is drastically diminished (cf. Smith 1997).

The power of external actors is determined in terms of their economic, political and/or military resources available for usage in the particular democratization case, and also by the significance of bilateral partner relations between the targets and the external actors (Reiber 2009: 220). Here, certain characteristics of the targets themselves, e.g. the availability of their own resources, the degree of the targets' dependence on external resources provided by democratizers, and the ability of targets to compensate these resources in case of being sanctioned, are of particular importance (Stokke 1995: 44). With regard to the latter, the existence of alternative offers from third actors, who are ready to provide comparable benefits to the targets without insisting on democratic norm compliance, must be accounted for. The availability of such alternative options to the target states may bring potential success of EU conditionality close to zero (cf. Kubicek 2003: 18; Reiber 2009: 220).

---

[19] Here, *effective* and *successful* are used interchangeably, in order to improve readability of the text.

Apart from that, there are some general implementation- or process-related factors (i.e. the way conditionality is applied) that must be taken under consideration. First of all, the use of incentives and sanctions can only be effective if they are credible, which implies a consistent way of the measures application (Schimmelfennig 2003: 413-414). If a democratizer fails to pursue a coherent and responsive conditionality strategy, its success will be minimized. The consistency in applying conditionality in turn can be influenced by the existence of competing issues on the external actor's foreign policy agenda. Thus, in the countries where economic or security interests of the EU or its Member States are at stake, the Union will hardly be able *"to maintain a consensus behind demands for political reform, thereby limiting the effectiveness of those demands"* (Levitsky and Way 2005: 21).

Regarding democracy promotion through dialogue based on normative suasion, success critically depends on the proximity (or compatibility) of values promoted by external actors with those of the targets (Checkel 2005: 813). The targets will commit to European values more readily if they can identify themselves with these values at least to some extent, or in other words, if the promoted values resonate with the targets' ones (cf. Payne 2001; Reiber 2009: 222).

Another crucial factor for the effectiveness of the dialogue-based instruments is the legitimacy of the democratizing actor and the promoted norms as perceived by socializees (cf. Gawrich 2006: 28). The central question here is whether the EU is seen as a moral authority and the promoted norms and values as a pattern to follow. The acceptance of the EU as a legitimate normative actor and moral authority is manifested through its ability to maintain open discussions addressing democratization issues with the target states (cf. Checkel 2005: 812-813; Warkotsch 2009: 252).

It is likely that EU-endorsed values will not be considered equally legitimate by all domestic groups (cf. Coppieters, et al. 2004: 14). Thus, in authoritarian states external democratization initiatives are commonly accepted as legitimate and welcome by pro-democratic opposition members and civil society representatives, but may be rejected by the existing governments (cf. Carothers 2009: 10). In these cases, the presence of pro-democratic domestic actors in the target countries could enhance broader acceptance of external (democratic) values and norms.

A broader acceptance of the EU's values and principles among the domestic groups also supposes not lecturing and demanding on the part of the

EU, but rather following those principles in practice and engaging in a deliberative argument with the socializees in *'in-camera'*, peer-to-peer settings (Checkel 2005: 813; Warkotsch 2009: 253). Here again, "*[t]he consistency of the messages conveyed by the different institutional structures of the EU will [...] affect the credibility of the EU's line, and how favorably it is received by local players*" (Coppieters, et al. 2004: 14).

Finally, as normative suasion is a long-term process based on interaction, the success of socialization will depend to a large extent on the density and the timeframe of institutional ties and contacts between the European Union and the target states (Warkotsch 2009: 253).

With regard to democratic empowerment, application of this instrument type implies the ability of external actors to provide relevant resources and expertise, for example financial support to democratic institution-building programmes. At the same time, there should be a demand for these programmes on the part of the recipients (Reiber 2009: 221-222). Here again, one needs to differentiate between governments and civil society organizations (CSOs) as beneficiaries of external democratization support. While pro-democratic CSO representatives will expectedly welcome external assistance that could strengthen their positions, authoritarian government members seeking to retain their power will be cautious of democratization-related programmes, as such programmes can challenge the existing power distribution (cf. Carothers 2009: 10; Warkotsch 2009: 264-265). The governments may express a greater interest in EU assistance, if they are aware of and can co-determine the flow and the contents of the assistance, in order to prevent damage to their power. Hence, such process-related factors as transparency of external assistance delivery vis-à-vis target governments and programme ownership can also affect programme implementation.

To sum up, there is an array of factors that can influence the process and outcome of external democratization. Drawing on the reviewed literature, a list of what Checkel (2005) and Warkotsch (2009) call *'scope conditions'* (or favourable factors) for successful democracy promotion may be generated (cf. also Reiber 2009). Table 3.2 summarizes scope conditions for the present analytical framework, distinguishing them along target-related, democratizer-related and process-related dimensions. This is not to suggest that each of the listed factors constitutes a necessary (and by no means sufficient) condition for success. Rather, based on the reviewed scholarly findings, it is assumed that, when present, these factors increase the likelihood of the application of democratization tools to be successful.

Table 3.2: Scope Conditions or Favourable Factors for Success of External Democratization Tools

	Democratizer-related	Target-related	Process-related
Conditionality-based tools	Ability to provide (meaningful) incentives and impose sanctions	Lack of own resources / dependency on external resources → Lack of alternative offers from external non-democratic actors	Credibility of measures application → consistent application → absence of competing interests on the foreign policy agenda
Dialogue-based tools	Legitimacy / moral authority → Ability to maintain dialogue on democratization-related issues	Compatibility of values and norms → Presence of pro-democratic domestic actors	Clear and consistent messages Deliberative, equality-based approach In-camera setting Length and intensity of institutional contacts
Democratic empowerment	Ability to provide relevant resources and/or expertise	Demand for the assistance (on the part of government and civil society)	Transparency of assistance delivery / joint ownership of assistance programmes

3.2.2 The EU Engagement in Central Asia: Main Assumptions

Now as the factors potentially influencing the outcome of external democratization efforts and scope conditions for success of each instrument type have been discussed, the next step is to assess whether they are relevant for explaining the results of EU democracy and human rights promotion in the Central Asian context. In order to do this, it first needs to be examined to what extent the above favourable factors are present in Kyrgyzstan and Uzbekistan, the two countries under study. The absence of these factors in the two country-cases would point at possible explanations for failure of EU democracy promotion efforts prior to investigation of the efforts themselves. The subsequent examination takes account only of democratizer- and target-related factors, as they constitute general external and domestic conditions for democratization. An analysis of process-related factors (or to what extent the process-related scope conditions are met in the case of EU democracy promotion in Central Asia) requires a detailed scrutiny of the implementation of each particular tool and is carried out in the empirical part of the work as part of case studies.

Conditionality-based tools

With regard to the democratizer-related factors for successful democracy promotion through conditionality, the EU cannot offer its strongest incentive of potential accession to the target states in Central Asia. Nor does the EU include the region into the closer cooperation framework under the European Neighbourhood Policy. Nevertheless, the Union has a set of other 'carrots' and 'sticks' that can be applied to the Central Asian states, such as developing (or ceasing) trade relations and providing (or withholding) economic assistance.

In applying political conditionality, the EU can draw on bilateral Partnership and Cooperation Agreements (PCAs) that were signed with Kyrgyzstan and Uzbekistan in the mid-1990s and constitute the legal basis for the relations between the Union and the Central Asian states. The texts of the agreements are almost identical and include respect for democracy and human rights as their *'essential element'* (cf. European Communities, their Member States and Kyrgyz Republic 1999: Art. 2; European Communities, their Member States and Republic of Uzbekistan 1999: Art. 2). This theoretically enables the EU to make implementation of the PCAs conditional on the compliance with the democratic and human rights standards. Thus, in the case of a violation of human rights and democratic principles by the governments of the Central Asian states, the PCAs could be (at least partially) suspended by the European Union as a sanctioning or coercive measure with a view to compel the target governments to adhere to the above principles. Such measures could affect both the political dialogue and trade relations between the EU and the target countries.

Another sanctioning measure of the EU could be a suspension of the development aid provided to the governments of the target states. The EU financial and technical assistance delivered to Central Asia is shaped by the

European Commission's Regional Strategy Papers that regulate funds allocation and distribution. According to the Commission's intent to mainstream *"human rights and democratisation issues into all aspects of EU policy decision-making and implementation, including external assistance"* (European Commission 2007e: 13), the Regional Strategy Papers should include an assessment of the situation regarding human rights and democratic development in the aid-receiving countries. The assessment results should in turn inform assistance strategy (European Commission 2008). Thus, the financial and technical support granted by the EU to the Central Asian states could be made conditional on their democratic and human rights progress.

In the 1990s through early 2000s, the EU provided bilateral and regional assistance to Central Asia through the Technical Aid Programme to the Commonwealth of Independent States (TACIS). Yet, the funding allocated though this programme to the region was very limited. The annual per capita support between 1995 and 2002 was around €4 on average (Emerson 2004: 43). In 2007, the TACIS was replaced by the EU's Development Cooperation Instrument (DCI) and the overall funding was increased. Over 2007-2010, the annual DCI assistance to Kyrgyzstan constituted €13.75 million and to Uzbekistan €8.2 million, while regional programmes for the whole of Central Asia were allocated €23.55 million annually (European Commission 2007a: 4-5). However, these amounts still appear to be inadequate when compared to the region's needs and EU assistance to its closer neighbourhood (Warkotsch 2009: 257).

In order to assess whether EU aid and trade associated incentives (and potential sanctions) are sufficient to shift Kyrgyz and Uzbek governments' cost-benefit calculations in favour of political change, it is necessary to examine to what extent the target-related conditions for success of conditionality-based tools are met in these countries.

The countries' domestic conditions vary in terms of their socio-economic development and resource availabilities. Along with Tajikistan, Kyrgyzstan is one of the poorest Central Asian republics with no hydrocarbon reserves that could help grow the economy.[20] The lack of industrial capacity and misfortunate economic reforms of the 1990s made the country highly dependent on foreign aid, including from the EU and its Member States (Anderson 1999: 79-83; Emerson et al. 2010: 16-22). Uzbekistan performs better in

---

[20] The country has some reserves of gold. Yet, its current production and export are not enough to significantly contribute to the economic growth (Tynan 2011a).

this regard. It is the world's sixth largest producer of cotton (UNCTAD n/a) and one of the top gas-producing countries in the post-soviet area (Melvin 2000: 78-79; U.S. Energy Information Administration n/a). While the country is not free of internal economic pressures, it is still considerably less dependent on external resources than Kyrgyzstan (Kassenova 2011: 52-59). This suggests that Bishkek would be more receptive to EU aid-related conditionality than Tashkent.

However, both countries have alternatives to the resources provided by the European Union from actors that do not pursue a democratization or human rights agenda. Particularly, Russia and China are important in these terms. Both Bishkek and (to a lesser extent) Tashkent are oriented towards Russia in their foreign relations, resulting from their historical political and economic ties to Moscow. While Kyrgyzstan continues receiving Russian economic aid, Uzbekistan is still dependent on the Russian pipelines for its natural gas exports (cf. Jackson 2010: 108-109; Urdze 2010: 216-219). In recent years, China has also established itself as an important investor and development assistance provider in Central Asia (Kassenova 2009).

Moreover, Russia and China are among the key trade partners and importers of resources from Uzbekistan (gold, cotton and gas) and Kyrgyzstan (gold and cotton). Table 3.3 below specifies the place and rank of the two regional actors and the EU in the external trade relations of the two Central Asian states.

Table 3.3: The Place of Russia, China, and the EU in Kyrgyzstan's and Uzbekistan's Imports, Exports and Total Trade in 2008 and Their Rank

	Imports	Exports	Total
Kyrgyzstan	China: 70,5% (1st) Russia: 13,9% (2nd) EU: 4,1% (3rd)	Russia: 29,6% (1st) China: 7,6% (5th) EU: 2,5% (8th)	China: 62,3% (1st) Russia: 15,9% (2nd) EU: 3,9% (4th)
Uzbekistan	Russia 27,6% (1st) EU: 17,9% (2nd) China: 16, 3% (3rd)	Russia: 25,3% (1st) EU: 11% (2nd) China: 6,1% (6th)	Russia: 26,7% (1st) EU: 15,2% (2nd) China: 12,2% (3rd)

Source: Emerson et al. 2010: 26.

The above numbers demonstrate the leading positions of Russia and China in imports and exports of Kyrgyzstan, while the EU lags behind. For Uzbekistan, the EU is one of the main trade partners. However, here Russia also clearly dominates trade relations.

To sum-up, although the instruments available to the EU—development aid and trade—have a value in themselves, one needs to consider how interested Central Asian elites really are in the limited European incentives (or fear European sanctions) given the alternative offers from other external players that are geographically and politically closer to the region and do not impose political preconditions for cooperation comparable to those of the EU. In view of the alternative opportunities provided by external non-democratic actors, the EU falls short of strong incentives and sanctions to promote democratization through conditionality in the Central Asian states.

Dialogue-based tools

The democratizer-related scope conditions for successful democracy promotion through dialogue include the legitimacy and moral authority of external actors manifested through their ability to maintain open democratization-related discussions with the targets (see Table 3.2). As demonstrated in chapter 2, the EU has clearly positioned itself as a value-based community and an actor willing to export its democratic and human rights norms to third countries. In its international affairs the Union has developed a variety of dialogue instruments. In Central Asia, the EU's normative suasion tool-kit relies mainly on interregional and bilateral political dialogue. Prior to 2007, the platform for this dialogue was provided solely through the Partnership and Cooperation Agreements that foresaw annual meetings at the ministerial level within the Cooperation Council, at the senior civil servant level within the Cooperation Committee, and at the parliamentary level within the Parliamentary Cooperation Committee framework (Art. 4-7). In the PCA with Kyrgyzstan, the goals and terms of the political dialogue are outlined rather vaguely: *"A regular political dialogue [...] shall support the political and economic changes underway [...] and contribute to the establishment of new forms of cooperation"* (European Communities, their Member States and Kyrgyz Republic 1999: Art. 4). While the Uzbek PCA stipulates that *"[t]he political dialogue [...] shall foresee that the parties endeavor to cooperate on matters pertaining to the observance of the principles of democracy, and the respect, protection and promotion of human rights [...] and shall hold consultations, if necessary, on relevant matters"* (European Communities, their Member States and Republic of Uzbekistan 1999: Art. 4).

In July 2005, a new post of European Union Special Representative (EUSR) for Central Asia was established, which was supposed to bring in a regional component in addition to the bilateral political dialogues. The duties of the EUSR include *inter alia* development of *"appropriate contacts and cooperation with the main interested actors in the region"* (Council of the European Union 2005b). Hence, the establishment of this post has enhanced the EU's capacity for dialogue not only with the governments of the Central Asian republics but also with other local stakeholders.

A further important step towards intensification and deepening of the dialogue was made with the adoption of the 2007 *'EU and Central Asia Strategy for a New Partnership'*. This document calls for a regular regional dialogue at the foreign minister level with the EU Troika and a bilateral human rights dialogue (HRD) with each of the Central Asian republics (Council of the European Union 2007c). The later format is particularly designed to *"discuss questions of mutual interest and enhance cooperation on human rights"* as well as to *"raise the concerns felt by the EU on human rights in the countries concerned, gather information and launch initiatives to improve the relevant human rights situation"* (European Commission 2009b: 1).

Apart from the human rights dialogue, the 'Strategy for a New Partnership' introduced another new instrument to EU democratization policy in Central Asia—a regional Rule of Law Initiative (RoLI). The initiative sought to include a three-level dialogue component: ministerial meetings intending to discuss and review policy developments in all Central Asian states and technical meetings on legal reform at regional and national levels (European Commission 2009c: 65).

The agreement of the Central Asian governments to participate in these dialogue formats, especially in the HRD and the RoLI, indicates their readiness to engage with the EU on matters of democratization and human rights. However, this does not mean that the governments (and the population) of the Central Asian countries accept democratic principles as a model to follow. Gleason, for instance, suggests that authoritarianism has become a political value and an ensconced social norm in Central Asia, which challenges legitimacy of the liberal democratic principles endorsed by the West (Gleason 2001). Warkotsch also argues that Central Asian socio-cultural idiosyncrasies drawing on historically developed personalistic and patrimonial-authoritarian patterns of political rule—especially apparent in Uzbekistan, but present in all countries of the region—stand in stark opposition to the democratic principles promoted by the EU. Being incompatible with European values, these patterns constitute one of the main impediments to external democratization efforts in Central Asia (Warkotsch 2008b: 66-68). Boonstra puts it even stronger: *"[D]emocracy is seen by the leaders of Central Asia as a direct threat to their existence"* and *"has a negative connotation among the general population in Central Asia because the concept is associated with the first decade of independence and thus linked to robber capitalism and uncertainty"* (Boonstra 2012: 2-3).

Finally, the legacy of the soviet period created difficult structural conditions for the development of democratic institutions, opposition movements and state-independent civil society in all Central Asian countries. Therefore, there is little existing internal support for democratic development. Nevertheless, there is a considerable difference between Kyrgyzstan and Uzbekistan in this regard. During the first half of the 1990s, the Kyrgyz president Askar Akaev chose a course toward political and economic liberalization of the country that went clearly beyond reforms of the other Central Asian republics (Zhovtis 2008: 21-22). Thus, Kyrgyzstan developed to a state with a relatively strong parliament, active opposition, to some extent independent mass media and a comparably open environment for civil society development (cf. Olcott 2005: 129-138; Hoffmann 2010: 91). At the later period, the country experienced a tightening of relations between the government on the one side and the opposition and non-governmental organizations on the other. However, the developments of the early 1990s have created a political culture that remained distinctly more liberal than in the rest of Central Asia (Emerson et al. 2010: 11-16). By contrast, Uzbekistan experienced only a very brief period of rather superficial pro-democratic reforms at the beginning of the 1990s, which was followed by a gradual consolidation of authoritarian rule, persecution of political opponents and establishment of control over media by state structures (Roy 2000: 132-134; Zhovtis 2008: 22). Furthermore, after 2003 the country went through a period of *'civil society counter-revolution'* that started in response to the 'coloured revolutions' in Georgia, Ukraine and Kyrgyzstan with the adoption of severe restrictions on NGO activities and resulted in *"the creation of a state-sponsored association of non-government, non-profit organizations"* (Buxton 2009: 46; cf.

Ilkhamov 2005). These measures have left little room for pro-democratic civil society and opposition movements in Uzbekistan.

Considering the democratizer- and the target-related conditions for success of the dialogue-based tools (Table 3.2), the EU's potential for successful democracy promotion through normative suasion is certainly limited in Central Asia. Although it has been possible to establish a number of dialogue platforms addressing democratization issues, European democratic and human rights values hardly serve as a point of reference for Central Asian political elites or the general populations (cf. Eckert 1996: 32-33; Omelicheva 2011; Boonstra 2012: 2-3). Nevertheless, due to the different political developments in the recent history of the two countries under study, the EU seems to have somewhat better chances for successful normative suasion in Kyrgyzstan than in Uzbekistan.

Democratic empowerment tools

With regard to democratic empowerment tools, the EU has established itself as a provider of democracy assistance through financing of democratic institutions and capacity-building programmes in its closest neighbourhood and in sub-Saharan Africa (Youngs 2008: 162-164). Yet, other regions, including Central Asia, also receive a smaller version of the EU's democratization support (European Parliament 2010).

In line with the European Commission's goal to mainstream human rights and democratization in its foreign affairs, EU development cooperation with third countries shall include programmes aiming to strengthen democratic institutions, good governance and the rule of law, which can target either state structures or the non-governmental sector (European Commission 2007e: 13). Thus, between 2001 and 2007 the already mentioned TACIS incorporated the so called Institution Building and Partnership Programme (IBPP) engaging with civil society organizations with the purpose to enhance their capacities as part of the post-soviet transformation process. During this period, 43 projects were supported through the IBPP in Central Asia, with grants varying from €100,000 to €200,000 (Giffen, et al. 2007: 4). The current Development Cooperation Instrument that replaced TACIS in 2007 includes a Non-State Actors and Local Authorities in Development (NSA/LA) programme also providing support to civil society. However, here the focus is on economic development and combating poverty (European Commission 2006b).

The main EU tool providing financial support to civil society actors particularly engaged in issues of human rights and democratic development is the European Instrument for Democracy and Human Rights (EIDHR). What distinguishes the instrument is that it draws on a separate budget line, complimentary to the mainstream cooperation programmes, and is supposed to operate independently without a need for consent from the target countries' governments (European Commission 2001a: 15). Created in 1994 upon an initiative of the European Parliament,[21] the EIDHR has become operational in Central Asia in the early 2000s (European Commission 2004a: Annex I). The instrument's overall annual budget varies between €100-135 million (Youngs 2008: 162; Boonstra and Hale 2010: 6). However, the amount allocated to Central Asia is very limited. Over 2005-2011, a total of €9 million was granted to both regional and country-specific projects implemented in the region (Emerson, et al. 2010: 98).

Concerning the targets' demands for EU assistance as one of the scope conditions for success of the democratic empowerment tools (see Table 3.2), it is necessary to differentiate between civil society and government actors as beneficiaries of this assistance. From the beginning of the 1990s, the development of a formal state-independent civil society in Central Asia—especially in the form of NGOs—has been associated with foreign funding (Babajanian, Freizer and Stevens 2005: 211-212). Twenty years after the break-up of the soviet system, civil society organizations are still rarely self-sustainable and their survival to a large extent depends on donor project support (cf. Ilkhamov 2005: 303; Abdusalyamova and Warren 2007: 24). The organizations working in the sphere of human rights and democratization are in a particularly difficult situation, as their operation is often constrained by state authorities, including the restriction of their financial opportunities. This provides for a continuous demand on the part of Central Asian pro-democratic NGOs for external assistance, also from the European Union. On the part of the governments, the need for external support of the democratic institution-building was more evident in the early 1990s, during their transformation following the collapse of the soviet regime. However, the governments currently demonstrate interest in economic assistance, security- and infrastructure-related programmes, especially those that could help maintain their regime stability (Warkotsch 2009: 256). At the same time, it must be noted that the Kyrgyz authorities have become more open

---

[21] At that time the instrument was named European *Initiative* for Democracy and Human Rights (Herrero 2009: 21).

to external democratic support after the coup of April 2010. This has been particularly demonstrated by Kyrgyzstan's requests for European expertise when the new state constitution was drafted in 2010 (Council of Europe 2010).

Thus, in view of the above scope conditions for success of democratic empowerment tools along the target- and democratizer-related dimensions (Table 3.2), the EU's potential to successfully promote democracy in the Central Asian states is again rather limited. While the Union has established a number of instruments and programmes to assist democratic institution-building, the funding provided to these programmes in Central Asia is hardly significant. Concerning the targets' demand for the assistance, it is clearly present on the part of the pro-democratic civil society, while very limited (or even absent) on the part of the governments. With regard to the latter, Kyrgyzstan still seems to be more receptive to EU democratic support than Uzbekistan.

Summarizing the above analysis, one should note the relative variance in domestic conditions in the two countries under study with somewhat better prospects for successful democracy and human rights promotion in Kyrgyzstan than in Uzbekistan. Yet, in general both countries do not provide a favourable environment for external democratization efforts. Simultaneously, the EU's strategic incentives, perceived moral authority and democratic assistance funding are limited. By looking at the target- and democratizer-related scope conditions for successful application of EU democratization tools, one can see that they are largely not present in the Central Asian context. The target- and democratizer-related factors revealed in section 3.2.1 can thus point at explanations for the failure of EU democracy and human rights promotion in Central Asia, especially in Uzbekistan. However, they cannot account for a relative success of the EU democratization policy, if it actually does have positive effects, for example at micro-level, bringing about certain changes in the targets' behaviour and attitudes towards democracy. Therefore, further factors potentially contributing to a more successful democracy promotion under challenging conditions are examined next.

Key hypothesis

A review of the recent literature specifically dedicated to external democracy promotion in Central Asia helps identifying such factors. Warkotsch, for instance, assumes that certain (micro-level) changes as part of a broader democratization process can be achieved in difficult environments by shifting the emphasis to promoting norms that do not directly challenge the target regimes' political survival (Warkotsch 2008b: 69). The main assumption is that in countries with unfavourable domestic and external conditions for democratization a relative success of external democracy and human rights promotion largely depends on what exactly is promoted, i.e. on the substance of promoted norms and changes.

In line with the strategic calculation logic, the targets' adaptation to the promoted norms can happen as the result of the application of conditionality-based tools only if political costs of the adaptation are low. To put it differently, pulled by incentives or pushed by sanctions, target elites in an authoritarian state will be more likely to comply with the demands of external actors, if the compliance does not endanger their power position. On the contrary, insistence on sweeping changes that directly aim at breaking up an authoritarian system will confront the interest of the target elites to preserve their authority and therefore will face strong resistance.

Along this line of argument, Golovko suggests a differentiation between *'politically sensitive'* and *'politically neutral'* externally promoted reforms, i.e. those that potentially threaten the target regime unchangeability and those that *"do not endanger political and economic power"* of the ruling elites (Golovko 2010: 107). According to the scholar, while politically sensitive reforms should be rejected by the governments, politically neutral ones could be accepted and successfully implemented in Central Asia.

This reasoning goes along with the rationalist approach. Yet, the assumption that the substance of promoted norms matters for success of external democratization efforts does not contradict the normative suasion logic. For instance, even in target societies, where ingrained practices are generally considered incompatible with European norms, certain EU claims might resonate with the targets' believes and hence be perceived as legitimate. In these terms, promotion of party competition and separation of powers will hardly correspond to the values of traditionally patrimonial societies (cf. Gleason 2001). In contrast, effective governance standards including accountability in the sphere of public administration or provision of certain equality rights can be quite appealing to the targets as a point of reference or even a way to bolster their legitimacy (cf. Warkotsch 2008b: 69-70). Hence, it would be easier to convince authoritarian governments to adhere to the latter norms in the process of dialogue.

At the same time, it has been pointed out that the differentiation between the strategic calculation and normative suasion mechanisms is rather analytical than empirical (cf. Kelley 2004: 428). In practice both mechanisms often work simultaneously without excluding one another. While the normative suasion is assumed to be the foundation of dialogue-based tools, strategic calculation of costs and benefits is never completely absent, especially if the dialogue concerns authoritarian governments that are urged to ease their power grip. Being persuaded in the appropriateness of certain norms during a dialogue process, political actors will not automatically stop calculating the potential costs of reforms in introducing those norms. Therefore, the underlying argument of what constitutes politically sensitive changes also would hold for the case of the EU dialogue-based tools.

Finally, as external democratic assistance—both targeting civil society and state structures—is usually channelled through governments, its acceptance by the governing actors (and hence the EU's ability to apply its democratic empowerment tools successfully) is highly dependent on the elites' goodwill and consideration whether these programmes are of their interest. While some democratization related assistance programmes may be perceived by governing elites as contributing to the modernization of state structures and functioning, others may be seen as endangering the position of those in power. Drawing on Golovko's terminology, it is arguable that the more politically sensitive the norms in focus of these programmes, the more reluctance they will evoke on the part of the target countries' governments, and hence the less successful the EU will be in applying its democratic empowerment tools.

These assumptions provide a foundation for the key hypothesis to be tested in the present study:

> In the countries with unfavourable domestic and external conditions for democratization, the EU conditionality, dialogue and democratic empowerment tools are more likely to be successful, if these tools promote less politically sensitive norms and changes.
> And vice versa: The more politically sensitive the promoted norms and changes are, the more likely the application of the EU democratization tools will fail.

These assumptions may seem logically obvious. Moreover, the practical application of EU democratization policy towards non-EU member states is argued to be shifting towards de-politicization of external democratic and human rights assistance and adjusting to local circumstances (cf. Carothers 2009; Wetzel and Orbie 2011b). Thus, the scope and substance of EU democracy support is already being adapted at the implementation level in a way that would supposedly make it work better. However, official EU documents by no means provide a link between the substance of promoted norms and the successful application of EU instruments. In fact, they commonly place various aspects of promoting human rights (political, economic and cultural), principles of good governance, rule of law and electoral democracy into one 'basket' (see chapter 2; cf. Kurki 2012). Based on its strategic documents, the EU does not seem to differentiate between 'politically sensitive' and 'politically neutral' changes or express awareness of possible effects of the substance of the promoted norms on the outcomes of its policy. Finding empirical evidence in support of the above hypothesis would thus reveal a need to reform the EU strategy in a way that accounts for the substance of what exactly is promoted.

In practical terms, a question remains how to identify which specific norms and changes are politically sensitive and which are politically neutral. In authoritarian environments, it may be assumed that fostering the core principles of liberal democracy, such as political contestation guaranteed through free and fair elections, horizontal separation of powers, and political rights of participation (cf. Wetzel and Orbie 2011a) would be politically sensitive, as these norms and principles would directly challenge authoritarian rule. On the contrary, the focus on what Wetzel and Orbie (2011a) call *'supporting conditions'* or the *'context of democracy'* (e.g. social and economic requisites) would be more politically neutral, as these would not directly interfere with the existing power relations. At the same time, it is assumed here that what matters is not the variance in the actual substance of externally promoted norms, but the substance as perceived by the target governments. Certain systemic factors, such as the characteristics of target states, their power constellations and historical developments, can have an effect on what norms and changes are considered more or less politically sensitive. Thus, the same norms can be perceived as extremely politically sensitive by authoritarian governments with a high degree of power concentration, while seen as rather politically neutral by the governments that are historically more open to democratic reforms. This is where the difference between Uzbekistan's and Kyrgyzstan's political regimes might become even more apparent. Hence, the degree to which the promoted norms are perceived as politically sensitive (or neutral) in the two countries under study is determined inductively, by looking at each particular case in the empirical part of the work.

Finally, while examining whether the perceived substance of externally promoted norms and changes has an effect on the outcome of external democratization efforts, it is also necessary to account for a possible influence of the process-related factors identified in the previous section. This is done as part of case studies in chapters 4, 5 and 6, in order to reveal possible alternative explanations of EU democracy promotion outcomes.

3.3 Further Methodological Considerations

As the understanding of causal mechanisms behind a social or political phenomenon *"almost always requires going beyond countable aspects and trends"* (Mabry 2008: 215), this research employs qualitative case study techniques, spanning the years 1991-2010 with a particular focus on the 2000s when the relevant EU democratization tools were introduced (following the ratification of the bilateral Partnership and Cooperation Agreements and the adoption of the 'EU-Central Asia: Strategy for a New Partnership'). The book offers three case studies of the EU instruments applied in Kyrgyzstan and Uzbekistan that are exemplary of each type of tools identified above—conditionality-based, dialogue-based, and democratic empowerment.

Concerning the first instrument type, it has been demonstrated above that the EU has a set of incentives related to aid and trade at its disposal. However, it has never linked them directly to democratization or human rights promotion in Central Asia. For instance, the EU's sector policy support programme in social protection and public finance management that provided €40 million to the Kyrgyz government relies solely on technical and financial governance indicators, without consideration of human rights standards or democratic governance conditions (European Commission, EuropeAid 2008; European Commission, EuropeAid 2011). Beyond rhetoric action, the only precedent of human rights related conditionality applied by the EU in the region throughout the whole period of 1991-2010 was the imposition of sanctions on Uzbekistan following a brutal suppression of protests by Uzbek authorities in the city of Andijan in 2005. As there have been no comparable instances of EU conditionality application in the region, it is not possible to undertake a cross-country comparison. Nevertheless, this case can provide valuable insights with regard to the two research questions of the current study. The sanctions enforcement against Uzbekistan is thus examined as a single case of EU conditionality-based tools in chapter 4.

For the second type of tools—dialogue-based—it is suggested to focus on the bilateral structured human rights dialogues (HRDs). Unlike other dialogue platforms (e.g. bilateral political dialogue under the Partnership and Cooperation Agreements or regional dialogue at the ministerial level) that only occasionally (if at all) covered the issues of human rights and democratic development, the HRDs were specifically introduced to address these concerns (European Commission 2009b: 1). Considering the EU's inclusive approach to conceptualizing democracy promotion (see chapter 2), the dialogue envisaged under the Rule of Law Initiative (RoLI) also appears to be of relevance for the current study. Yet, the Rule of Law Platform—the actual dialogue component of the RoLI—was established only in 2011 (Schuster 2011: 3), which is beyond the time span of this research. The human rights dialogues have been in operation for a longer period of time—since 2007 in Uzbekistan and since 2008 in Kyrgyzstan (Council of the European Union n/a)—and therefore can offer more useful insights with regard to changes observed over time. In addition, the case of HRDs allows for a cross-country comparison of results of the application of dialogue-based tools in Central Asia. The implementation and outcomes of the dialogues are examined in chapter 5.

Finally, concerning democratic empowerment tools, over the years the EU has provided little democratization-related support to the Central Asian governments under the aforementioned TACIS programme and the later Development Cooperation Instrument (DCI). While TACIS largely emphasized economic aspects of post-soviet transition, DCI has mainly focused on assistance in combating poverty (cf. Boonstra and Hale 2010; EU-Central Asia Monitoring n/a). Institution- and capacity-building programmes targeting civil society on the other hand are more relevant for the present research. The focus on civil society support is also well justified in view of the prominence of the concept of civil society in EU governance (Kohler-Koch 2012: 810-814) and its external relations, especially in EU democratization policy (Wichmann 2007: 107-110). Of particular interest for this study are the Institution Building and Partnership Programme (IBPP) that was part of TACIS, and the European Instrument for Democracy and Human Rights (EIDHR), the EU's specific tool for external democratization support. While the former programme provided funding to civil society organizations, it was a component of the EU's mainstream assistance negotiated with the Central Asian governments. The EIDHR, on the contrary, is intended to assist the non-governmental sector without the need for consultation with or agreement by state authorities. The two instruments differ with regard to a key aspect that can have an effect on their outcomes in view of the above assumptions concerning process-related favourable factors for success of the democratic empowerment tools. Here, it is therefore suggested to scrutinize the implementation of both these tools, as they represent two distinct kinds of assistance—channelled through the government consent and granted directly to civil society. The above mentioned Non-State Actors and Local Authorities in Development (NSA/LA) programme that provides funding to civil society under the DCI is excluded from this analysis, as it has been established rather late (the NSA/LA projects have started only in 2009) and therefore can hardly provide useful insights under the timeframe of the current study. Chapter 6 examines the IBPP and EIDHR implementation and outcomes in both Kyrgyzstan and Uzbekistan.

Methodologically, the subsequent analysis draws on process-tracing with embedded elements of the congruence method (in accordance with George and Bennett 2005). Process-tracing is described as *"an indispensable tool for theory testing and theory development"* (George and Bennett 2005: 207) used to examine *"the processes unfolding in the cases at hand as well as the outcomes in those cases"* (Hall 2003: 393). With the focus on causal chains and causal mechanisms, the method serves to identify intervening causal processes between independent and dependent variables. It helps to narrow the list of potential causes and identify convergence or interaction of several causal variables (George and Bennett 2005: 206-213). In this study process-tracing takes the form of an *'analytic explanation'* (cf. George and Bennett 2005: 211) guided by the key hypothesis. This is complimented by the congruence method which starts from theoretical assumptions and then assesses their *"ability to explain or predict the outcome in a particular case"* (George and Bennett 2005: 181). This is particularly used to scrutinize the ability of the theoretically derived process-related factors (see Table 3.2) to explain the outcomes of the EU tools application, i.e. for testing the applicability of possible alternative explanations.

The analysis relies on data collected from various sources, including EU and Central Asian documents (agreements, strategy papers, statements, programme and project reports, etc.), human rights reports by national and international agencies and watchdog organizations (e.g. Freedom House and Human Rights Watch), government press-releases, and news coverage. In order to secure access to the information that is not publicly available, expert interviews have been used as a complimentary method of data collection.[22]

Overall, 33 anonymous semi-structured interviews have been conducted with the relevant European and Central Asian stakeholders, including policy-makers, practitioners and civil society representatives.[23] The interviews drew on guidelines prepared in advance that allowed spontaneous follow-up questions depending on the interview situation and interviewees' responses. The validity of data obtained through this method was checked by juxtaposing information from individual interviews against each other and against the background of the further information sources mentioned above.

The interviews were conducted in several rounds, with the first one (accomplished in June-August 2009) serving as an initial orientation to provide an *'exploratory tool'* (cf. Bogner and Menz 2009: 46). The subsequent rounds in 2010-2011 included *'systematizing'* expert interviews aiming to gain access to the specific knowledge possessed by experts. The interviewed experts were not seen as the object of the analysis here but rather as a *"source of information with regard to the reconstruction of sequences of events and social situations"* (Bogner and Menz 2009: 47; cf. Vogel 1995: 77; Gläser and Laudel 2004: 10).[24] This method proved to be essential for obtaining information necessary for the present research that could not be retrieved from publicly available documents. The specific use of these data is explicated in the subsequent case studies.

---

[22] For the relevance of expert interviews to evaluation studies see Wroblewski and Leitner 2009.
[23] A complete list of all interviews can be found in Annex I.
[24] This type of expert interview is distinguished from *'theory-generating interviews'*, a methodology developed by Meuser and Nagel (1991; 2009) that aims at *"communicative opening up and analytic reconstruction of the subjective dimension of expert knowledge"* (Bogner and Menz 2009: 48).

4. The EU Sanctions Against Uzbekistan

This chapter examines the application of sanctions imposed by the European Union upon Uzbekistan in the wake of the events in the Uzbek city of Andijan in May 2005. The case is exemplary in a sense that so far it has been the only precedent of sanctions enforcement as part of EU external democracy and human rights promotion in relations with Central Asia. Moreover, this was the first time in the European Union's history that a decision was made to partially suspend a Partnership and Cooperation Agreement with a post-soviet state. This makes it a crucial case for investigation of the performance of EU conditionality-based tools in the region.

The first section of the chapter traces implementation of the sanctions and identifies their effects in an attempt to assess whether and to what extent the EU efforts were successful. The next section turns to the possible explanations of the outcomes of the European engagement in accordance with the assumptions stated in chapter 3.

As discussed in section 3.1, the success of EU conditionality-based tools is defined in terms of the achievement of changes occurred in the target's behaviour in response to European demands, i.e. compliance with the EU conditions. The absence of the expected changes in behaviour would hence signify a failure of the EU conditionality. Another possible outcome of the EU engagement could be that only some aspects of the expected change occur (e.g. not all EU demands are fulfilled). In this case, the EU efforts would be only partly successful (see Table 3.1). In order to identify the changes, attribute them to EU engagement and verify the assumptions concerning explanatory factors stated in chapter 3, the study draws on an extensive analysis of EU sanctions related documents and relevant reports produced by international and Uzbek NGOs, government agencies, and media for the purposes of data triangulation. To access information that is not publicly available, these sources are complimented by expert interviews with European and Uzbek authorities and civil society actors.

4.1 Tracing Implementation of the Sanctions

As it has been previously mentioned, the Partnership and Cooperation Agreement between the European Union and the Republic of Uzbekistan, includes respect for democracy and human rights as *'an essential element'* (Art. 2). This enables the EU to suspend the agreement in the event of a severe violation of human rights and democratic principles by the Uzbek state authorities. The first and (so far) the only attempt to assume restrictive measures, including a partial suspension of the PCA with Uzbekistan, was made by the European Union in response to the severe human rights breach by the Uzbek authorities during the riots in Andijan in May 2005 and the refusal of the Uzbek government to permit an independent international investigation of the events.

According to the preliminary report issued by the OSCE Office for Democratic Institutions and Human Rights, 300-500 mostly unarmed civilians may have been killed during the violent suppression of protests by the Uzbek military and law enforcement bodies in Andijan on 13 May 2005[25] (OSCE Office for Democratic Institutions and Human Rights 2005: 23). In addition to the disproportional use of force during the riots, the authorities are reported to have reacted with numerous arrests and harassments of Uzbek activists in connection with the disturbances (Front Line 2007; Human Rights Watch 2005).

In the wake of the events, the European Union together with the UN, the OSCE, and the USA repeatedly called on the Uzbek authorities to allow an international inquiry into what had happened in Andijan (Council of the European Union, External Relations Council 2005a; Council of the European Union, External Relations Council 2005b). Yet, the Uzbek government refused. Only an internal investigation was pursued by a special Uzbek parliamentary commission on the order of the president Islam Karimov, which was criticized by human rights defenders as intransparent and biased (Fergana News Information Agency 2006).

In response to the Uzbek authorities' refusal to allow an independent international inquiry and *"[i]n light of the excessive, disproportionate and indiscriminate use of force by the Uzbek security forces during the Andijan events"*, the Council of the European Union decided to impose the so called 'smart sanctions' on Uzbekistan at the Council's 2679th session on 3 October 2005 (Council of the European Union, External Relations Council 2005c). The respective Common Position (2005/792/CFSP) was adopted by the Council on 14 November 2005 (Council of the European Union 2005a).

---

[25] The reported number of casualties, the development of the events and their causes vary significantly in different sources. An alternative view on the events is provided e.g. by Akiner (2005).

4.1.1 The EU Sanctions and Conditions for Their Withdrawal

The sanctions included the following three elements: (1) a suspension of all scheduled technical meetings[26] under the Partnership and Cooperation Agreement; (2) an *"embargo on exports of arms, military equipment and other equipment that could be used for internal repression in Uzbekistan"* as well as the related technical assistance and military training; and (3) restrictions on admission to the European Union of *"those individuals directly responsible for the indiscriminate and disproportionate use of force in Andijan"* (Council of the European Union, External Relations Council 2005c). The admission restrictions (or the visa ban) concerned twelve Uzbek top officials believed to be responsible for the use of force against the demonstrators in Andijan, including *inter alia* the (former) interior minister Zokirjon Almatov, his deputy at the time Tohir Mullajonov, defence minister Qodir Ghulomov, head of Uzbekistan's National Security Service Rustam Inoyatov, Andijan governor Saydullo Begaliyev, and commander of the interior ministry special forces Vladimir Mamo (Council of the European Union 2005a).

The measures were initially introduced for the period of one year. As it was announced in the Council Conclusions of 3 October 2005 and in the Common Position 2005/792/CFSP, within this period of time the enforced restrictions would be held *'under close review'* according to developments in certain areas (Council of the European Union, External Relations Council 2005c; Council of the European Union 2005a). This would allow the European Union to alter or repeal the measures in case the position of the Uzbek government changed.

Translating the areas for 'close review' that were listed in the Council Conclusions and in the Common Position into more concrete EU demands, the following conditions for the sanctions withdrawal were identified:

- Uzbek authorities' consent for an independent international investigation into the Andijan events;
- fair and transparent conduct of Andijan-related trials;
- release of human rights defenders and critics of the Uzbek government's actions from detention and cessation of their harassment; and
- actions on the part of the Uzbek authorities demonstrating their willingness to commit to the principles of respect for human rights, rule of

---

[26] These are not to be confused with the political meetings under the PCA such as Cooperation Councils that were still allowed to be held after the introduction of the EU sanctions.

law and fundamental freedoms (cf. Council of the European Union, External Relations Council 2005c; Council of the European Union 2005a).

Based on the review process during the next years, the sanctions were gradually eased by the European Union and finally eliminated in October 2009. In the following, each round of the review process and changes undertaken by the Uzbek government with respect to EU demands are scrutinized with the aim of evaluating success of the EU measures.

4.1.2 The EU Sanctions at Work

The 2006 Review Round

The first review of the sanctions by the Council of the European Union took place in November 2006. By this time point, none of the European demands stated in the Common Position 2005/792/CFSP were fulfilled by the targeted Uzbek authorities to the extent that would have allowed significant alleviation of the measures. The Uzbek government continued rejecting an independent international inquiry into the Andijan disturbances. Repressions against opposition and government-critical media and activists, who presented a different from the Uzbek government's version of the events, were reported by Western observers and international watchdog organizations (e.g. Stroehlein 2006; International Crisis Group 2006b; European Forum for Democracy and Solidarity n/a).

According to the International Crisis Group, over 200 people received prison sentences related to the Andijan protests within one year following the events; most of these trials were held behind closed doors (International Crisis Group 2006b: 4-5). Several processes against persons accused of Islamic extremism and organization of the riots were open for the public. All defendants in these cases were found guilty upon their testimonies. The cases were dismissed by human rights groups as based on confessions allegedly extracted through torture (Radio Free Europe/Radio Liberty 2005; Stroehlein 2006). The defendants received considerably mitigated sentences, as compared to the tendency of prior trials involving accusations in religious extremism (cf. Embassy of Uzbekistan to the United States, Press Office 2005c; Saidazimova 2005). However, no serious litigations were initiated against the high-ranking officials believed to be directly responsible for the use of force against the Andijan protestors. Some of them (e.g. Ghulomov, Begaliyev and Almatov) were removed from their posts for officially different reasons, not necessarily related to the Andijan events.[27] On the whole, the above does not suggest that the EU demand for fair and transparent trials was fulfilled by the Uzbek authorities.

By the end of 2006, the initial reaction of the Uzbek government to the EU sanctions, which had led to the temporary cessation of political dialogue between the two parties,[28] changed in a way that Tashkent started actively seeking a renewal of contacts with the European Union and pushing for alleviation of the restrictions. At the Cooperation Council that was held on 8 November 2006 (one day before the Political and Security Committee's meeting where the sanctions were to be reviewed), the Uzbek government proposed opening of a bilateral human rights dialogue and holding a joint meeting of experts to discuss the Andijan events. These propositions were conceived by the EU officials as the first steps of the Uzbek authorities demonstrating their willingness to commit to human rights (Presidency of the Council of the European Union 2006).

In view of these developments, on 17 November 2006 the Council of the EU decided to reinstate the suspended technical meetings under the PCA *"with the aim of bringing about, through dialogue, compliance by Uzbekistan with the principles of respect for human rights, rule of law and fundamental freedoms"* (Council of the European Union 2006). The arms embargo and the visa ban remained in place to be reviewed in another twelve and six months respectively (Council of the European Union 2006). Thus, the next review round was supposed to take place in two steps—in May 2007 for the admission restrictions, and in November 2007 for the arms embargo—with regard to the same demands initially stated in the Council Conclusions of 3 October 2005 and the Common Position 2005/792/CFSP.

The 2007 Review Round

Throughout 2007, the Uzbek authorities continued opposing an independent international inquiry. Nevertheless, in December 2006 and April 2007 they organized two rounds of the EU-Uzbek Experts talks on the events in Andijan, which were proposed by the Uzbek side earlier at the Cooperation

---

[27] While Begaliyev was accused of being partly responsible for the Andijan events by President Islam Karimov (Stroehlein 2006; Najimova and Kimmage 2006), Almatov retired on health grounds and was replaced by Anvar Salihbaev, who was also subject to the EU visa ban (Radio Free Europe/Radio Liberty 2006).

[28] Thus, Uzbekistan chose not to participate in the Cooperation Council that had been scheduled for February 2006 (International Crisis Group 2006b: 4).

Council. The talks were conducted in Tashkent and Andijan with the participation of experts from the European Commission, the Presidency, the Council Secretariat, and from four Member States, i.e. Germany, Great Britain, France, and Sweden (Presidency of the Council of the European Union 2006). The outcomes of the talks were not made publicly available though. In addition, the format of the talks was very different from that of an international investigatory mission. The EU demand for an independent inquiry into the Andijan events thus remained unfulfilled.

State repressive actions against opposition, government-critical media and human rights activists reportedly continued throughout the year (Freedom House 2008). International organizations, including UNHCR, which experienced difficulties in their activities in 2006, were eventually forced to close their offices in Uzbekistan after working with Andijan witnesses, and they did not regain access to the country (International Crisis Group 2006b: 7). Several further closures of foreign-based organizations, especially NGOs, occurred in 2007 (Freedom House 2008).

The situation with those detained and convicted in relation to the Andijan riots, including human rights activists, also did not change. Following pressure from the European Union, only two well-known human rights defenders—Umida Niazova and Gulbahor Turaeva—were conditionally released from custody (in May and June 2007 respectively), while the other activists remained under arrest (cf. Council of the European Union, External Relations Council 2007a,b; Freedom House 2008).

At the same time, on 8-9 May, shortly before the review of the visa ban was supposed to take place, the first round of the bilateral EU-Uzbek human rights dialogue was held in Tashkent upon the invitation of the Uzbek side. During the meeting, Uzbek representatives expressed their commitment to the further long-term engagement in the dialogue (Council of the European Union, External Relations Council 2007b). This was characterized as one of the *'positive developments'* in the EU-Uzbek relations by the Council of the European Union. Further human rights developments that were welcomed by the EU included decisions of the Uzbek government to abolish the death penalty and to introduce *habeas corpus* into Uzbek law (Council of the European Union, External Relations Council 2007a).

In view of these mixed developments, the first phase of the 2007 sanctions review resulted in the Council's Common Position 2007/338/CFSP of 14 May 2007, which renewed the admission restrictions for another six months but shortened the list of individuals subject to the visa ban to eight Uzbek top officials (Council of the European Union 2007b).[29] In the second phase that followed in November 2007, the Council adopted its Common Position 2007/734/CFSP, which suspended application of the visa ban *"[w]ith a view to encouraging the Uzbek authorities to take positive steps to improve the human rights situation and taking into account the commitments of the Uzbek authorities"* (Council of the European Union 2007a). The arms embargo was to be maintained for another 12 months.

Most importantly however, the Common Position introduced significant changes to the conditions that needed to be fulfilled by the Uzbek government for the EU sanctions to be lifted. Uzbekistan was urged *"to implement fully its international obligations relating to human rights and fundamental freedoms as well as rule of law"* (Council of the European Union 2007a). More specifically, the altered EU demands included the following:
- permission of unimpeded access by relevant international bodies, i.e. the International Committee of the Red Cross (ICRC), to prisoners;
- effective engagement with the UN Special Rapporteurs[30] to Uzbekistan;
- allowing all NGOs, including Human Rights Watch, to operate without constraints in Uzbekistan;
- release of human rights defenders from detention and cessation of their harassments;
- positive engagement on human rights issues in the framework of the EU-Uzbekistan Cooperation Committee; and
- reforms of the judiciary, law enforcement and police law (Council of the European Union 2007a).

Two of the four initial requirements stated in the Common Position 2005/792/CFSP that imposed the sanctions—open and fair conduct of trials related to the Andijan disturbances and the Uzbek authorities' consent for an independent international investigation into the events—were absent in the new Common Position of 13 November 2007, despite the fact that these

---

[29] The document provided no references to the reasons why four of the twelve Uzbek officials, who had initially been subject to the EU restrictions, were removed from the list.

[30] This particularly refers to the UN Special Rapporteur on extrajudicial, summary or arbitrary executions and the Special Rapporteur on torture and other cruel, inhuman or degrading treatment or punishment, who both repeatedly requested visits to Uzbekistan since 2005 and 2006 respectively (Office of the United Nations High Commissioner for Human Rights n/a).

requirements were not fulfilled. At the same time, the originally very broadly formulated condition—actions on the part of the Uzbek authorities demonstrating their willingness to commit to the principles of respect for human rights, rule of law and fundamental freedoms—was transformed into a set of more specific demands. The only initial requirement that remained unchanged was the release of human rights defenders from custody and cessation of their harassment. Hence, the next sanctions review rounds in 2008 and 2009 were based on the revised set of conditions.

The 2008 Review Round

In 2008, the sanctions review was again accomplished in two steps—in April and October—with the visa restrictions considered twice. The review process revealed a rather mixed picture regarding the changes undertaken by the Uzbek government in response to the EU's demands.

Already in March 2008, Tashkent permitted ICRC prison visits to resume after a three-year post-Andijan break, thus fulfilling the first EU condition for revision of the sanctions (International Crisis Group n/a). At the same time, with respect to the demand for effective engagement with the UN Special Rapporteurs, neither the Special Rapporteur on extrajudicial, summary or arbitrary executions, nor the Special Rapporteur on torture could secure an invitation to visit Uzbekistan by the end of 2008, despite several requests to the Uzbek government (Office of the United Nations High Commissioner for Human Rights n/a; cf. Fitzpatrick 2010). Domestic and international NGOs based in Uzbekistan, including Human Rights Watch, continued experiencing bureaucratic obstruction to their work by the Uzbek authorities (Freedom House 2009: 583).

The demand for the release of human rights defenders from detention and cessation of their harassment was only partly fulfilled. In February 2008, three human rights activists Saidjahon Zainabiddinov, Karim Bazarbaev and Ikhtior Hamroev were granted amnesties and released from jail. Under a general prison amnesty, all charges were dropped against independent journalist Umida Niazova (Institute of War and Peace Reporting 2008; Freedom House 2009: 10). Two further activists were released from custody in June 2008. At the same time, on 15 April a dissident poet Yusuf Juma was sentenced to five years of forced labour for organizing a protest against Islam Karimov in December 2007. Later, in June and August 2008, several further independent journalists and activists were detained on different grounds (International Crisis Group n/a).

With regard to the condition of positive engagement on human rights issues in the framework of the EU-Uzbekistan Cooperation Committee, an inference whether it was fulfilled could be made only based on expert interviews with the EU officials, as the Cooperation Committees took place behind closed doors. The interviewees, however, could not provide a clear answer to this question, partly due to their reluctance to go into detail and partly to the broad original formulation of the requirement that left a lot of room for interpretation (e.g. of what could be characterized as 'positive'). The responses thus provided a mixed picture, which led to the conclusion that the condition was only partly fulfilled by the Uzbek authorities (cf. Interviews 10, 12, 15 and 16, Annex I).

Finally, in response to the EU demand for reforms of the judiciary, law enforcement and police law, several amendments to the Criminal Code were approved by the Uzbek parliament in 2008 (Legislative Chamber of the Olyi Majlis of Republic of Uzbekistan n/a). However, most of these amendments addressed procedural issues related to the previously scheduled reforms— abolition of the death penalty and introduction of habeas corpus. In addition, they left many practical problems of implementation unresolved (Bureau of Human Rights and Rule of Law Uzbekistan 2009). No significant actions were taken by the Uzbek government or the legislature to enhance independence of the court system and its judges from the executive branch (Freedom House 2009: 14-15). On the positive side, the Uzbek state officials indicated their willingness to cooperate with the EU in the framework of the regional Rule of Law Initiative (RoLI) that had been proposed by the 2007 'EU-Central Asia: Strategy for a New Partnership'. Therefore, the EU demand for reforms of the judiciary, law enforcement and police law was partly fulfilled by the Uzbek authorities.

In the Council Conclusions on Uzbekistan of 24 April 2008, both positive and negative developments with regard to the fulfilment of the EU's demands by the Uzbek government were noted. In view of these mixed developments, the Council decided to keep the visa restrictions suspended until the second review phase in October 2008 (Council of the European Union 2008b). Then, the progress was supposed to be evaluated against the six conditions that had been set out in the above Common Position 2007/734/CFSP of 13 November 2007.[31] In addition, the prior generally

---

[31] With regard to the prior demand for effective cooperation of the Uzbek government with the UN Special Rapporteurs, the Council Conclusions of 24 April 2008 specifically referred to the Special Rapporteurs on torture and on freedom of the media (Council of the European Union, External Relations Council 2008b).

formulated demand for actions demonstrating the willingness of the Uzbek authorities to adhere to the principles of respect for human rights, rule of law and fundamental freedoms was re-introduced (Council of the European Union, External Relations Council 2008b).

The second phase of the 2008 review was thus based on an updated set of seven conditions for lifting the sanctions. It resulted in the final withdrawal of the admission restrictions and prolongation of the arms embargo for another twelve months (Council of the European Union, External Relations Council 2008a; Council of the European Union 2008a).

The 2009 Review Round

For the final review in October 2009, the updated conditions stipulated in the Common Position 2007/734/CFSP of 13 November 2007 and in the Council Conclusions of 24 April 2008 were considered.

With regard to the demand for the ICRC prison visits, the agreement that had been reached between the Committee and the Uzbek authorities in 2008 remained in place. In August 2009, the initial six-month pilot program allowing ICRC to enter and evaluate prisons was extended for an unlimited period of time (U.S. Department of State 2010b).

Regarding the demand for cooperation of the Uzbek government with the UN Special Rapporteurs on torture and on freedom of the press, they could not obtain official invitations to visit the country in 2009 (Office of the United Nations High Commissioner for Human Rights n/a). The demand thus remained unfulfilled.

Throughout the year, human rights activists and journalists who criticized the government reportedly continued being subject to harassment, arbitrary arrest and politically motivated prosecution (Freedom House 2010: 575). Although several activists were released from prison, at least fourteen human rights defenders remained in custody on different charges by the end of the year (Human Rights Watch 2010). Reports of their torture and other ill-treatment continued (Amnesty International 2010).

The situation with international and domestic NGOs in Uzbekistan also remained unchanged. In 2009, only two domestic human rights NGOs were officially registered with the Uzbek Ministry of Justice. They continued experiencing bureaucratic obstruction to their work. Human Rights Watch that was particularly mentioned in the Council Conclusions of 24 April 2008 remained registered, but still could not resume its operations since the Uzbek government refused to accredit the organization's country director. On the positive side, the government approved several proposed OSCE projects, including in the 'human dimension', i.e. human rights related projects, to which the Uzbek authorities had objected since 2006 (U.S. Department of State 2010b; International Crisis Group n/a). This fact alone, however, does not allow concluding that the EU demand for unconstrained operation of NGOs was at least partially fulfilled.

With regard to the condition of positive engagement on human rights issues in the framework of the EU-Uzbekistan Cooperation Committee, the conducted expert interviews again could not provide deeper insights, due to the reluctance of the interviewees to go into detail about the meetings. The answers of the interviewees largely depended on what they perceived as 'positive engagement' and resulted in mixed assessments (cf. Interviews 10, 12, 15 and 16, Annex I).

In response to the EU requirement for reforms of the judiciary, law enforcement and police law, further amendments to national legislation were approved by the Uzbek parliament in 2009, including a law that allowed the human rights ombudsman unhampered access to prisons to monitor conditions and obliged authorities at certain pre-trial detention facilities to arrange meetings between a detainee and a representative of the Human Rights Ombudsman's Office upon the detainee's request (Legislative Chamber of the Olyi Majlis of Republic of Uzbekistan n/a). At the same time, amendments to the Law on Advocacy abolished private defence attorney organizations, including the independent Association of Advocates of Uzbekistan and the Tashkent Bar Association, substituting them with a state-controlled Chamber of Lawyers (overseen by the Ministry of Justice). According to these amendments, all Uzbek defence attorneys were required to be certified by the Chamber, which resulted in a loss of licenses by several prominent human rights defenders (Freedom House 2010: 580; U.S. Department of State 2010b). No significant actions were taken by the Uzbek government or the legislature to enhance independence of the court system from the executive (Freedom House 2010: 579–580). Nevertheless, Uzbekistan continued active participation in the regional Rule of Law Initiative and hosted an expert seminar on 'Compliance with Defence Rights in Criminal Proceedings' in September 2009 (Interview 23, Annex I). These developments left the EU demand for reforms of the judiciary, law enforcement and police law only partly fulfilled.

Finally, concerning the EU's very generally formulated criterion for revision of the sanctions—actions of the Uzbek authorities that would demonstrate their willingness to adhere to human rights, rule of law and fundamental freedoms—in addition to the above developments, ratification of conventions against child labour was particularly noted by the EU as one of the positive changes undertaken by Uzbekistan (Council of the European Union, External Relations Council 2009).

In view (or in spite) of these ambiguous developments, the 2009 sanctions review round resulted in the withdrawal of the remaining arms embargo by the Council of the European Union. The decision was explained with the aim *"to encourage the Uzbek authorities to take further substantive steps to improve the rule of law and the human rights situation on the ground"* (Council of the European Union, External Relations Council 2009).

4.1.3 Summary of the Results

Table 4.1 brings together the EU demands and the results of the sanctions according to the annual review rounds from 2006 to 2009. As demonstrated in the table, only two of the nine conditions were continuously stated by the EU during the whole period of the sanctions: the release of human rights defenders from custody and cessation of their harassment, and actions on the part of the Uzbek authorities demonstrating their willingness to adhere to human rights, rule of law and fundamental freedoms. Both of these demands were only partly fulfilled by the Uzbek government, according to each round of the review process. The two further conditions initially set by the EU in relation to the Andijan disturbances—consent for an international independent inquiry into the events, and fair and transparent conduct of Andijan-related trials—were not renewed after 2007, despite the fact that none of them was accommodated by the target government. Instead, a new set of requirements was introduced. Two of them—positive engagement on human rights issues in the framework of the EU-Uzbekistan Cooperation Committee and reforms of the judiciary, law enforcement and police law—were partly met by the Uzbek government in 2008 and 2009. The three further conditions introduced after the 2007 review showed very different results. While the demands for effective engagement with the UN Special Rapporteurs and unrestricted functioning of foreign and domestic NGOs were not met, the requirement to permit unimpeded access by relevant international bodies (i.e. the International Committee of the Red Cross) to prisoners was complied with. The latter condition was the only one that was fulfilled by the Uzbek government over the entire period of EU application of sanctions.

Table 4.1: Results of the EU Conditionality Application

EU conditions for sanctions to be lifted	Results of annual reviews			
	2006	2007	2008	2009
Consent for independent international inquiry into the Andijan events	-	-	n/a	n/a
Fair and transparent conduct of Andijan-related trials	-	-	n/a	n/a
Release of human rights defenders from custody and cessation of their harassment	+/-	+/-	+/-	+/-
Demonstration of willingness to adhere to human rights, rule of law and fundamental freedoms	+/-	+/-	+/-	+/-
Unimpeded access by relevant international bodies to prisoners	n/a	n/a	+	+
Effective engagement with the UN Special Rapporteurs	n/a	n/a	-	-
Allowing all NGOs to operate without constraints	n/a	n/a	-	-
Positive engagement on human rights issues in the framework of the EU-Uzbekistan Cooperation Committee	n/a	n/a	+/-	+/-
Reforms of the judiciary, law enforcement and police law	n/a	n/a	+/-	+/-

Note: (+)   condition fulfilled
 (-)   condition not fulfilled
 (+/-) condition partly fulfilled
 (n/a) condition not applied

4.2 Explaining the Outcomes of EU Sanctions

According to the general hypothesis stated in chapter 3, success of conditionality-based tools in such regions as Central Asia can be influenced by the substance of the norms and reforms promoted by the European Union. Governing elites in the target countries are expected to be more likely to comply with EU demands when they perceive these demands as less politically sensitive, i.e. not endangering their power positions or the political status-quo. While testing this hypothesis on the example of EU sanctions against Uzbekistan, it is necessary to account for a possible influence of the process-related factors identified in chapter 3 (see Table 3.2), as they can provide an additional explanation to the results discussed above. Hence, the subsequent sub-sections investigate the role of process-related factors and scrutinize the empirical evidence in support of the main hypothesis. The final sub-section accounts for potential interfering effects of other external actors' conditionality against Uzbekistan, in order to allow for effect attribution and to eliminate alternative or confounding explanations.

4.2.1 Lack of Credibility as an Explanation for Failure

Credibility of incentives and sanctions has been identified as the key process-related factor for their successes (Table 3.2). It implies consistency in delivery of the measures, which can be negatively affected by the presence of competing interests on the external actor's foreign policy agenda. Hence, this sub-section looks at the lack of consistency in the application of EU sanctions against Uzbekistan as a possible explanatory factor for their limited successes and examines how foreign policy interests of the EU and its Member States influenced the measures' applications.

To begin with, the way the EU sanctions were enforced throughout 2005-2009 threatened the credibility of European conditionality. As demonstrated in the previous section, the sanctions were gradually alleviated with each review round and finally lifted in 2009, in spite of the fact that most of the EU requirements were not or were only partly fulfilled by the Uzbek authorities. The change in scope of EU demands after the 2007 review further testifies to the lack of consistency in the application of sanctions. While the introduction of the new specific requirements by the EU is understandable in view of the reportedly degrading human rights situation and constraints to the work of civil society organizations in Uzbekistan, it is not self-evident why the demand for an independent international inquiry into the Andijan events was officially dropped after 2007.[32] It is especially questionable, considering that the necessity of such an inquiry continued to be part of the public debate about the situation in Uzbekistan throughout the later period (Stroehlein 2008).

---

[32] With regard to the removal of the requirement for the fair and transparent conduct of the Andijan-related trials after the 2007 review round, the official justification was that the majority of the trials had been conducted within the first two years after the disturbances in May 2005, i.e. they were concluded by the end of 2007 (Interviews 10 and 16, Annex I).

As the interviews with the EU officials revealed, there were serious contradictions in the positions of EU Member States concerning enforcement of the sanctions. Every time the Council of the EU was supposed to review the restrictions, tough negotiations started between the two camps led by 'pragmatically oriented' Germany on the one side, who argued in favour of the necessity of a constructive political dialogue with Uzbekistan and the withdrawal of sanctions, and by Sweden and the UK on the other, who wanted to maintain the measures (Interviews 10, 11 and 12, Annex I). As the Council had to act by unanimity in order to extend the sanctions, the decision each year was a compromise between these two counterpositions. Two years after the sanctions were introduced it became apparent that the position of the Uzbek side regarding the possibility of an independent inquiry into the Andijan events would not change. Thus, the main condition for the withdrawal of the restrictions would not be fulfilled, which would have signified a clear failure of the EU measures. In this situation, a compromise was achieved in the Council to make the lifting of sanctions conditional on other changes, primarily improvements in the general human rights situation in Uzbekistan (Interview 10, Annex I).

The inconsistency of EU sanctions is further illustrated by the actions of the German government concerning the (at that time) Uzbek interior minister Zokirjon Almatov and the head of Uzbekistan's National Security Service Rustam Inoyatov. Although both of these officials were on the EU's blacklist of persons assumed to be directly responsible for the Andijan violence and thus subject to EU admission restrictions, Almatov was allowed to undergo cancer treatment at a German hospital at the end of 2005 and Inoyatov was invited to visit Germany in November 2006. During their stays in Germany, the Human Rights Watch and a group of Uzbek activists filed a complaint seeking to bring the German government to investigate Almatov and Inoyatov for crimes against humanity. Yet, the opening of the investigation was rejected by the German federal prosecutor, which was characterized by the Human Rights Watch as a breach of the German Criminal Code against International Law (European Center for Constitutional and Human Rights n/a; Human Rights Watch 2006).

Another noteworthy example concerns Germany's alleged violation of the EU embargo on arms export and related technical assistances. Thus, the German Defence Ministry is reported to have provided military training to 35 Uzbek servicemen between 2005 and 2009, which was in contradiction of the official EU line (Uznews.net 2010).

Only a year after the sanctions had been introduced and shortly before they were supposed to be reviewed by the Council of the European Union in November 2006, the German foreign minister Frank Walter Steinmeier travelled to Tashkent to meet the president Islam Karimov and discuss the possibility of gradually eliminating the sanctions with the condition that *'concrete measures'* would be implemented by the Uzbek government (Ryan 2006; McDermott 2006). Thus, already in 2006 Germany assumed the role of a mediator between Tashkent and Brussels. This move was rooted in the growing significance of the bilateral relations with Uzbekistan and Berlin's interests in the region, especially in view of the German chairmanship of the EU in the first half of 2007, which included adoption of a regional European strategy towards Central Asia—prepared by Germany in 2006—as an important element of its agenda.

The interests of Berlin in maintaining stable relationships with the region, and with Uzbekistan in particular, are at least twofold. First of all, Central Asia is a steadily growing market, to which German companies are keen on securing greater access. Thus, during the above mentioned visit of Frank Walter Steinmeier to Uzbekistan in 2006, he took his delegation to Bukhara to discuss the prospects of strengthening the existing cooperation with local businessmen, including potential diversification of economic activities in the areas of industry, tourism, medicine and education, as well as further investment projects (McDermott 2006). As a result of these efforts, the Uzbek-German trade rose from roughly US $330 million in 2005 to over US $470 million in 2008, with German exports amounting to up to 90% of this sum (Deutsche Botschaft Taschkent 2010).

Another (probably even more influential) factor in the bilateral relations derives from Berlin's security considerations and the geographic proximity of Uzbekistan to Afghanistan. The commitment to the stabilization of Afghanistan and the deployment of Bundeswehr troops as part of the NATO-led International Security Assistance Force (ISAF) has remained high on the German government's agenda since 2001. In this regard, Uzbekistan has been perceived as a key partner of Germany and NATO in the region, not least because both U.S. and German troops were stationed there before 2005, ensuring delivery of the ISAF supplies and humanitarian aid to Afghanistan (Interview 1, Annex I). However, following open criticism by the U.S. of the Andijan violence and their intercession for the political refugees from Uzbekistan, the Uzbek government demanded termination of the U.S. operations at the Karshi-Khanabad (K2) military base (Nichol 2010: 36).

Furthermore, after the introduction of EU sanctions, Uzbekistan restricted over-flight rights for those European NATO members that criticized human rights abuses by the regime and insisted on the maintenance of the sanctions (Schmitz 2009). This and the closure of K2 significantly reduced NATO's room for manoeuvring to support the ISAF troops in Afghanistan. In the meantime, the Uzbek government signed a defence agreement with Russia, which left open the possibility of the establishment of a Russian military base in the Central Asian state (Blagov 2005).

The freezing of Uzbekistan's relations with the USA and the EU and the new Russian-Uzbek defence pact signified an increased strategic reorientation of the Central Asian republic towards Russia, which stood in stark contrast to Germany's intensions to enhance its engagement with all countries in the region. In this context, Germany had to assume a very careful approach as a mediator between the EU and the Uzbek government, aiming to enhance the political dialogue in the framework of the new regional strategy and pushing for the suspension of the EU sanctions immediately after they had been introduced (Interviews 1 and 10, Annex I). In addition, during the period of 2005-2009, the Bundestag considerably increased payments to the Uzbek Ministry of Finance for leasing the Termez military airbase near the Afghan border. In 2008, these payments reached €15,2 million (Tynan 2011b). Unlike the case of K2, the Termez airbase was left at the disposal of German forces throughout the entire sanctions period demonstrating that Berlin was successful in protecting its security interests.

The above contradictions among EU Member States and the resulting inconsistency in the sanctions implementation undermined credibility of the EU measures. Owing in part to German meddling, this gave a signal to the Uzbek government that the official EU line was soft and flexible. This eventually contributed to the failure of the restrictions to bring about significant changes in Uzbekistan.

Yet, the inconsistency in sanction enforcements as such does not explain why some of the EU conditions were at least partly fulfilled by the Uzbek authorities, while others were opposed throughout the entire period of the sanctions. Considering that favourable factors for success of conditionality-based tools (including democratizer-, target- and process-related dimensions, as identified in chapter 3) were practically absent in the case of the EU's engagement in Uzbekistan, the sanctions were expected to fail completely. The variance in Tashkent's compliance with the different EU requirements suggests that the decisive factor for the fulfilment of these requirements was their substance, i.e. the degree to which they were perceived as more or less politically sensitive by the Uzbek government.

4.2.2 Substance of the EU Demands and Their Implications as Explanatory Factors

This section takes a closer look at what compliance with the norms promoted by the EU and the specific conditions for removal of the sanctions would have implied. First, the implications of the demands that were not met by the Uzbek authorities are examined.

One of the four originally stated conditions—allowing an independent international inquiry into the Andijan events—not only remained unfulfilled, but was openly opposed by the Uzbek government from the very start of the external pressure. It was argued that the disturbances in May 2005 were a state-internal affair and that agreement with the international investigation would undermine national sovereignty (Embassy of Uzbekistan to the United States, Press Office 2005b). Here, it is suggested that it was the legitimacy of the existing political regime and leadership that could be undermined by the independent inquiry.

Following Fish, *legitimacy* is conceived as *"a generally positive orientation among the populace toward the political regime. A regime is legitimate to the extent that populace regards it as providing satisfactory order and believes that no available alternative would be vastly superior"* (Fish 2001: 27). In accordance with the empirical approach to the concept, it is distinguished between input (or process) legitimacy, output (or performance) legitimacy, legitimacy drawing on shared beliefs, and international (or external) legitimacy. Hence, democratic elections are regarded as only one of the possible sources of regime legitimacy. Non-democratic regimes draw instead on delivery of certain public goods (such as security) or shared beliefs (e.g. based on common traditions) as their sources of legitimacy (Organization for Economic Co-operation and Development 2010).

Coming back to the EU demand, an international investigation into certain events in the territory of a state can be launched only upon an official invitation by the state, if it is not regarded as fragile or failed. In accordance with the established practice, the state inviting such an inquiry is obliged to guarantee an extensive freedom of action to the investigation commission, which includes:

- Freedom of movement throughout the territory of the country;
- Free access to all places and establishments relevant to the work of the commission;
- Freedom of access to all sources of information, including documentary material and physical evidence; and
- Freedom to interview government representatives and community leaders, as well as representatives of civil society and other institutions and, in principle, any individual whose testimony is considered (cf. Kyrgyzstan Inquiry Commission n/a).

Although the inviting state mandates the international inquiry commission,[33] it has very limited control over the commission's actions and the final results of the investigation. The outcomes of such an investigation and recommendations for further actions are made available to a broader global public and discussed at international forums, e.g. within the framework of the UN and (if relevant) the OSCE. As the commission is commonly composed of respected international experts and well-known politicians, the outcomes of their inquiry are perceived as a credible official source of information and providing a kind of final judgement for a particular event (Interview 31, Annex I). Hence, if the investigation outcomes provide a negative picture of the authorities and severely criticise their actions, they can generate high political costs for the established regime by undermining its international (and internal) legitimacy.

Throughout the whole period of sanctions, the Uzbek government maintained a certain official version of the Andijan happenings. They presented them as riots organised by extremist groups associated with the banned Hizb-ut-Tahrir party and supported from outside the country with the aim of destabilizing constitutional order and creating an Islamic state in Uzbekistan (Embassy of Uzbekistan to the United States, Press Office 2005a; cf. Najimova and Kimmage 2006). According to this account, armed 'bandits' attacked a police station, military barracks and a prison, eventually capturing the oblast's administration building on the night of May 12. The organizers of the disturbances were thus described by Tashkent as Islamists connected with international terrorist organizations, who took hostages, attract-

---

[33] If a state is regarded as fragile or failed, an international inquiry commission can be mandated by the UN. Reacting to the international pressure, Tashkent repeatedly reminded that this was not the case in this particular situation, and an international inquiry into the Andijan events could be started only upon an official invitation of the Uzbek government (Polat 2007: 19).

ed their relatives and supporters to Andijan's central square in front of the administration building and ultimately used them as a human shield when pressing the government to fulfil their demands. This formally justified the authorities' reaction and use of force to end the riots (Embassy of Uzbekistan to the United States, Press Office 2005a; cf. Burnashev and Chernykh 2007: 68-69). Such presentation of the events was also in line with the Uzbek government's prior legitimacy claims, which according to Schatz, were *"rooted in the logic of combating radical Islamism"* (Schatz 2006: 269), i.e. drew on providing security as the main public good.

The government's version of the disturbances contrasted sharply with the very critical Western media reports and watchdog organizations' statements that pictured the Andijan events as a massacre of peaceful civilian demonstrators by the Uzbek military and law enforcement bodies (e.g. Human Rights Watch 2005). These reports and statements called for an enhanced international pressure on Tashkent and an initiation of the independent inquiry. While the evidence provided later by some researchers (e.g. Polat 2007) suggested that the Uzbek government's version corresponded at least to some extent with what had actually happened, it was the version of the human rights groups that was primarily considered by the Council of the European Union in its decision to impose sanctions (cf. Interviews 4, 12 and 15, Annex I). This apparently created an impression in Karimov's administration that the international investigation—should it be launched—would be affected by an already formed negative image of the Uzbek leadership in the West and produce biased results.

In fact, if the findings confirmed the disproportionate and indiscriminate use of force by the Uzbek security forces during the Andijan disturbances, i.e. if the government was shown to have engaged in major human rights breaches, then it would have significantly challenged the Uzbek leadership. First, as the observance of the fundamental human rights standards became a condition for the international recognition of state sovereignty and regime legitimacy (cf. Organization for Economic Co-operation and Development 2010: 29), criticism of Tashkent in the outcomes of the investigation would have extremely negatively affected the government's external legitimacy. Second, such outcomes would have also essentially undermined the regime's domestic output legitimacy, as they would mean that the Uzbek leadership failed to deliver two main public goods, i.e. security and the guarantee of basic human rights (cf. Eckert 1996: 31-32). The legitimacy of power is the necessary component of its authority, which provides ability to rule by consent (cf. Weber 2009). The diminished legitimacy of the Uzbek government and the president, who was personally in charge of the Andijan operation (Embassy of Uzbekistan to the United States, Press Office 2005a), could have weakened their authority and thus challenged the regime stability.

The Uzbek authorities seem to have been aware of such possible effects of the international inquiry findings (Interview 31, Annex I). This explains their position to oppose the launch of the independent investigation. At the same time, the Uzbek government initiated the EU-Uzbek Experts talks on the Andijan events in December 2006 and April 2007. Thus, they secured a more extensive control over the proceedings than the format of an international investigation would have allowed. Furthermore, the outcomes of the talks were not made available to the general public, and hence could not affect the legitimacy of the Uzbek leadership, as the findings of the independent inquiry otherwise could have done.

Unlike the case of the international investigation, the EU demand for fair and transparent conduct of the Andijan-related trials was not openly opposed by the Uzbek government. Yet, it still remained unfulfilled. While several trials held in the aftermath of the events were open for public, one could hardly characterize them as fully transparent and fair, as they were based on the defendants' confessions that had allegedly been coerced. The outcomes of the trials fully supported the official government's line, which was severely criticized by the western media and human rights groups. Conducting the trials in a truly fair and transparent manner could have revealed certain details contradicting the officially presented version of the events, thus creating an even broader platform for the critics of the Uzbek government. At the same time, initiation of lawsuits against those in charge of suppressing the Andijan disturbances would have meant an acknowledgement of the responsibility for the disproportionate use of force by the highest political and military figures. This again could undermine legitimacy of the Uzbek leadership, especially considering that the security and military authorities had acted on behalf of the president Islam Karimov (Embassy of Uzbekistan to the United States, Press Office 2005a).

The further EU requirement of effective engagement of the Uzbek government with the UN Special Rapporteurs introduced after the 2007 review round also was not met. The demand concerned cooperation with the Special Rapporteurs on extrajudicial, summary or arbitrary executions, on torture and other cruel, inhuman or degrading treatment or punishment, and on the promotion and protection of the right to freedom of opinion and expression. Despite their repeated requests, none of the Rapporteurs could obtain an official invitation to visit Uzbekistan from 2007 to 2009.

Notably, the UN Special Rapporteur on torture Theo van Boven had previously visited the country in late 2002. As the result of his mission, a report that was extremely critical of the situation in Uzbekistan was published (United Nations Special Rapporteur on Torture and Other Cruel, Inhuman or Degrading Treatment or Punishment 2003). The report enjoyed a high level of visibility and was discussed at various forums, including the UN, which contributed to the negative image of the Uzbek government among the international community. This evoked a corresponding reaction of the Uzbek leadership. Being aware of the possible consequences of the Special Rapporteurs' missions, the Uzbek government saw the fulfilment of the EU demand as potentially too damaging for the regime's international legitimacy, which had already been undermined (Interview 31, Annex I).

Finally, the EU requirement to allow all (domestic and foreign) NGOs to operate without constraints was also ignored by the Uzbek authorities. At the time when the demand was put to the fore by the Council of the EU (after the 2007 review round), Uzbekistan's legislation obliged all civil society organizations to be officially registered with the Ministry of Justice in order to carry out their activities in the country. In addition, initiation of specific projects was required to be reported to the state authorities. Unauthorized projects and activities of NGOs that failed to obtain a registration were considered to be illegal and could be sanctioned in accordance with established legal provisions. At the same time both domestic and international NGOs active in Uzbekistan were vulnerable to various inspections by the Uzbek state agencies. This created a functional mechanism of state control over the civil sector, which allowed closure of many NGOs that were critical of the existing regime (Ilkhamov 2005: 300-301).

While the civil sector was controlled by the state throughout the entire period of Uzbekistan's independence (and certainly prior to it as part of the soviet system), the 1990s saw relative liberalization with the establishment of numerous non-governmental organizations primarily supported with foreign funding. The notable tightening of the state grip on the NGOs started after 2003, in response to the 'coloured revolutions' in Georgia, Ukraine and Kyrgyzstan and continued after the events in Andijan. All three revolutions resulted in the swift change of political elites and ouster of previous leaders. All three were regarded as facilitated by Western efforts through training and financial support of opposition parties and civil society (primarily human rights related) organizations (cf. Polat 2007: 9). The disturbances in Andijan were also perceived by the government as an attempt by foreign actors to overthrow the established regime (Embassy of Uzbekistan to the United States, Press Office 2005a). Hence, the Uzbek authorities became suspicious of any NGOs' activities that went beyond social services provision, as they were regarded as potentially threatening to the regime status quo. This made the EU demand for unrestricted operation of all NGOs politically sensitive for the Uzbek leadership.

In contrast to the above, the EU requirement to allow unimpeded access for the relevant international bodies (i.e. the International Committee of the Red Cross) to detainees was quickly fulfilled by the Uzbek government. Within only six months after the condition had been officially stated, the ICRC received permission to resume prison visits. In order to explain this quick compliance, one needs to consider the aims of the visits and the general terms on which the ICRC work is based.

As Aeschlimann and Roggo put it, the ICRC visits *"serve primarily to 'establish the facts': to understand how the place of incarceration and the system work, to detect problems in the daily lives of detainees, and to document any abusive practices or violations of the rights of detainees defined by the regulations in force and international standards"* (Aeschlimann and Roggo 2007: 1). On the basis of these findings, the ICRC approaches the authorities to ensure that the respective measures are taken to improve the prisoners' conditions. Before such a visit is carried out, the situation, problems and operation of the detention facility are carefully documented and analysed. The actual visit comprises an inspection of the entire premises and interviews with both the detainees and the prison staff. The ICRC delegates are thus able to tour the detention facilities, talk with the prisoners in private, repeat visits as often as they deem necessary, and maintain constructive dialogue with the authorities. Yet, what is decisive here is that the ICRC findings and recommendations are confidential; they are discussed only with the authorities concerned (Aeschlimann and Roggo 2007). In other words, however critical these findings may be, they are not made available to the general public, and hence cannot be damaging to the regime legitimacy. Moreover, the ICRC visits to prisons do not directly challenge the political elites and the status quo of the power distribution. Therefore, the EU demand for the resumption of prison visits by the ICRC was not regarded as highly politically sensitive and was met relatively quickly by Tashkent.

For the four EU conditions that were partly met by the Uzbek government, it is necessary to consider to what extent they were fulfilled (i.e. what exactly was accomplished and what was neglected by the targets) and how precisely (or vaguely) the demands were formulated.

With regard to the latter, only one of the conditions contained a concrete requirement—release of human rights defenders from custody and cessation of their harassment. The mentioned defenders were mainly associated with state-independent media or human rights organizations supported through foreign funds. Imprisonment of the activists often followed their criticisms of the Uzbek government's actions, including the suppression of the Andijan disturbances. In view of the above discussion, criticisms were regarded by the Uzbek authorities as damaging their image and herewith the regime legitimacy, prompting action to lockdown the dissident voices (cf. Interviews 7 and 8, Annex I).

In response to EU pressure, several activists were released from custody throughout 2006-2009. The amnestied were mainly the persons whose cases were specifically addressed during the bilateral Human Rights Dialogues. Moreover, the releases often happened shortly before the sanctions review rounds or the EU-Uzbekistan Cooperation Councils, when the issue was high on the bilateral agenda and enjoyed greater publicity. At the same time, the amnesties mostly provided for the suspension of the sentences (and not their complete termination), which significantly limited the activists' freedoms after they had been released from custody. This allowed Tashkent to demonstrate certain acts of compliance with this EU condition, while maintaining control over the actions of the human rights defenders and journalists.

The other three EU requirements were formulated in a way that left a lot of room for interpretation of whether and to what extent the conditions could be fulfilled, but also whether and to what extent they were politically sensitive. The requirement for *'actions of the Uzbek government that would demonstrate the willingness to adhere to human rights, rule of law and fundamental freedoms'* is probably the most illustrative in these terms. This formulation meant that almost any steps taken by Tashkent to meet the other EU demands could be conceived as (at least) a partial fulfilment of this requirement. Moreover, such broad formulation gave an opportunity for the Uzbek authorities to claim compliance with this condition after undertaking only minor, less politically sensitive changes.

The EU demands for the positive engagement of the Uzbek government on human rights issues in the framework of the EU-Uzbekistan Cooperation Committee and for the reforms of the judiciary, law enforcement and police law were similarly vague. With regard to the former, the conducted interviews have revealed that there was no consensus among EU officials on what 'positive engagement' actually implied (cf. Interviews 10, 12, 15 and 16, Annex I). The latter condition also did not provide any references about the quality and the extent of the required reforms. Hence, initiation of comprehensive changes that could potentially challenge the established power system was not necessary in order to demonstrate that the EU demand was at least partly fulfilled. As a result, even the limited steps taken by the Uzbek authorities allowed them to claim compliance with the EU conditions.

4.2.3 Possible Interfering Effects

While evaluating and explaining the outcomes of the EU sanctions application, it is necessary to consider possible interfering effects of other external actors' engagement. In the wake of the Andijan events, the European Union was the only international actor that introduced sanctioning restrictions against Uzbekistan. While Tashkent continued participating in international forums in the framework of the UN and the OSCE, none of these organizations went beyond official condemnation of the Uzbek government's actions. As the coercive power of sanctions is deemed greater than that of rhetoric action (cf. Warkotsch 2008a: 229), the effects of the EU measures are expected to be significantly more powerful than those of the above international organizations.

However, it is important to note that when the EU sanctions entered into force in late 2005, the U.S. already had its restrictive measures in place. The restrictions were imposed by the U.S. Congress in response to Uzbekistan's lack of progress on democratic reforms and a deteriorating human rights record in 2004 (i.e. prior to the Andijan events). The Congress particularly barred military aid provided by the U.S. to the Uzbek government. Suspension of the measures was conditional upon a *"substantial progress in meeting commitments to respect human rights; establish a multiparty system; and ensure free and fair elections, freedom of expression, and the independence of the media"* (Nichol 2012: 17). After the Andijan unrest, the Uzbek authorities' actions were severely criticized by the U.S. government and the debate around further sanctions intensified. However, it was not before 2008 that the U.S. introduced admission restrictions applied to the persons allegedly responsible for the human rights violations in Andijan. Additionally, progress in investigating and prosecuting officials responsible for the deliberate killings of civilians in Andijan was stipulated. Yet, already in 2009 (and in the years after) the State Department issued waivers for Uzbekistan, so that practically no U.S. sanctions have been enforced since (Nichol 2012: 5).

While effects of the U.S. measures cannot be fully disregarded, the fact that they were in place prior to Andijan and did not result in the Uzbek government's compliance, but instead provoked rigorous counter-actions on the part of Uzbekistan (cf. Nichol 2010: 36) hardly suggests that the coercive power of the U.S. sanctions was significant. At the same time, the U.S. conditions for the withdrawal of sanctions were even more generally formulated than that of the European Union. This allows at least partly accommodating the problem of effect attribution by looking at the (lack of) compliance with each of the EU conditions individually, as it has been done in this study. Finally, the U.S. demands that intersected with some of the EU requirements were also not fulfilled by the Uzbek authorities (cf. Nichol 2012: 1-7), which is consistent with the above explanations of the sanctions application outcomes.

4.3 Concluding Remarks

This chapter evaluated successes and failures of the enforcement of sanctions by the European Union against Uzbekistan and examined possible explanations of EU conditionality outcomes. The success of the measures was assessed in terms of observable behaviour adaptations, i.e. compliance by the Uzbek government with the EU demands (cf. Table 3.1). As demonstrated in section 4.1, only limited changes were achieved as the result of the application of coercive measures. Of the nine EU conditions for the sanctions withdrawal, only one saw full compliance by the Uzbek authorities. The further four requirements were only partly fulfilled, whereas the other four were completely neglected by the targets.

While these effects appear to be very limited, there is a potential indirect impact that the sanctions might have had on the general human rights developments in Uzbekistan. Thus, several interviewed EU officials and civil society representatives have suggested that although the measures proved to be more symbolic, they signalled European concerns about the events in the country and revealed potential political costs that the Uzbek government would face in case of a further deterioration of the human rights situation. This might have had a *'preventive'* effect with regard to a possible violent suppression of future protests in Uzbekistan (cf. Interviews 10, 16 and 18, Annex I).

As suggested by the empirical evidence scrutinized in the second section of this chapter, the lack of credibility and consistency in the sanctions implementations, derived from the conflicting foreign policy interests of the EU Member States, apparently contributed to the failure of EU conditionality to achieve greater results. Yet, the lack of credibility could not explain the variance in Uzbekistan's compliance with the different EU conditions. Hence, as hypothesized in chapter 3, the substance of the changes demanded by the EU (i.e. the degree to which they were perceived as more or less politically sensitive by the targets) was examined as a possible explanatory factor.

Politically sensitive changes were defined here as those that could endanger, or be perceived as endangering the power position of target elites and the existing regime status quo. The findings have demonstrated that the EU demands that could potentially undermine the regime legitimacy and thus threaten its stability were neglected or openly opposed by the Uzbek leadership; whereas the conditions that were seen as less damaging or—due to their vague formulation—allowed a certain room for interpretation were at least partly fulfilled by the targets. Hereby, the key hypothesis of the current study that the substance of externally promoted norms and changes matters for success of the application of democratization tools by the EU has been confirmed for the case of EU conditionality measures against Uzbekistan.

Furthermore, as assumed in chapter 3, the degree to which certain EU demands were seen as more or less politically sensitive proved to be context-dependent. The EU sanctions against Uzbekistan was the only case of the EU human rights-related conditionality in Central Asia meaning that the present study does not allow for a cross-country comparison. However, it has demonstrated that certain externally promoted reforms and changes, which do not necessarily lead to immediate regime liberalization and hence to a loss of power by authoritarian elites, can still be seen as highly politically sensitive by the target governments, depending on country-specific developments. In the case of Uzbekistan, the need to maintain external and internal regime legitimacy proved to be decisive as to which EU demands were considered politically sensitive.

5. Structured Human Rights Dialogues

This chapter examines the implementation of EU bilateral human rights dialogues (HRDs) with the Central Asian states, and evaluates and explains their effects, where present. The first section traces the dialogue process, in order to assess whether the EU efforts drawing on normative suasion were successful. Such an evaluation appears to be quite a challenging task in terms of operationalizing and measuring effects of the dialogue. So far theoretically-oriented studies of normative suasion have not been able to fully resolve this challenge (cf. Wetzel 2013), while empirically grounded research on the effects of human rights dialogues has been largely missing (probably due to the fact that HRDs are a rather new format). In accordance with the discussion in chapter 3, the success of the dialogue-based tools is defined in terms of the internalization of promoted norms and values by the targets and corresponding 'sustained', long-term changes in the targets' behaviours (cf. Checkel 2005: 804; Warkotsch 2009: 252). An evaluation based on this definition would need to consider a possibility that the targets strategically adapt their behaviours rather than alter their beliefs and internalise new norms (cf. Checkel 2001: 566). In order to operationalize the latter (partly intangible) alterations and exclude possible intervening influences, this study uses a launch of relevant long-term initiatives and reforms proposed by the targets in connection with the dialogue process as an indication of success of the dialogue-based tools, while controlling for possible effects of external conditionality pressures.

Hence, section 5.1 examines whether and what long-term, forward-looking initiatives, programmes and legislative reforms were started by the governments of Kyrgyzstan and Uzbekistan in connection with the HRDs. First, the thematic scope of the HRDs is specified. Then, the long-term initiatives by the Central Asian governments related to the dialogues are identified. The analysis covers the period of the first three years after the establishment of the structured HRDs with Uzbekistan and Kyrgyzstan in 2007 and 2008 respectively. For the purpose of effect attribution, the study accounts for possible intervening influences of other EU measures (e.g. application of sanctions) and efforts of third actors in the region. Finally, section 5.2 scrutinizes possible explanations of the outcomes of the European engagement in accordance with the assumptions stated in chapter 3.

5.1 Tracing Implementation of the Dialogues

As mentioned in chapter 3, the structured human rights dialogues were introduced in EU democratization policy for the region after the adoption of the EU 'Strategy for a New Partnership' with Central Asia in June 2007 (Council of the European Union 2007c). The dialogues are conducted on a bilateral basis with each of the five Central Asian republics and are designed to *"discuss questions of mutual interest and enhance cooperation on human rights, inter alia in multilateral arena such as the United Nations and the OSCE"*, as well as to *"raise the concerns felt by the EU on human rights in the countries concerned, gather information and launch initiatives to improve the relevant human rights situation"* (European Commission 2009b: 1).

Originally, the structured HRDs included formal meetings of the senior and/or middle-range human rights officials of the European Commission,[34] Council Secretariat[35] and the EU Presidency[36] with the representatives of relevant departments of the Central Asian republics, usually ministers or deputy ministers of the interior and justice (Axyonova 2011). After the Lisbon Treaty's entry into force in December 2009 and the subsequent establishment of the European External Action Service (EEAS), the latter institution took over the organization of the official dialogue rounds. The rounds are supposed to be held annually with all five Central Asian countries (Interview 30, Annex I).

In accordance with the EU general guidelines on HRDs (Council of the European Union 2009c), the dialogues also involve human rights activists, NGO members, and academic representatives from both Europe and Central Asia through the civil society seminars held in between the official HRD sessions. The purpose of this exercise is to provide a platform for discussion to civil society and generate recommendations feeding into the official dialogue sessions (Axyonova 2011). Hence, the issues in focus of the civil society seminars are also included into the scope of the present analysis.

The EU-Uzbekistan human rights dialogue, held in the framework of the Subcommittee on Justice and Home Affairs, Human Rights and Related Is-

---

[34] E.g. policy officers from the DG RELEX, Human Rights Unit.
[35] E.g. at the level of the Head of the Human Rights Unit of the Council Secretariat.
[36] Generally with the incumbent presidency in the position of chair.

sues, was the first one to be established on a regular basis.[37] The opening round took place in 2007 following preparatory negotiations that had started one year earlier (even before the adoption of the 'Strategy for a New Partnership').[38] The EU-Kyrgyzstan human rights dialogue was launched several months later with the first official session conducted on 28 October 2008 (Council of the European Union n/a).

By the end of 2010, four official rounds of dialogues were conducted with Uzbekistan and only two with Kyrgyzstan. The third HRD round with the later state was deferred from autumn 2010 to June 2011, due to the absence of a functional government in the country after the overthrow of President Kurmanbek Bakiyev in April 2010 and the subsequent parliamentary elections on 10 October 2010 that did not immediately lead to successful coalition building (Interviews 19 and 20, Annex I). Over 2008-2009, one civil society seminar was organized in each of the countries and a regional seminar with participants from all five Central Asian states was held in Brussels in 2010.

The following sub-section reviews the issues discussed during the HRD rounds and civil society seminars, in order to specify the thematic scope of the dialogues. As the HRDs take place behind closed doors and the reporting on internal discussions is commonly limited to very concise press releases by the organizing institutions, the current analysis also relies on data collected during expert interviews with European and Central Asian civil society representatives and EU officials involved in the dialogue process. The latter group of interviewees includes officials from the former European Commission's DG RELEX, Human Rights Unit of the Council Secretariat, EEAS, and the EU Delegation in Kazakhstan (which prior to 2010 was a joint delegation of the European Commission to Kazakhstan, Kyrgyzstan and Tajikistan).

5.1.1 The Issues in Focus of the HRDs

The official HRD sessions include several hours of intensive, focused discussions on human rights related matters. The adoption of an agenda for each dialogue round follows a standard procedure of preliminary exchange of notes between the EU representatives and the respective ministry of for-

---

[37] Prior to it, *ad hoc* consultations on human rights-related matters had been undertaken with Turkmenistan (European Commission 2009b).

[38] The negotiations were initiated in response to the human rights violations in Andijan in 2005.

eign affairs on the issues to be discussed during the official session (Interviews 11 and 15, Annex I). The discussions usually cover general human rights concerns and specific developments in each country.

Uzbekistan

Over 2007-2010, the official rounds of the EU-Uzbekistan human rights dialogue commonly focused on the national legislative reforms, engagement in the international forums for the protection of human rights, and cooperation with international human rights mechanisms in the following areas:

- possibility of an international inquiry into the Andijan events of 2005;
- access to justice for all citizens, particularly through the implementation of *habeas corpus* in law enforcement practices and insurance of equal, unimpeded access of citizens to legal assistance;
- abolition of the death penalty;
- general situation of human rights defenders and civil society development;
- freedom of thought, conscience and religion, including in the fight against religious extremism;
- freedom of expression, information and media, especially in terms of legislation leading to liberalization of the media;
- children's rights and combatting of child labour, particularly forced work in Uzbekistan's cotton fields; and
- reform of prison conditions, including elimination of torture, and access to detention places by the relevant international bodies, i.e. the International Committee of the Red Cross (cf. Council of the European Union 2010c; Council of the European Union n/a; European Union 2008: 17; European Union 2007: 22-23; Interviews 11, 15, and 20, Annex I).

The civil society seminar held in Uzbekistan in October 2008 concerned liberalization of mass media as part of the democratization process, whereas the above mentioned regional seminar organized in Brussels in June 2010 covered different aspects of women's rights (European Commission 2009b; Bick 2010).

Kyrgyzstan

By comparison, during the first two rounds of the EU-Kyrgyzstan HRD, the focus was on the development of a national framework for the protection of human rights and enforcement of national human rights legislation concerning the following issues:

- freedom of association and assembly, including civil society development;
- freedom of thought, conscience and religion;
- freedom of expression, information and media, including cessation of violence against journalists and provision of guarantees for their safety;
- democratic elections;
- reforms related to the judicial system and the abolition of the death penalty;[39]
- protection of refugees, migrants and asylum-seekers;
- rights of prisoners, including elimination of torture and cruel, inhuman and degrading treatment;
- women's rights; and
- rights of children (cf. Swedish Presidency of the European Union 2009; European Union, External Action 2010: 130; Interviews 11, 15, and 20, Annex I).

The first civil society seminar held in Bishkek in March 2009 focused on the protection of children's and prisoners' rights. As it has been indicated above, the regional seminar of 2010 covered women's rights in all Central Asian republics, including Kyrgyzstan (European Commission 2009a; Axyonova 2011: 2).

In addition to the discussions on the general human rights developments in Kyrgyzstan and Uzbekistan, the EU regularly raised a number of individual cases with regard to the protection of human rights defenders, journalists and their family members against arbitrary or oppressive treatment (e.g. detention or other limitation of their rights) by state authorities in both countries. A list with the names of persons concerned was handed over by the European representatives to the respective Central Asian government officials during each HRD round with an expectation that the cases would be followed-up by the next dialogue session (Interviews 11, 15, 19 and 20, Annex I).

---

[39] In Kyrgyzstan, the death penalty was abolished by law in June 2007. A moratorium on executions was in place already since 1998 (Radio Free Europe/Radio Liberty 2007).

5.1.2 Evaluating the Results: What Has (Not) Been Achieved

This sub-section examines whether the governments of Kyrgyzstan and Uzbekistan responded to the issues in the scope of the above mentioned HRDs by launching any long-term initiatives, programmes or legislative reforms.

Notably, to date there has been no publicly available evaluation of the implementation and effects of the HRDs in the Central Asian countries.[40] According to officials of the European Commission and the Council Secretariat, internal discussions on the HRDs take place on a regular basis as part of the preparation and follow-up of the official sessions. Yet, no extensive internal evaluation has been conducted so far (Interviews 11, 15 and 20, Annex I), which also indicates methodological challenges of such a study in the absence of clearly stated objectives and benchmarks for the dialogues (Interview 19, Annex I).

In order to identify the long-term initiatives by the Central Asian governments in the spheres related to the HRDs, the current research draws on reports by the Freedom House, particularly *'Nations in Transit'*, which cover both Kyrgyzstan and Uzbekistan, and the very detailed *'Country Reports on Human Rights Practices'* prepared annually by the U.S. Department of State. This is further complemented by an analysis of press releases of the Uzbek and Kyrgyz state agencies and state-independent media reports facilitated by the online *'Crisis Watch Database'* that is maintained by the International Crisis Group (International Crisis Group n/a).

The presence of long-term initiatives and reforms however does not imply that they resulted from the normative suasion process within the framework of the EU human rights dialogues. In other words, there might have been other (domestic and external) factors that could lead to the reforms. Therefore, the current research also draws on expert interviews with EU officials and civil society representatives involved in the HRDs that help identify whether the respective changes connect with the dialogues. The study further takes account of possible intervening influences of the other EU measures (e.g. application of sanctions in the case of Uzbekistan) and efforts of third parties that also pursue democratization or human rights agendas in Central Asia.

---

[40] This is despite the EU's own guidelines for human rights dialogues that call for a regular assessment of the HRDs' performance and added value (Council of the European Union 2009c: 28).

Uzbekistan

With regard to the issues in focus of the EU-Uzbekistan HRD identified in section 5.1.1, the main changes undertaken by the Uzbek government that were associated by some interviewees with the dialogue process were the abolition of the death penalty in law and practice, the ratification of the ILO *Worst Forms of Child Labour Convention* and *Minimum Age Convention*, and the introduction of *habeas corpus* as part of the judiciary reform (Interviews 18 and 23, Annex I). However, as most of these changes occurred in 2008-2009 after only one or two official rounds of the HRD, some suggested that the reforms resulted from other internally and externally driven processes instead. Uzbekistan had experienced international pressure to undertake the above changes, e.g. through the UN channels, prior to the establishment of the EU-Uzbekistan human rights dialogue (Interviews 6, 11, 15 and 16, Annex I).

Some of the interviewees also connected the above improvements with the response of the Uzbek government to the EU sanctions rather than the HRD, especially in view of the conditions for the sanctions withdrawal that included *inter alia* very generally formulated demands for reforms of the judiciary, law enforcement and police law, as well as other actions demonstrating willingness of the Uzbek authorities to adhere to human rights, rule of law and fundamental freedoms (Interviews 9, 10 and 19, Annex I). Nevertheless, the interest of Uzbek officials and their information requests concerning practices related to the *habeas corpus* during official HRD rounds suggest that the dialogue played a facilitating role at least with regard to the introduction of *habeas corpus* (Interview 15, Annex I).

The HRD discussions concerning a possible reform of prison conditions in Uzbekistan and access to detention places by the relevant international bodies could be regarded as partly successful, as access by the International Committee of the Red Cross to prisoners was made possible by the Uzbek authorities. Yet, this possibility was also immediately related to EU conditionality, as allowing the ICRC prison visits was explicitly stated as one of the conditions for the EU sanctions withdrawal after the 2007 review round (see chapter 4).

Likewise, the release of several human rights activists from custody, which was in focus of the HRD sessions, has sometimes been associated with the positive effects of the dialogue process (Interview 18, Annex I). However, it was also among the EU requirements that were officially stated during the whole period of the EU sanctions (see Table 4.1 in chapter 4). The fact that the release of human rights defenders happened immediately prior to the review of the restrictions by the Council coupled with the fact that the Uzbek government was interested in demonstrating human rights progress in order to foster the withdrawal of sanctions suggests that the HRD alone would not have led to this improvement (Interviews 16 and 19, Annex I). In addition, the individual cases of political amnesty do not necessarily signify a long-term change or internalization of human rights values by the Uzbek government authorities, especially considering that the harassment of human rights activists has not stopped after 2009 (U.S. Department of State 2011b).

Attempts of EU officials to persuade the Uzbek government of the necessity for an international inquiry into the Andijan events were also backed-up by EU sanctions. Yet, in this case it could be partly possible to distinguish the effects of conditionality from those of the dialogue. The demand for investigation was not officially stated by the EU after the 2007 sanctions review (Council of the European Union 2007a). Yet, it continued being in focus of the EU human rights dialogue with Uzbekistan even at a later stage (Interviews 11 and 20, Annex I). Hence, if the position of the Uzbek government had changed after the start of the HRDs in 2007 and especially after the withdrawal of the EU sanctions in 2009, the change could be (at least to some extent) associated with the dialogue process. However, the normative suasion appeared to be fruitless, as the Uzbek authorities remained opposed to the possibility of an international investigation and no long-term initiatives or reforms related to the Andijan events could be identified.

With regard to the further issues in focus of the bilateral HRD—the freedom of thought, conscience and religion, and the freedom of expression, information and media—the dialogue process cannot be considered successful. From the very beginning of the HRD, these issues appeared to be among the most difficult to discuss with the Uzbek government and state-led civil society (Interview 15 and 27, Annex I). A good example is the failure of the first civil society seminar titled *'Liberalization of mass media—an important component of the democratization of society'*, held in Tashkent in 2008 (Babadjanov 2008), which turned out to be a *'very unpleasant experience'* for both the Uzbek and European sides (Interview 15, Annex I). The participating European human rights NGOs, mainly based in Brussels, expressed harsh critique with regard to the lack of freedom of mass media in Uzbekistan. The Uzbek side was represented by government-organized NGOs

(GONGOs), who responded by presenting primarily positive statistics and progressive developments in the country. This left no room for a serious, constructive discussion during the first round of seminars and eventually led to the cancellation of the next civil society seminar in 2009 (Interviews 18 and 19, Annex I). In general, no reforms or initiatives could be identified in Uzbekistan in 2008-2010 that would have signified improvements in the freedom of thought and conscience and the freedom of expression and media.

To sum up, many of the issues in focus of the EU-Uzbekistan HRD were closely related to EU sanction conditionality. This is particularly true for the possibility of an international inquiry into the Andijan events of 2005, reforms of the judiciary and criminal law (introduction of *habeas corpus*), treatment of human rights defenders and civil society development, as well as the reform of prison conditions and access to detention places by the relevant international bodies (cf. Table 4.1 in chapter 4). It is therefore very difficult to distinguish effects of the dialogue process from those of the EU political conditionality. As the identified reforms and changes took place shortly prior to the sanctions review rounds, they apparently were triggered by the coercive measures rather than normative suasion. This suggests that taken as a tool in its own right the HRD would not have led to any significant improvements in Uzbekistan. Nevertheless, the human rights dialogue seems to have played a facilitating role as an additional channel of European concerns and expectations and thus intended to reinforce the application of EU sanctions (Interview 15, Annex I).

Kyrgyzstan

Interestingly, while all of the interviewed civil society representatives and EU officials characterized the EU-Kyrgyzstan human rights dialogue sessions as very open and constructive (especially in comparison to the EU-Uzbekistan HRD), they found it difficult to point at concrete effects of the dialogue process (Interviews 9, 11, 15, 16, 19, 20 and 27, Annex I). This is particularly true if one regards government initiatives and reform proposals as an indication of success. In Kyrgyzstan, reform processes in many spheres identified in sub-section 5.1.1 followed the ratification of international human rights treaties in the 1990s and early 2000s, i.e. long before the establishment of the bilateral HRDs (Interview 15, Annex I; cf. University of Minnesota, Human Rights Library n/a). The only relevant international treaties that entered into force in Kyrgyzstan between 2008 and 2010 were the ILO *Migration for Employment Convention* and *Maintenance of Social Security Rights Convention* (International Labour Organization n/a). Yet, both of them were ratified by Kyrgyzstan already in September 2008, before the first official session of the EU-Kyrgyzstan HRD that was held on 28 October 2008 (Council of the European Union n/a).

Nevertheless, some positive developments that were associated with the effects of the human rights dialogue could be identified during the interviews. One of the main examples concerned the recommendations elaborated at the first civil society seminar *'Co-operation to protect and promote children's rights and prisoners'*, which took place in Bishkek in March 2009. As a follow-up of the recommendations during the 2009 dialogue session, the Kyrgyz government representatives proposed to prepare a national action plan in the sphere of children's rights. According to an interviewed EU official, this demonstrated the Kyrgyz authorities' responsiveness and commitment to the dialogue process but also their constructive cooperation with civil society (Interview 20, Annex I). The preparation of the action plan however could not proceed in 2010 due to political turmoil in the country. Hence, this development can be regarded as only a partial success of the HRD.

Another example of positive developments that were allegedly facilitated by the dialogue related to the suspension of charges and release from custody of individuals whose prosecution was politically motivated (Interview 18, Annex I). However, such cases were rare, whereas a number of persons facing politically motivated charges remained in custody during the Bakiyev presidency (cf. U.S. Department of State 2010a; International Crisis Group n/a). Hence, the individual cases of amnesty could not be regarded as an indication of a long-term change or a general trend towards improvement of the human rights situation between October 2008, when the dialogue process started, and April 2010, when President Kurmanbek Bakiyev was forced to resign. The political liberalization and release of further political prisoners that followed Bakiyev's resignation were associated by interviewees with more democratically oriented policies of the new interim government rather than with the bilateral dialogue process (Interviews 16, 19 and 30, Annex I).

Other than that, no noteworthy improvements or government initiatives related to the issues in focus of the HRDs (specified in sub-section 5.1.1) could be identified in Kyrgyzstan after the start of the HRD process and prior to the coup of April 2010. The later more significant political developments of 2010-2011 (e.g. constitutional reform that allowed for more accountability of the government) can hardly be regarded as resulting from the bilateral dialogue, as the HRD process was interrupted between October 2009 and June 2011 due to the internal events in Kyrgyzstan, and from 2008 to 2009 only two HRD sessions took place.

To sum up, the general dialogue atmosphere in the case of Kyrgyzstan was much more open than in Uzbekistan, which provided a positive environment for productive discussions both during official HRD rounds and civil society seminars. However, similarly to the HRD with Uzbekistan, it was difficult to identify the actual effects of the dialogue. The only example of a long-term initiative by the Kyrgyz government that was directly associated with the HRD process was the proposal to develop a national action plan for the protection of children's rights. However, this can be regarded only as a partial success, because the preparation of the action plan could not proceed due to the political instability in the country throughout 2010.

In general, in both country-cases the human rights dialogues cannot be regarded as successful, as they have not led to any concrete initiatives or reform proposals by the governments (with the exception of the proposed action plan in Kyrgyzstan). This however is not surprising considering that normative suasion tools are expected to produce results in the long run, while the recent establishment of the HRD format and the time span of the current study do not allow tracing effects in the longer term. In the given timeframe, the dialogues have been viewed mainly as complementary tools for obtaining or sharing information and facilitating changes triggered by other internal and external processes (cf. Interviews 15 and 30, Annex I).

5.2 Explaining the Outcomes: Multiple Causes of Failure

As hypothesized in chapter 3, the success of the EU dialogue-based tools in such regions as Central Asia can be influenced by the degree to which the promoted norms and changes are politically sensitive for the targets, i.e. are perceived as endangering the existing political status quo. The hypothesis seems to be controversial, as the dialogue-based tools are supposedly based on the normative suasion mechanism (following the constructivist logic of appropriateness), while the above definition of politically sensitive norms draws on the rationalist mechanism of strategic calculation. However, the rationalist-constructivist distinction between the two mechanisms is more analytical than empirical. In reality both mechanisms often work simultaneously (cf. Checkel 2001: 581; Kelley 2004). While the theoretical differentiation between various democratization tools refers to their underlying logics (see chapter 2), the operationalization of their success in the current study reflects the practices of applying the tools (see chapter 3). The presence (or absence) of reform proposals by target governments as an indication of success (or failure) can be a result of both strategic calculation and normative suasion. As the latter mechanism is expected to work mainly in the long run (Warkotsch 2008b: 64), the short time span of the EU human rights dialogues suggests that the involved Central Asian government actors were rather guided by the strategic calculation logic, especially because they were simultaneously affected by other tools of external actors (e.g. international pressure through the UN and U.S. or EU sanctions conditionality) to which the dialogues were complimentary. Hence, the above formulation of the key hypothesis is still valid for the case of the HRDs.

In addition to the substance of promoted norms and changes, factors related to the implementation of the dialogues may also affect their results. The review of these factors in chapter 3 allowed building a set of process-related scope conditions (or favourable factors) for success of the dialogue-based tools (see Table 3.2 in chapter 3). The conditions include 'in-camera' settings, deliberative and equality-based approach, clear and consistent messages by the democratizer, as well as a long-term and intensive dialogue process (cf. Checkel 2005). The absence of these favourable factors in the case of the HRDs with Kyrgyzstan and Uzbekistan could have contributed to their very limited effects. Before turning to the main hypothesis, it is therefore necessary to take a closer look at the HRD implementation modalities.

5.2.1 Process-related Factors

With regard to the 'in-camera', not open for public settings, they were provided for official dialogue rounds that generally took place behind closed doors. Participants were limited to a number of selected senior and/or middle-range officials of the EU and the respective Central Asian state. As it has been mentioned above, the reporting on the course and contents of the HRD sessions was limited to very concise press releases by the organizing institutions. Following each dialogue round, the European Commission (and later the EEAS) organized briefings with European civil society organizations (CSOs) with the purpose of information sharing and exchange. Yet, the briefings were open to a very limited number of mainly Brussels-based NGOs active in human rights promotion, and the information distributed and discussed during such events was to be treated as confidential (Interviews 18 and 19, Annex I).

By comparison, civil society seminars held in-between the official dialogue rounds enjoyed much more transparency and visibility. Not only were they open to a considerable number of European and Central Asian NGOs and human rights defenders, in the case of Kyrgyzstan the detailed reports on the course of the seminars were made publicly available by the European Commission (Axyonova 2011). While in Kyrgyzstan such transparency and the involvement of civil society in the dialogue process in general proved to be rather positive (considering the readiness of the Kyrgyz government to accept recommendations of the CSOs), in Uzbekistan it turned out to be *'a disaster'* and a *'lesson learning experience'* after the failure of the first civil society seminar (cf. Interviews 19 and 15, Annex I).

The assumption that the dialogue settings mattered was also confirmed by the fact that during the official HRD rounds, held behind closed doors, specific cases of human rights violations could be raised and very critical issues were addressed directly. Whereas in the case of more open-for-public civil society seminars, there was a general tendency towards opting for 'softer', less controversial issues, especially after the first seminar with Uzbekistan (Interviews 15 and 19, Annex I).

Concerning the deliberative and equality-based approach as a further scope condition for success of the dialogue-based tools, it was hardly met by the European Union. According to the involved EU officials, the HRD sessions were usually structured as follows: European representatives offered thematic presentations on the 'best practices' to follow (e.g. abolition of the death penalty or *habeas corpus*), and representatives of the respective Central Asian government presented (follow-up) reports on the recent human rights developments in the country. Human rights violations or shortcomings in the EU Member States were commonly not part of the dialogues (Interviews 11, 15 and 20, Annex I). This appears to resemble a teacher-student relationship rather than a peer-to-peer deliberation. Only in the case of the EU-Uzbekistan dialogue, human rights related issues in the European states were partly discussed. This, however, was not originally initiated by the EU, but demanded by the Uzbek authorities, who agreed to participate in the dialogue only if it was based on the principle of equality of the both parties (Interview 15, Annex I).

Regarding the clarity and consistency of the democratizer's messages, it is very difficult to assess whether they were provided for by the EU in the framework of the closed-to-public HRD sessions. While it was impossible to secure an agreement for interviews with Central Asian government representatives who were involved in the dialogue process, reliance solely on responses of the respective EU officials could have led to biased results. Nevertheless, what generally could be observed was that messages sent during the bilateral human rights dialogues were not necessarily reinforced through the other official dialogue formats. Thus, the EU Member State officials often avoided human rights related questions during formal meetings dedicated to economic or security cooperation, which was justified by the existence of the HRD as a specific platform for raising human rights concerns. This was particularly demonstrated during the EU-Central Asia Ministerial Conference in September 2009, when the human rights and democratization-related issues were deliberately excluded from the agenda. This fact signifies the lack of coordination and consistency among the different dialogue formats of the EU with the Central Asian states (Interview 19, Annex I).

Finally, with regard to long-term and intensive institutional contacts as a scope condition for success of dialogue-based tools, it has yet to be met. The HRD process started in 2007 and took place only once a year (or even less frequently in the case of Kyrgyzstan). This is hardly enough to lead to an internalization of the promoted norms and a long-term change. The low intensity of the human rights dialogues and the insufficient inter-institutional contacts were clearly demonstrated by the inability of the EU officials to follow-up on the development of the national action plan in the sphere of children's rights that had been proposed by the Kyrgyz government in 2009 (Interview 20, Annex I). In these terms the lack of effects of the human rights dialogues is not surprising.

On the whole, the process-related factors favourable for success of the dialogue-based tools were only partly present in the case of the EU human rights dialogues with both Kyrgyzstan and Uzbekistan. While the 'in-camera' setting was provided for the official dialogue rounds (unlike for the civil society seminars), the deliberative, equality-based approach was only partly employed in the case of Uzbekistan and absent in the case of Kyrgyzstan.

Concerning the other factors, neither the consistency of messages throughout various dialogue formats, nor the length and intensity of the HRD processes were ensured. This has apparently contributed to the poor results of the dialogue-based tools.

5.2.2 Substance of the Promoted Norms

The main hypothesis of this study assumes that in authoritarian environments such as in Central Asia, EU democratization tools are more likely to be successful if they promote less politically sensitive norms and changes. Applying this to the human rights dialogues, they too are assumed to be more likely to result in government initiatives and reform proposals when the contents of the dialogue are not expected to shift the political status quo or endanger existing power relations.

In Uzbekistan, no long-term initiatives or reforms directly associated with the HRD process could be identified. This is not surprising considering that favourable factors for success along the democratizer-, target- and process-related dimensions were largely absent. According to interviewed EU officials, the dialogues with the Central Asian states from the very beginning were expected to play a facilitating role rather than trigger concrete changes. In Uzbekistan, the HRD was supposed to complement other EU democratization tools, serving as an additional channel for explicating demands related to the imposed sanctions (Interviews 15 and 30, Annex I). The short-term changes and limited reforms initiated by the government were mainly associated with the coercive measures, which were reinforced through general international pressure by the UN and the United States. With regard to these changes, the above hypothesis has been tested and confirmed for EU conditionality-based tools in the previous chapter. However, in the absence of government initiatives and reforms that could be detached from external conditionality there is not enough empirical evidence to test the hypothesis for the case of the EU-Uzbekistan human rights dialogue.

The HRD with Kyrgyzstan offers more useful insights. Unlike Uzbekistan, the country did not experience international sanctions. At the same time, it provided a more fertile ground for external democratization and human rights promotion. The EU human rights dialogue with Bishkek was partly successful resulting in the government's proposition to elaborate a national action plan to protect the rights of children. It is therefore necessary to take a closer look at this initiative, its context and implications.

While the rights of children were an important matter covered by the EU-Kyrgyzstan HRD, the European Union was neither the first nor the only external actor to promote the issue. The UN agencies, especially the United Nations Children's Fund (UNICEF) and also the United Nations Development Programme (UNDP), have been active on this issue for a much longer period of time. The protection and promotion of children's rights have been in the centre of the UNICEF engagement in Kyrgyzstan since the mid-1990s, when the organization opened its office in Bishkek. Following the ratification of the international *Convention on the Rights of the Child* by the Kyrgyz Republic in 1994, UNICEF has assisted the government in implementing its key provisions (UNICEF n/a).

As it is part of this Convention, the Kyrgyz Republic has regularly reported to the UN Committee on the Rights of the Child.[41] As a follow-up to the 1990 World Summit for Children and in preparation for the 2002 UN Special Session on Children, the government also prepared a progress report on the implementation of the World Summit Declaration (Kyrgyz Republic 2000). In 2000, in cooperation with UNICEF, Kyrgyz authorities developed the national *'New Generation'* programme to protect children's rights. In 2006, the Code of the Kyrgyz Republic on Children was adopted (United Nations Committee on the Rights of the Child 2007). Thus, the action plan in the field of children's rights proposed by the Kyrgyz government during the HRD with the EU was by no means a new development, but rather a continuation of the previous experience of similar programmes and initiatives developed in cooperation with international actors.

At the same time, the rights of children in Kyrgyzstan have never been politicized to the extent that they have been for instance in Uzbekistan, where the state has continuously been accused by international organizations, watchdogs and rights groups of using forced child labour in the cotton fields (e.g. Cotton Campaign n/a; Uzbek-German Forum for Human Rights 2012). The use of child labour has also been reported in Kyrgyzstan, yet it has never taken a form or extensiveness that is comparable to its western neighbour and has been regarded as a product of increasing poverty rather than the government's deliberate policies (International Labour Organization 2001).

---

[41] The reports can be retrieved from *Refworld*, an online database supported by the UNHCR, the UN Refugee Agency (UNHCR Refworld n/a).

In Kyrgyzstan, children's rights are commonly associated with social service provisions, foremost health care and education, which are placed under a shared responsibility of the state and the society. For instance, the Constitution of the Kyrgyz Republic, as well as the Children's Code, the Family Code and the Civil Code provide for the *"responsibility of society as a whole for caring for families and children"*, specifying that the *"responsibility for children and their education is the natural right and civil duty of parents and that the State must ensure the support, instruction and education of orphans and children whose parents have lost custody"* (Child Rights International Network 2010). The above mentioned initiatives and documents (especially the progress report on the implementation of the World Summit Declaration and the 'New Generation' programme) also emphasise social protection aspects (Kyrgyz Republic 2000). Finally, the international actors engaged in the promotion of children's rights in Kyrgyzstan have also traditionally concentrated on social rights and human security concerns. For instance, UNICEF activities have predominantly focused on child health and nutrition, poverty reduction, early childhood development and education, as well as disaster response and crisis-related assistance (Government of the Kyrgyz Republic and UNICEF 2012: 5-6).

In view of the general perception of children's rights as part of the social domain and the government's previous experience of developing child support programmes in cooperation with international organizations, children's rights are not attributable to the category of highly politically sensitive issues in Kyrgyzstan. The protection and promotion of children's rights (predominantly related to the improvement of living conditions, health care and education) could hardly endanger the existing regime or power relations. On the contrary, the development of programmes to support children as a vulnerable group meant a potential increase in the inflow of international financial assistance, which in the end would benefit state structures involved in the programme's implementation. This explains why the Kyrgyz government easily agreed to follow the recommendation of the 2009 civil society seminar to develop a national action plan in the sphere of children's rights.

As the action plan proposal was the only case of the government's initiative that could be attributed to the dialogue process, there is not enough empirical evidence to fully confirm or refute the key hypothesis of the current study. Nevertheless, the above analysis provides some evidence in support of the assumption that the substance of promoted norms and changes matters for success of the EU dialogue-based tools.

5.3 Concluding Remarks

This chapter evaluated successes and failures of the EU's human rights dialogues with Kyrgyzstan and Uzbekistan and examined possible explanations of their results, which were very limited. The success of the dialogues was assessed in terms of the launch of legislative reforms, long-term initiatives and state programmes proposed by the target governments within the HRD framework. As demonstrated in section 5.1, the dialogues have not resulted in any major changes. In Uzbekistan, the HRD served as a tool to compliment EU sanctions. While the latter measures have been regarded as triggers of some limited reforms, the dialogue proved to be largely unsuccessful as a stand-alone tool. In Kyrgyzstan, the HRD process was partly successful with regard to one issue under discussion. Following civil society recommendations, the Kyrgyz government proposed to develop a national action plan in the sphere of children's rights, which unfortunately could not be accomplished in the following years due to the political turmoil in the country.

As suggested by the empirical evidence scrutinized in section 5.2, the process-related factors coupled with other (target- and democratizer-related) factors have contributed to the very limited effects of the HRDs. Among the process-related factors, the short time span and the low intensity of the dialogues seem to be decisive for the absence of positive changes, considering that normative suasion is expected to work in the long run. Concerning the key hypothesis of the current study (that the substance of promoted norms and changes matters for the success of the EU democratization tools), it could not be fully tested for the human rights dialogues, as the only positive development that could be attributed to the HRDs was the above mentioned proposal by the Kyrgyz government. Nevertheless, the evidence provided for this particular case is consistent with the assumption that the changes that are not regarded as politically sensitive for the established regime are more likely to occur as the result of the application of dialogue-based tools.

In view of the absence of several (target-, democratizer- and process-related) favourable conditions, the failure of the HRDs appears to be overdetermined, especially in the case of Uzbekistan. Also, interaction between different types of interventions (e.g. between EU sanctions and HRD in Uzbekistan) and various actors (e.g. UNICEF and EU in Kyrgyzstan) hinders isolation of individual causes. Nevertheless, certain interaction patterns and their effects could be revealed. Thus, in the case of Uzbekistan, the EU sanctions and the human rights dialogue were supposed to be mutually reinforcing. The Uzbek government agreed to participate in the HRD in an attempt to show its readiness to engage with the EU on human rights issues and thus show compliance with EU conditions for withdrawal of sanctions. At the later stage, the dialogue served as an additional channel for explicating EU concerns and sanctions-related demands. Yet, this still did not lead to significant improvements. While in the case of Kyrgyzstan, the UN engagement in the sphere of children's rights apparently prepared the ground for the Kyrgyz government initiative proposed in the framework of the EU human rights dialogue, thus contributing to the partial success of the HRD.

6. The Institution Building and Partnership Programme and the European Instrument for Democracy and Human Rights

This chapter scrutinizes the application of the EU's democratic empowerment tools in Central Asia. It particularly evaluates the Institution Building and Partnership Programme (IBPP), which was part of the EU mainstream assistance prior to 2007, and the European Instrument for Democracy and Human Rights (EIDHR), the specific EU tool for external democratization and human rights promotion through direct civil society support. According to the discussion in chapter 3, the success of the democratic empowerment tools is defined in terms of the EU's ability to fully implement its democratization related assistance, which depends on the target government accepting EU support. Hence, the first part of this chapter examines to what extent the IBPP and the EIDHR could be implemented in Kyrgyzstan and Uzbekistan and whether the programmes were constrained by the countries' governments. The second section turns to possible explanations of the EU engagement outcomes in accordance with the assumptions stated in chapter 3.

6.1 Tracing Implementation of the Programmes

The Institution Building and Partnership Programme (IBPP) 'Support to Civil Society and Local Initiatives' was established as part of the Small Projects Programme within the broader framework of the EU's TACIS programme in 2001. The IBPP was designed to support a democratic institution-building process through partnership of non-governmental organizations, local/regional authorities and not-for-profit professional organizations in the TACIS countries, including Central Asia, with their counterparts in the European Union. Notably, the operation of the programme is based on financing agreements negotiated between the European Commission and the target countries' governments, which makes the IBPP implementation dependent on these governments' consents.

This is different in the case of the European Instrument for Democracy and Human Rights (EIDHR) that provides financial support directly to non-governmental organizations and thus is supposed to circumvent governmental interference with the instrument. Moreover, EIDHR focuses in particular on civil society organizations that seek to preserve their independence from state authorities and is specifically designed to cover issues of human rights and democratic development to which target governments would be reluctant to consent.

6.1.1 The IBPP at Work

This sub-section scrutinizes the IBPP implementation in Kyrgyzstan and Uzbekistan. Prior to examining the actual application of the programme, it introduces the general IBPP programming and operation procedures in more detail. This information provides an understanding of how the programme works and is relevant for the subsequent evaluation of the IBPP performance in Central Asia.

Programming and Operation Background

The ground for establishing the Institution Building and Partnership Programme was prepared by Council Regulation (99/2000) of 29 December 1999 concerning the provision of assistance to partner states in Eastern Europe and Central Asia (through the TACIS programme). Although the regulation did not explicitly mention the IBPP, it identified support for civil society as one of its focus areas (Council of the European Union 2000: Annex II) and provided for the possibility of financing small-scale projects (Council of the European Union 2000: Art. 2/2). The regulation set priorities for the European Commission's assistance to the Central Asian states, which were later reflected in the multi-annual EU's Strategy Paper for Central Asia for 2002-2006 and the respective Indicative Programmes (IPs) for 2002-2004 and 2005-2006. None of the documents specified the details of the Institution Building and Partnership Programme (cf. European Commission 2002; European Commission 2004b). Yet, the latter Indicative Programme stated that the IBPP was supposed to offer *"a comprehensive thematic approach towards civil society issues, integrating activities in a specific sector with democracy building activities and through a direct dialogue and cooperation at the grass roots level with a wide range of partners: civil servants, professionals, young people, women, consumer groups, trade unions, farmers associations, regional or communal bodies"* (European Commission 2004b: 35-36).

The IBPP operation is steered by state-specific Annual Action Programmes (AAPs), which are based on the European Commission's financing decisions and are part of financing agreements negotiated by the Commission with the target countries' governments. The financing decisions contain Action Fiches (AFs), which elaborate the context, specific objectives, implementation issues, budget, timing, and monitoring and evaluation methods of the IBPP. As already noted, the fact that the AAPs/AFs need to be approved by the target governments through signing of financing agreements makes the IBPP's launch and implementation dependent on these governments' approval (Interviews 21 and 26, Annex I).

The Institution Building and Partnership Programme operates through calls for proposals that are issued in regular intervals. European civil society organizations in partnership with their counterparts from target countries may submit their project proposals directly to the European Commission headquarters. The IBPP relies on the so called *'direct centralized management'* (e.g. European Commission 2010a: 7). This means that the European Commission's EuropeAid Co-operation Office (AIDCO)[42] in Brussels is in charge of the overall IBPP operation, preparing the AAPs, negotiating them as part of financing agreements with target countries' governments, launching calls for proposals, selecting projects for grant support, managing contracts, and finally monitoring and evaluating implementation.[43] The Commission's delegations[44] in the target countries only assist AIDCO with communication and project monitoring on the ground (Interviews 21 and 26, Annex I).

The initial stage of the IBPP implementation—the AAP preparation and negotiation of financing agreements with the target countries' governments—is usually quite a long process. It may take up to one year, depending on the beneficiary countries' internal review procedures and the necessity to integrate potential amendments to Action Fiches proposed by the governments (Interviews 21 and 26, Annex I). Only after signing a financing agreement can AIDCO launch a call for proposals to select projects for IBPP support. The calls for proposals and the subsequent selection pro-

---

[42] In 2010, AIDCO was merged with the Directorate-General for Development to form the new EuropeAid Development and Cooperation DG (DEVCO), which is now responsible for external assistance programmes under centralized management. Here it is still referred to as AIDCO in order to avoid confusion. Also for the time period covered in this study the formation of DEVCO was not yet completed.

[43] In addition to the AIDCO's internal monitoring and evaluation, external consultants are usually engaged to provide independent, impartial assessment of individual project results and overall performance of the programme (Interview 21, Annex I).

[44] After the Lisbon Treaty entered into force in December 2009, the Commission's delegations became delegations of the European Union.

cesses commonly take another six months before the contracts with successful applicants (i.e. organizations carrying out the projects) are signed. Hence, the actual implementation of IBPP projects may start two years after the relevant AAP was prepared by AIDCO (or even later).

In view of the above operation procedures, difficulties in the IBPP implementation may emerge at least at two stages: (1) during the process of AAP negotiation and signing of financing agreements, and (2) at the stage of delivery of the IBPP projects. In the following, the IBPP performance in Central Asia is evaluated accordingly, by scrutinizing these two stages.

The IBPP Implementation in Kyrgyzstan and Uzbekistan

For the evaluation of the IBPP functioning at the stage of financing negotiation, this study relies on the information obtained through expert interviews with EU officials at AIDCO and the Commission's Delegation in Kazakhstan, which prior to 2010 was also partly responsible for the EU engagement in Kyrgyzstan (see Annex I). With regard to the analysis of the IBPP project implementation on the ground, specific project compendia have been collected for this research (Annexes II-III). For the on-going projects the current information provided on the European Commission's website was used, while for the completed ones the data were extracted from an internal IBPP evaluation prepared for the Commission in 2007 (Giffen et al. 2007). These data were complimented by information requests to the implementing organizations and expert interviews with EU officials and Central Asian civil society representatives.

In the case of Kyrgyzstan, the expert interviews conducted with EU officials at AIDCO and the Commission's Delegation have not revealed any major difficulties during the negotiation and signing of financing agreements (cf. Interviews 6, 16, 21 and 26, Annex I). According to one of the officials, the process of negotiation *"went quite smoothly throughout the whole period of the IBPP functioning"* and the Kyrgyz authorities were *"always very open and quick to sign financing agreements",* mostly without proposing any amendments (Interview 21, Annex I). This indicated the Kyrgyz government's willingness to work with the EU in the sphere of democratic institution-building and civil society support (Interviews 23 and 26, Annex I).

This was very different in the case of Uzbekistan, where the programme operation was interrupted several times. The first complications started with the abeyance of the 2005 AAP, when EU sanctions were imposed on Uzbekistan following the Andijan unrest in May 2005. As a result, AIDCO could not proceed with IBPP implementation in 2006 (Interview 21, Annex I). Nevertheless, a year later the programme could be continued (European Commission, EuropeAid 2010).

Another suspension of the Institution Building and Partnership Programme in Uzbekistan resulted from a failure to sign a financing agreement for the 2008 Action Programme in a timely manner. According to the EU financing procedures (Council of the European Union 2002), the so called *'year n + 1'* rule applies to the deadlines for financing commitments. This means that a financing commitment to a certain action to be pursued within one year (e.g. AAP) must be agreed upon with the beneficiary state not later than 31 December of the year following the adoption of the respective European Commission's decision. Hence, a financing agreement for the 2008 AAP needed to be signed by the Uzbek government by 31 December 2009. However, the signature was delayed due to the late adoption of the respective Commission's decision (in November 2008) and the necessity to integrate comments and changes suggested by the Uzbek side into the agreement. By the time the amended agreement reached Uzbekistan (in September 2009),[45] the National Coordinator, who was in charge of signing the agreement, had changed and there was a short vacuum of power, after which a new coordinator was appointed. Yet, according to the Uzbek government's internal procedures, the new coordinator could not sign the agreement with the name of the previous coordinator on it. In order to change the name, the agreement had to be sent back to AIDCO again. This eventually led to an additional delay and failure to sign the agreement before the end of 2009, in spite of the fact that the issue had been taken to the level of the Director General by then (Interviews 23 and 26, Annex I). Consequently, the funding foreseen for the 2008 AAP was lost and had to be re-committed at a later stage. This was done with the 2010 AAP, which contained two blocks, including programmes under the actual 2010 AAP–2010/I AAP—and programmes financed under the ex-2008 AAP–2010/II AAP (Interviews 21 and 26, Annex I).

The interviewed EU officials generally characterized the Uzbek procedures related to the signature of financing agreements as *'very bureaucratic'* and *'long-lasting'* with a tendency to a *'last minute consent'*, which created an impression that the EU's assistance was *'accepted but not very welcome'* in the country (Interviews 21 and 26, Annex I). Yet, there was no common

---

[45] As there was no EU delegation in the country at that time, the official correspondence with the Uzbek government was carried on through the Uzbek embassy in Brussels.

opinion among EU officials, whether the failure of 2008 was the result of the *'bureaucracy used to the maximum'* or *'bureaucratic procedures instrumentalized not to sign the agreement'* (cf. Interviews 21, 23 and 26, Annex I).

At the same time, it was noted that since 2009 the situation had started to change. According to interviewed European Commission officials, both agreements for the 2009 and 2010 AAPs were signed very quickly and without major amendments or complications (Interviews 23 and 26, Annex I). This was exactly the time period when the EU lifted its sanctions against Uzbekistan. This suggests that Uzbekistan's readiness to accept IBPP support was associated with the withdrawal of EU sanctions and the general normalization of the bilateral relations.

With regard to the IBPP projects on the ground, their actual implementation did not start before 2002, despite the preparation of the first AAPs steering the programme already in 2001. The delay resulted from the above procedures related to the adoption of the Commission's decisions, negotiation of bilateral financing agreements and contracting civil society organizations. Thus, the projects that started in Kyrgyzstan and Uzbekistan in 2002-2003 were still financed under the country-specific Action Programmes for 2001 (Interviews 21 and 26, Annex I).

In Kyrgyzstan, the IBPP projects were operating between 2002 and 2009, with the last projects starting in 2007 (Annex II). During this time period 14 projects were supported with small grants varying from €100,000 to €200,000. In Uzbekistan, the IBPP projects are still running in the time of writing, with the latest call for proposals issued in February 2011 (European Commission, EuropeAid n/a).[46] Over 2003-2010, 21 projects were allocated small grants varying from €49,000 to €200,000 (Annex III). The difference in the number of IBPP projects in the two countries is puzzling, as Uzbekistan appears to be a more difficult environment for the IBPP implementation compared to Kyrgyzstan. This difference however may be explained by a greater overall amount of TACIS (and IBPP) funds provided by the EU to Uzbekistan (European Commission 2004b).[47]

According to the interviewed EU officials and the Commission's internal evaluation, none of the IBPP projects conducted in Kyrgyzstan in 2002-

---

[46] This is due to the above re-commitment of 2008 AAP funds to 2010/II AAP.

[47] Thus, for the IBPP projects implemented in Kyrgyzstan between 2002 and 2009 the EU granted roughly €2.3 million in total, while for the projects running in Uzbekistan between 2003 and 2010 over €3.7 million were provided (cf. Annexes II and III).

2009 ended prematurely or experienced registration difficulties or other problems resulting from their work with the authorities (cf. Giffen et al. 2007: 35-36; Interviews 21 and 26, Annex I). Furthermore, the 'tulip revolution' of 2005 leading to the government change in Kyrgyzstan did not appear to have had a significant impact on IBPP implementation. The only difficulty that could be identified as an effect of the political crisis was a start delay of one of the projects—'Green Agenda in Kyrgyzstan'. Yet, after only three months, the project activities could begin and were fully implemented (Giffen et al. 2007: 36).

In Uzbekistan, two (out of total 21) projects could not fully realize their activities as originally planned. One aiming at capacity-building and networking of NGOs and conducted by the LAS Legal Aid Society and the Organisation Mondiale contre la Torture intended *inter alia* to undertake a research of human rights in the country, including the legislation and the judicial process. However, the publication of the final report on the topic was hindered by the Uzbek authorities. A second project, 'Regional integration, governance and headway training', pursued capacity-building for NGOs working with and advocating for refugees and displaced persons. It was conducted by an Uzbek NGO Hamroh-Consulting and the Christian Outreach Relief and Development but had to stop its activities after six months of work, following a closure of the Uzbek partner organization (Giffen et al. 2007: 51).

Summarizing the above, the results of the IBPP implementation varied among the Central Asian states. In Kyrgyzstan, the programme was fully operational and did not experience any major problems at the stage of negotiating and agreeing upon financing or during project delivery. By contrast, in Uzbekistan the IBPP work was challenged by the government's actions several times at both stages of its operation. Nevertheless, one can conclude that the programme was at least partly implemented in the country.

6.1.2 The EIDHR at Work

Now as the IBPP implementation in Kyrgyzstan and Uzbekistan has been discussed, this sub-section turns to the analysis of the European Instrument for Democracy and Human Rights. First, the relevant programming and operation procedures are reviewed based on the information provided in the EU documents. Next, the instrument's application in the Central Asian countries is examined. For the latter, the analysis relies on data retrieved from the EIDHR global and regional project compendia and databases available on the European Commission's website, as well as on responses to information requests and expert interviews at AIDCO, the Delegation of the European Commission in Kazakhstan and with representatives of civil society organizations implementing the projects. Similarly as in the case of the IBPP, special compendia of EIDHR projects that covered Kyrgyzstan and Uzbekistan have been put together as part of this research (Annexes IV-V).

Programming and Operation Background

Originally, the EIDHR operated on the basis of annual programming documents adopted by the European Commission (Herrero 2009). In order to provide a legal framework for the Commission's actions in the field of democracy and human rights assistance, in April 1999 the Council adopted two Regulations (975/1999 and 976/1999) on the development and consolidation of democracy and the rule of law and respect for human rights and fundamental freedoms (Council of the European Union 2003: 42). With the preparation of the new Financial Perspectives in 2006, a new Regulation (1889/2006) was adopted by the European Parliament and the Council, which established the current European Instrument for Democracy and Human Rights (European Parliament and Council of the European Union 2006a).

These regulations set the requirements and priorities for the European Commission's actions in the field of democracy and human rights promotion, providing the basis for the multi-annual programming documents, which guide the implementation of the EIDHR assistance. So far, four such documents have been issued by the Commission: EIDHR programming documents for 2002-2004 and 2005-2006 and EIDHR strategy papers for 2007-2010 and 2011-2013. For the time period covered in this study, the first three documents are of particular relevance.

For identifying projects to be supported through the EIDHR funds, the instrument relies on the following three procedures:

1) Calls for proposals at global and regional levels organized by the European Commission's EuropeAid Co-operation Office (AIDCO)[48] for cross-country or cross-regional (macro-)projects to be implemented

---

[48] As already mentioned, in 2010 AIDCO was merged with the Commission's Directorate-General for Development to form the new EuropeAid Development and Cooperation DG (DEVCO), which is now responsible for administrating EIDHR global and regional projects.

by international governmental or non-governmental organizations and networks;
2) Local calls for proposals for micro-projects (since 2007—Country-Based Support Schemes/ CBSS), which are supported through small grants[49] made available to local civil society actors and administered directly by the Commission's delegations[50] on the ground;
3) Funds allocated without calls for proposals to targeted projects, e.g. for joint programmes with partners that can include international governmental organizations or for election observation missions, but also individual support provided to human rights activists in the countries where they are under most pressure (cf. European Commission 2001c; European Commission 2004a; European Commission 2007c).

As the third category includes support to election observation (which is carried out in the Central Asian states with the involvement of the European Parliament but under the auspices of the OSCE), funding of very specific projects (e.g. the Venice-based European Inter-University Centre for Human Rights and Democratization) and undisclosed assistance to human rights defenders, the EIDHR interventions under this category either are irrelevant for the scope of the current section or cannot be analysed due to a lack of publicly available information. The subsequent analysis will therefore focus on the projects identified within the first two categories of the EIDHR procedures.

EIDHR Implementation in Kyrgyzstan and Uzbekistan

Central Asian countries became eligible for the EIDHR support in 2001, when funds were allocated for regional (macro-)projects as well as country-specific micro-projects to be conducted in Kyrgyzstan, Kazakhstan and Tajikistan. Although Uzbekistan and Turkmenistan could be targeted by regional projects, they were excluded from the list of countries eligible for EIDHR micro-project allocations (European Commission 2004a: Annex I). Due to a suspension of the micro-project facility between 2002-2003 for administrative reasons, no EIDHR funds were provided to micro-projects in Central Asia in 2002-2004 (European Commission 2004a: Annex I). The EIDHR programming document for 2005-2006 confirmed Central Asia as a region eligible for macro-project support (European Commission 2004a:

---

[49] The maximum small grants size varied over time as follows: 1999-2001 – €50,000; 2002-2006 – €100,000; 2007-2010 – €300,000 (Herrero 2009: 11).
[50] After the Lisbon Treaty, delegations of the European Union.

26). Kyrgyzstan, Kazakhstan and Tajikistan were again identified as countries qualifying for both macro- and micro-project assistance, whereas Uzbekistan and Turkmenistan were among the countries entitled only for macro-project funding. The same approach continued with the 2007-2010 EIDHR Strategy Paper, which identified Kyrgyzstan, Kazakhstan and Tajikistan as the only Central Asian countries where the Country Based Support Scheme replacing the micro-project facility was supposed to be launched (European Commission 2007c: Annex II).

Over 2003-2010, seven regional projects were conducted in Central Asia with the support of the EIDHR funds (Annex IV).[51] However, not all of the countries concerned were equally covered by the projects' activities. Thus, Kyrgyzstan was targeted by all seven projects, whereas Uzbekistan was covered only by four of them (Annex IV).

In addition to the regional projects, numerous country-specific projects were conducted with the EIDHR support in Central Asia. Yet, their number also varied significantly among the countries. Thus, the official EIDHR projects compendia list 50 macro- and micro-projects implemented in Kyrgyzstan over 2004-2010 (European Commission 2010b; European Commission n/a; cf. Annex V). At the same time, the documents contain no records of EIDHR projects in Uzbekistan (cf. European Commission 2010b; European Commission n/a).

According to Crawford, in 2006 a project aiming at *'strengthening critical social and political reporting'* in Uzbekistan proposed by the Konrad Adenauer Foundation received an EIDHR macro-grant with funding of €900,240 (Crawford 2008: 183). However, the foundation could not start implementing the project due to a refusal of registration by the Uzbek authorities (Interview 21, Annex I). This needs a further clarification, as it has been stated above that the EIDHR is supposed to operate independently of consent of the target countries' governments. Indeed, unlike the projects supported through mainstream assistance (e.g. IBPP), which are officially approved by beneficiary governments through previously signed financing agreements, the launch of EIDHR projects does not depend on such agreements. Yet, according to the Uzbek legislation, NGOs implementing their projects in Uzbekistan are required to register and report their activities to the Ministry

---

[51] The lists of regional and country-specific projects in Annexes IV and V begin with the projects, for which the EIDHR funds were allocated in 2001. However, the actual implementation of the first projects did not start before 2003 and 2004 respectively for procedural and administrative reasons.

of Justice (International Center for Non-for-Profit Law n/a). Thus, the actual permission to start an EIDHR project still stays in the competence of national authorities.

Based on the experience of the Konrad Adenauer Foundation, no further attempts to initiate EIDHR projects in Uzbekistan were made between 2006 and 2009. The situation started slowly changing only in 2010, when a Slovenian NGO managed to pass the registration procedure to conduct an EIDHR-supported project aiming at capacity-building (including fund-raising and management training) of local civil society organizations. However, some EU officials described this as a special case rather than a new tendency, because the leader of the Slovenian NGO had a long-term experience of engagement in Uzbekistan and was 'very well-known' in the country and 'trusted by the authorities' (cf. Interviews 21 and 24, Annex I).

Considering the number of EIDHR projects in Kyrgyzstan over 2004-2010, the state of affairs was obviously different. Within this time period, 12 EIDHR macro- and micro-projects were implemented by international NGOs in the country, e.g. by Internews, Soros Foundation Kyrgyzstan, Eurasia Foundation of Central Asia, Folkekirkens Nodhjaelp Danchurchaid, and Pro NGO (Annex V). Another 38 projects were conducted by Kyrgyz civil society organizations. As stated by EU officials, neither foreign nor local NGOs implementing EIDHR projects in the country experienced registration problems comparable to those in Uzbekistan. In fact, the registration process was quite quick and uncomplicated. On the whole, state authorities did not constrain project activities or interfere with the work of implementing NGOs to the extent that would have led to the projects' termination (Interviews 17 and 24, Annex I).

At the same time, over the years one can observe an apparent tendency of a gradual decrease in the overall number of EIDHR projects in Kyrgyzstan (Annex V; see also Table 6.2 below). However, this is not explained by a worsening of the political environment or a growing resistance of Kyrgyz authorities to EU engagement (cf. Interview 24, Annex I). Rather, the EU raised the maximum grant size for individual small projects considerably, especially after the CBSS launch in 2007,[52] while the overall EIDHR budget allocation to the country was not growing proportionally. Thus, in 2004 thirteen grants provided to micro-projects in Kyrgyzstan varied from €12,829 to

---

[52] The maximum grant size for micro-projects increased in 2007 from €100,000 to €300,000 (Herrero 2009: 11).

€49,478. Whereas in 2008 seven CBSS grants varied from €53,820 to €149,994. Finally, the two CBSS grants received by international NGOs—Eurasia Foundation of Central Asia and Pro NGO—in 2010, constituted €187,305 and €209,452 respectively (Annex V). Hence, the number of the EIDHR country-specific projects decreased, as the funding for each individual project was increasing.

To sum up, over 2003-2010 Kyrgyzstan benefited from 57 regional and country-specific projects. All of them could be implemented and did not experience any major difficulties originating from state authorities. Uzbekistan was targeted by only 4 regional EIDHR projects. The interviewed EU officials expected these projects to have a greater potential for full implementation of their activities, as the Uzbek authorities would have fewer possibilities to interfere in their operation compared to the country-specific microprojects (Interview 21, Annex I). At the same time, it was impossible to identify actual difficulties in the regional projects' deliveries due to the complexities of the projects and multiplicity of actors involved. Therefore, an unambiguous conclusion concerning their success or failure could not be drawn. The attempts to launch country-specific projects could not be realized in Uzbekistan during the period under study. According to the interviewed officials and civil society representatives, Uzbekistan was generally considered an *'extremely difficult country'*, where it was nearly impossible to talk about democracy or human rights assistance (cf. Interviews 7, 9, 10, 21, 23 and 26, Annex I).

6.1.3 Summary of the Results

Summarizing the main findings of the above sub-sections, a considerable difference in the application of the EU's democratic empowerment tools in Kyrgyzstan and Uzbekistan could be observed. In the former country, both the IBPP and the EIDHR could be fully implemented and did not experience any significant complications or hurdles resulting from the target government's actions. In this sense, one can regard the EU democratic empowerment in Kyrgyzstan as successful.

In Uzbekistan, the IBPP and the EIDHR performed differently. The Institution Building and Partnership Programme (that relied on the prior consent of the target country's government through the signing of financing agreements) could be largely implemented, although it experienced considerable difficulties during both negotiation and delivery. Thus, with the IBPP the EU could achieve at least partial success. The EIDHR that was supposed to provide support directly to the non-governmental sector and hence operate independently of the government was less successful. The country-specific assistance failed to be implemented, while only few regional projects that partly targeted Uzbekistan could be realized.

Table 6.1 below summarizes the results of the application of EU democratic empowerment tools in the two countries under study. As it was unclear whether the regional EIDHR assistance experienced any constraints resulting from the authorities' actions, it is not included in the table.

Table 6.1: Results of the IBPP and EIDHR Application in Kyrgyzstan and Uzbekistan

Programmes	Programme results by country	
	Kyrgyzstan	Uzbekistan
IBPP	+	+/-
EIDHR (country-specific)	+	-

Note: (+)   programme successfully implemented
 (+/-) programme partly successful
 (-)   programme application failed

6.2 Explaining the Outcomes of the IBPP and EIDHR Application

As suggested in chapter 3, the success of EU democratic empowerment (i.e. institution- and capacity-building programmes) can be influenced by the substance of norms and changes promoted. Thus, the instruments are more likely to be successfully implemented by the EU (without experiencing constraints on the part of the target countries' governments), if they focus on less politically sensitive norms that do not directly challenge the existing regime. While testing this hypothesis, it is also necessary to consider the process-related factors that might affect the EU tools application. This allows for identification of possible alternative explanations. For the democratic empowerment instruments, the transparency of assistance delivery vis-à-vis target governments and joint ownership of the programmes in the sense that the governments are aware of the programmes' details and can co-determine their scope have been identified as the main process-related factors (see Table 3.2 in chapter 3). Hence, the subsequent sub-sections investigate whether the latter factors or the substance of promoted norms account for the results of the IBPP and EIDHR implementation in Kyrgyzstan and Uzbekistan.

6.2.1 Assistance Transparency and Ownership

While looking for empirical evidence in support of the assumption that transparency and ownership of the assistance programmes mattered, it is necessary to specify to what extent the Kyrgyz and Uzbek authorities could actually follow and co-determine IBPP and EIDHR implementation. As the instruments were successful in Kyrgyzstan, but had different results in Uzbekistan, the variance in transparency and ownership of the programmes in the two countries could provide an explanation for the varied outcomes.

At first sight, the two programmes seem to differ in these terms. The IBPP implementation is basically agreed with the governments through the signing of financing agreements. In addition, the majority of the IBPP projects in both countries cooperated with various local and national state bodies and institutions at some point of their implementation (Interview 21, Annex I). Thus, state authorities had an opportunity to closely follow the IBPP operation and interfere in it at different stages, if deemed necessary.

In turn, EIDHR assistance appears to be less transparent to the target countries' governments, as it is provided directly to state-independent non-governmental organizations and does not require preliminary financing agreements. Yet, the EIDHR projects also cooperate with state structures as part of their activities (Interviews 5 and 8, Annex I). To illustrate, two EIDHR projects conducted by the Kyrgyz Public Association of Soldiers' Mothers in 2006-2008 and 2009-2011 specifically aimed at working with the Ministry of Defence to promote the observance of human rights in the military (Annex V). Furthermore, the Kyrgyz and Uzbek authorities have a possibility to keep a close watch on the projects through the registration and reporting procedures for implementing NGOs (although these procedures certainly vary in the two countries). Thus, both the IBPP and the EIDHR operations can be monitored by the governments. This leaves it up to the governments in a way, to determine how much they will meddle beyond simple monitoring.

At the same time, in both cases the actual project contents and activities cannot be co-determined by state authorities in advance, as the IBPP and the EIDHR function through calls for proposals aiming at NGOs. While the general thematic scope of the two programmes is pre-set by the European Commission and specified through the calls for proposals, the concrete projects are designed by the applying civil society organizations. Thus, in both cases state authorities have little influence on the projects at the stage of their initiation, yet they can interfere in the CSO activities at the later stage of project implementation.

Summarizing the above, the process-related factors—assistance transparency and ownership—did not differ significantly in the cases of the IBPP and EIDHR implementation in the two countries under study. As the programmes were equally successful in Kyrgyzstan, but revealed different results in Uzbekistan, the process-related factors do not provide valid outcome explanations. Hence, the subsequent part investigates empirical evidence in support of the main assumption of the present study, i.e. that the substance of promoted norms accounts for the outcomes of the EU democratic empowerment tools in Central Asia.

6.2.2 Substance of the Promoted Norms

As the IBPP and the EIDHR featured different results in Kyrgyzstan and Uzbekistan, it is necessary to examine the normative substance of the programmes in the two countries separately. A closer look should be taken at the contents of the IBPP and EIDHR projects.

In Kyrgyzstan, the majority of the IBPP projects focused on social reforms and social services provision, especially to vulnerable groups of people, including women, elderly people, children, persons with disabilities, and unemployed adults. One of the earlier projects related to local economic development through promoting entrepreneurship at the grassroots level. Later, there were four projects concentrating specifically on improving capacities of either Kyrgyz NGOs or local administrations. Two of them aiming at the *'development of participation in public policy and social cohesion in Kyrgyzstan'*, and at the *'improvement of quality of services of local self-government bodies'* (both launched in 2007) were related to administrative reforms and governance issues (Annex II).

While focusing on social reforms, many projects sought to introduce new attitudes or methods of working (e.g. through the integration of the disabled, providing opportunities for youth and women's social participation and their involvement in economic activities, and brining in the principles of sustainable environmental management). Notably though, none of the projects directly aimed at the promotion of the core principles of democracy, including electoral processes, democratic public institutions, citizens' political participation and representation, or observance of political freedoms and rights (cf. Giffen et al. 2007: 50-51).

This was different in the case of the EIDHR implementation in Kyrgyzstan. According to the EU's own categorization, the general thematic foci of the projects varied from issues related to governance, rule of law and justice to human rights and fundamental freedoms to civil society development. More specifically, the projects targeted such areas as: political participation by citizens and democratic political representation; support to electoral processes; independence of media and freedom of press; human rights monitoring, education and awareness raising, including observance of the rights of women, children and persons with disabilities; justice and penal system; torture prevention; and strengthening of civil society through capacity building (Annex V).

Notably, the projects categorization in the official EIDHR compendia does not use the term *'democracy'* for labelling thematic fields of the projects or areas of their application. Instead, almost all projects related to citizen political participation and democratic representation, electoral processes, and freedom of press are attributed to the category *'Governance'* (European Commission 2010b; European Commission n/a). Of the 50 EIDHR projects conducted in Kyrgyzstan over 2001–2010, 17 projects are ascribed to this category. Another 13 projects are found under the thematic field *'Promotion and protection of human rights and fundamental freedoms'*. The projects supporting observance of the rights of women (6), children (2), persons with disabilities (1), and persons belonging to minorities and ethnic groups (1) are detached into separate categories. The projects aiming at prevention of torture (2) and trafficking in human beings (1) are also distinguished from the general thematic field of human rights and fundamental freedoms. Finally, 6 projects relate to the category *'Strengthening civil society'* and only 1 to the *'Rule of law and justice including penal system'* (Annex V).

Yet, such categorization does not always take account of specific activities and contents of the projects, when attributing them to certain thematic fields. Thus, a project 'Support Centre of National Minority Rights' launched by the Youth Publication Union 'Golden Goal' in 2008 is put under the category *'The rights of persons belonging to minorities and ethnic groups'* of the EIDHR Compendium 2007-2009 (European Commission 2010b). At the same time, the project's activities aimed at *"[s]trengthening minority group interaction with State bodies and NGOs, political representation and participation at local and national levels and involvement in democratic reforms"* (European Commission 2010b: 46). Therefore, the project could be also ascribed to the category *'Governance'*.

In order to avoid such ambiguity, the subsequent analysis of the EIDHR projects in Kyrgyzstan is based not on the EU's categorization but on the consideration of particular projects' contents and activities. Accordingly, 21 projects are identified as addressing the core principles of democracy, including electoral processes, democratic public institutions, citizens' political participation and representation, and observance of political freedoms and rights. Capacity-building projects for civil society organizations and projects promoting human rights other than political ones are not included into this number (Table 6.2). Thus, almost a half of all EIDHR projects implemented in Kyrgyzstan over 2001–2010 aimed at the establishment or reinforcement of the principles of democracy that would supposedly be regarded as politically sensitive in an authoritarian regime (cf. chapter 3).

Table 6.2: EIDHR democracy-related projects in Kyrgyzstan in 2004-2010[53]

Starting year	Overall number of projects	Number of democracy-related projects
2004	13	4
2005	9	9
2006	9	2
2007	6	2
2008	7	3
2009	4	0
2010	2	1
Total	50	21

Sources: European Commission 2010b, European Commission n/a.

To sum up, while the IBPP implementation in Kyrgyzstan was predominantly socially oriented, the EIDHR to a large extent involved the promotion of certain democracy components. Nevertheless, both programmes could be fully implemented and did not experience hurdles stemming from state authorities' actions aimed at termination of project activities. The results allow drawing two alternative conclusions. First, as the implementation of the

---

[53] The table includes EIDHR projects, whose implementation started prior to March 2010. Precise information about later projects is not available in the time of writing.

substantively different IBPP and EIDHR programmes was equally successful in Kyrgyzstan, the substance of externally promoted norms does not necessarily determine the outcome of the application of democratic empowerment tools. An alternative conclusion would be that in the country under study the external promotion of the core principles of democracy through capacity- and institution-building programmes was not perceived as highly politically sensitive by the ruling elites.

As in the case of Kyrgyzstan, the IBPP projects in Uzbekistan were oriented towards poverty reduction and social services provision. The main focus was on assisting or educating various vulnerable groups, e.g. persons with disabilities, women, children or young adults. None of the projects aimed directly or indirectly at the enhancement of the core democratic principles. The only project that could be partly attributed to the 'Governance' category was a project titled 'Support of municipality (re-)management of power grid' jointly implemented by the administrations of the cities of Tashkent and Mannheim (Annex III). Yet, the project mainly concentrated on technical aspects of governance.

Notably, projects supporting persons with disabilities or providing health education (in the sphere of HIV/AIDS prevention) were particularly welcomed by state authorities (Interview 21, Annex I). Thus, implementing organizations of the project 'Environmental education - learning for life'—the Public Centre for Healthy Life and the Field Studies Council—were approached by the Uzbek Ministry of Public Education with a suggestion to conduct additional HIV/AIDS awareness trainings for state institutions in Tashkent (Giffen et al. 2007: 53).

At the same time, two projects addressing the general human rights situation and the rights of refugees and displaced persons in Uzbekistan had to terminate their activities following interference by state authorities, as described in the previous section of this chapter. In the case of the former project aiming at improving capacities and networking of NGOs in Uzbekistan the authorities reacted to an attempt of the implementing CSOs to publish a report on the human rights situation and the judicial process, which would have been very critical of the present state of affairs (Interview 33, Annex I). The European Commission's Monitoring Report of 2005 stated that *'the specific Uzbek context was insufficiently considered in the project design'* and *'the exercise* [the research into the human rights situation, V.A.] *should have been discussed with the Uzbek authorities before launching the pro-*

ject' (cited in Giffen et al. 2007: 51). In addition, the project was to be implemented between 2003 and 2005—the time when the 'coloured revolutions' led to a change of governments in Georgia, Ukraine and Kyrgyzstan. The fact that the 'revolutions' were largely associated with NGOs' actions receiving foreign funding and the discussed project was supposed to contribute to the strengthening of NGOs' capacities would explain why the project activities were politically sensitive for the Uzbek authorities, who at that point saw promotions of any independent and government-critical NGOs as potentially revolutionary. The latter project addressing the rights of refugees and displaced persons in Uzbekistan also intended to pursue capacity-building for NGOs (working on migration issues). Started in 2005, it was supposed to engage with civil society organizations that also worked with those who sought refuge abroad following the Andijan protests. Considering the highly politically sensitive nature of the events and the refugee issue (see chapter 4), the Uzbek authorities did not want the project to proceed. These facts support the assumption that the substance of external assistance can influence its implementation.

Another fact in support of this assumption is the inability to implement EIDHR country projects that generally tend to focus on the issues of human rights and democratic development in Uzbekistan. The project aiming at the strengthening of critical social and political reporting that was initiated by the Konrad Adenauer Foundation but could not start its activities, as described in the previous section, serves as an illustration. As discussed in chapter 5, the issue of media freedom is a very politically sensitive one in Uzbekistan. And the fact that the project was supposed to start in 2006— only one year after the Andijan and amid the EU sanctions—was hardly favourable for the project to commence its activities.

The above examples allow concluding that in the case of Uzbekistan the substance of assistance programmes and the norms that they promoted did determine the EU's ability to implement them. The programmes and specific projects that focused on social rights and service provisions could be fully implemented and were even welcomed by state authorities. While the programmes and projects that aimed at enhancing or monitoring the observance of political rights or strengthening state-independent civil society organizations critical of the government were terminated or could not even start their activities. The projects focusing on investigating human rights violations, capacity-building for NGO activists and independent media reporting were particularly constrained by the government. The promotion of political rights and freedoms (e.g. the freedoms of association and expression)—that are among the core attributes of liberal democracy (cf. Wetzel and Orbie 2011a)—appeared to be highly politically sensitive for the Uzbek elites, especially against the background of the internal and external events associated with a possible regime change (e.g. the Andijan disturbances and the 'coloured revolutions').

6.3 Concluding Remarks

This chapter evaluated the application of EU democratic empowerment tools of the Institution Building and Partnership Programme and the European Instrument for Democracy and Human Rights in Kyrgyzstan and Uzbekistan. It also examined possible explanations of successes and failures of these programmes. The success was defined in terms of the EU's ability to fully implement the programmes without experiencing constraints on the part of the target countries' governments.

The IBPP and the EIDHR featured different results in the two countries under study. While in Kyrgyzstan both programmes could be successfully implemented, in Uzbekistan the IBPP was only partly successful and the EIDHR country-specific support completely failed.

As demonstrated in section 6.2, the identified process-related factors—transparency and ownership of the assistance programmes—could not fully account for the variance in the above results. Hence, the key hypothesis of the current study (that the substance of what is promoted matters for the success of the application of EU democratization tools) was tested. While in the case of Uzbekistan the hypothesis could be confirmed, in the case of Kyrgyzstan the examination of the empirical evidence resulted in two alternative conclusions. On the one hand, it suggested that the substance of promoted norms and changes did not necessarily determine the success of the EU democratic empowerment tools. On the other, it could be concluded that—although the IBPP and EIDHR substantially differed—the issues in scope of these programmes were (equally) not seen as highly politically sensitive by the Kyrgyz authorities. The latter conclusion however does not exclude the possibility that the substance of what is promoted may still matter for the success of EU tools. The two conclusions may thus be regarded as contradictory.

While the empirical evidence available for the case of Kyrgyzstan does not rule out one of these options, a comparison between the two countries' domestic conditions may provide a clue. As pointed out in the introduction to this study, the political regime in Uzbekistan is commonly associated with a strong and stable authoritarian rule (cf. Warkotsch 2008b: 62). In this context, it is not surprising that the issues in scope of the EIDHR (aiming to foster political rights and democratic reforms of governing structures) were highly politically sensitive for the regime in Tashkent, which resulted in a failure of the EU to implement the programme. Kyrgyzstan, in its turn, is a semi-authoritarian regime that is more open for a political change (cf. Gumppenberg and Steinbach 2004: 156). This fact coupled with the successful implementation of the EIDHR in the country suggests that the issues in scope of the programme that were highly politically sensitive for the regime in Uzbekistan, were not seen equally so by the Kyrgyz government. This is consistent with the second aforementioned conclusion and the assumption stated in chapter 3 that the degree to which the same norms are seen as more or less politically sensitive is context-dependent and may be determined by the nature of the political regime in question.

7. Conclusion

This study evaluated and explained successes and failures of EU democratization policy in environments challenging for external democracy promotion, i.e. in authoritarian states that are excluded from potential EU membership and not part of closer political and economic cooperation with the Union. The study did not undertake assessment at the level of polity, but rather looked at the effects of EU democratization policy at the micro-level, tracing the application of specific EU instruments and changes that they may or may not have triggered (or facilitated) in the target countries. The geographical scope of the research was post-soviet Central Asia. More specifically, the analysis focused on two divergent examples of Kyrgyzstan and Uzbekistan. The countries represented two groups of states in the region—semi-authoritarian north-eastern tier and dictatorially governed south-western tier (cf. Warkotsch 2008b: 62; Zhovtis 2008: 26)—and were selected as the most- and least-likely cases for success of EU democratization efforts respectively.

In view of the unfavourable domestic and external conditions for democratization in Central Asia, the main questions guiding the research were: (1) whether EU democracy and human rights promotion was successful in the region (at the micro-level), and if so, to what extent, and (2) what factors made the EU efforts more (or less) successful, i.e. what accounted for the variance in the outcomes of the EU policy.

With regard to the first research question, the success of EU efforts was defined in terms of the achievement of expected changes as the result of the application of specific EU democratization tools, based on theoretical considerations about the tools' underlying logics of functioning. The success was operationalized individually for each type of tools that the Union used. Three types of EU instruments were identified: conditionality-based (drawing on incentives and sanctions), dialogue-based (relying on normative suasion), and democratic empowerment tools (i.e. assistance provided for democratic institution- and capacity-building). The success of the conditionality-based tools was evaluated in terms of observable changes in the short-term behaviour of the target governments, i.e. their compliance with EU demands. The success of the dialogue-based tools was operationalized as relevant long-term initiatives and reforms that were proposed by the target governments themselves in the framework of a particular dialogue platform. Hereby, the evaluation accounted for possible intervening effects of the other actors' engagements and the influence of EU coercive measures. Finally, the performance of the democratic empowerment instruments was evaluated based on the EU's ability to fully implement its capacity-building programmes in the target countries (see Table 3.1 and discussion in chapter 3).

With regard to the second research question, a number of factors that could generally influence the outcomes of the EU political engagement were identified, based on the literature review. Drawing on these factors, a list of scope conditions (or favourable factors) for success of the EU democratization tools application was developed, distinguishing them along the target-, democratizer-, and process-related dimensions (see Table 3.2 in chapter 3). The subsequent analysis revealed that the target- and the democratizer-related favourable factors were largely absent in the context of EU engagements in Central Asia. Hence, the factors identified along these two dimensions could hardly account for relative success of EU democratization policies.

The review of the literature specifically dedicated to external democracy promotion in Central Asia helped identify another factor that could potentially explain the variance in the outcomes of EU efforts, namely the substance of what exactly was promoted in each setting (cf. Warkotsch 2008b). Accordingly, it was hypothesized that, in unfavourable for democratization environments, EU conditionality, dialogue, and democratic empowerment tools would be more likely to be successful, if they promoted less politically sensitive norms and changes. In line with Golovko (2010), politically sensitive norms and changes were defined as those that potentially threatened the power position of the target elites and the target regime status quo. It was assumed that in autocracies the promotion of the core principles of liberal democracy (e.g. political contestation guaranteed through free and fair elections, horizontal separation of powers, and political rights of participation) could be generally regarded as politically sensitive, as these norms would directly challenge the authoritarian rule. On the contrary, the focus on what Wetzel and Orbie (2011a) called *'supporting conditions'* or the *'context of democracy'* (e.g. social and economic requisites) would be rather politically neutral, as it would not directly interfere with the existing power relations. At the same time, it was suggested that what mattered was not the variance in the actual substance of the norms, but the substance as perceived by the target governments. This perception could be influenced by certain contextual factors, such as characteristics of the target states, their power constellations and historical developments (e.g. prior experiences of political reforms). Hence, the degree to which certain norms and changes were considered politically sensitive was expected to be context-dependent and was to be determined inductively as part of the case studies.

The empirical part of the work comprised three case studies of EU instruments that were exemplary for each of the identified types of tools. The examination focussed on the enforcement of EU sanctions against Uzbekistan between 2005 and 2009, the bilateral EU human rights dialogues with Kyrgyzstan and Uzbekistan, and the implementation of two EU civil society support programmes—the Institution Building and Partnership Programme (IBPP) and the European Instrument for Democracy and Human Rights (EIDHR)—in both countries. The case studies examined successes and failures of the EU efforts and tested the key hypothesis, while also accounting for the influence of the analytically derived process-related factors (Table 3.2) and possible intervening effects of the other external actors' engagement.

The empirical investigation revealed rather limited results of the EU efforts. Thus, EU sanctions against Uzbekistan were only partly successful. Of the nine EU conditions for the withdrawal of sanctions, one was fulfilled, four were partly complied with and the other four were ignored by the targets. The human rights dialogues mainly played a facilitating role in both Kyrgyzstan and Uzbekistan, with very limited success in the former and no direct effects in the latter. According to the interviewed EU policy-makers, the HRDs were expected to compliment other EU instruments rather than produce immediate results. The civil society support programmes performed differently in the two countries. In Kyrgyzstan, both the IBPP and the EIDHR operated successfully. In Uzbekistan, the former programme could be partly implemented, while the implementation of the country-specific support under the latter instrument failed completely.

With regard to an explanation of the above results, provided empirical evidence supported the stated hypothesis in the case of EU sanctions: The application of the EU's conditionality-based tools proved to be more successful in achieving compliance with EU demands when promoting less politically sensitive changes. The EU demands that could potentially undermine established regime legitimacy and thus threaten its stability were neglected or openly opposed by the Uzbek leadership. On the contrary, the demands that were seen as less damaging or—due to their vague formulation—allowed certain room for interpretation were at least partly met by the targets. The need to maintain external and internal regime legitimacy proved to be decisive for which EU demands were considered more or less politically sensitive by the Uzbek government.

Concerning the human rights dialogues (HRDs), their extremely limited effects and the relatively short time span covered by the current study meant that the hypothesis could not be fully tested. Nevertheless, evidence provided for the HRD with Kyrgyzstan was consistent with the assumption that the substance of what was promoted mattered for the outcomes. Here, the EU proved to be more successful in facilitating changes that were associated with the social domain rather than political reforms, while the prior positive experience of external actors' engagement in Kyrgyzstan enhanced EU efforts.

Finally, the results of the EU's civil society assistance programmes in Uzbekistan fully supported the key hypothesis. The EU failed in implementing the programmes and projects that focussed on fostering politically sensitive norms and changes. The promotion of the core attributes of liberal democracy (cf. Wetzel and Orbie 2011a), e.g. political rights and freedoms, appeared to be highly politically sensitive for the Uzbek authorities, especially against the background of internal and external events associated with a possible regime change (Andijan disturbances and 'coloured revolutions' in Georgia, Ukraine and Kyrgyzstan). In the case of Kyrgyzstan, the available empirical evidence did not allow for a clear conclusion. Yet, the comparison of the results of the two substantially different programmes, the IBPP and the EIDHR, in the two countries (with varying degrees of power concentration) went in line with the initial assumptions suggesting that the degree to which the norms were seen as more or less politically sensitive was context-dependent and was determined by the nature of the political regime in question.

In all three cases (the EU sanctions, human rights dialogues, and civil society support programmes), the identified process-related factors had considerable explanatory value for the failure of democracy and human rights promotions. Yet, these factors could not fully account for the variance in outcomes, which underpinned the validity of this study's main hypothesis.

Constraints such as restrictions in time and data availability, along with the complexity of interactions between various factors prevented this research from providing a conclusive determination of the outcomes of EU engagement in each particular case under study. This especially concerns the EU human rights dialogues. Nevertheless, the empirical evidence provided in the three case studies supported the assumption that the substance of what was promoted mattered for the outcomes of the EU's application of democratization tools. While the results of the EU efforts were rather limited, in general the Union proved to be more successful in advancing less-politically sensitive norms and changes, i.e. those that did not directly challenge the power position of the authoritarian elites and the regime status quo (cf. Golovko 2010). In the case of Uzbekistan, the promotion of the core principles of liberal democracy (cf. Wetzel and Orbie 2011a), but also the changes that directly or indirectly threatened its regime legitimacy appeared to be highly politically sensitive. The promotion of what Wetzel and Orbie (2011a) titled *'supporting conditions'* or *'the context of democracy'*, e.g. social welfare, on the contrary, was regarded as rather politically neutral. In the case of Kyrgyzstan, the analysis did not allow a clear inference as to what norms and changes were politically sensitive (or neutral) for the government. Yet, the EU was equally successful in promoting the core attributes and the supporting conditions of democracy, at least when using its democratic empowerment tools.

These observations allow drawing several complimentary conclusions about EU engagement in Central Asia.

First, the variance in the results in Kyrgyzstan and Uzbekistan—two states with varying degrees of power concentration—validates the relevance of domestic conditions for democratization. In Uzbekistan, the EU efforts were clearly challenged by the regime's stance. Even the changes that did not directly damage the government's position were difficult to enforce. Kyrgyzstan however seemed to offer a window of opportunity, especially with regard to the EU's democratic empowerment tools. The successful operation of the EIDHR, the EU's specific instrument for promoting political rights and freedoms, free and fair elections, and democratic governance, signified a relative openness of the country's government to the EU's democratization agenda. This offers a possibility for enhancing democracy and human rights promotion through the democratic empowerment tools in Kyrgyzstan.

Second, the above analysis suggests that the same norms and changes that may be seen as politically sensitive in the context of one state can be politically neutral for another. This affirms the assumption that the degree to which the promoted norms and changes are considered politically sensitive is context-dependent and may be influenced by the political regime in question. As the target governments are supposedly more receptive of the externally promoted norms that they see as less politically sensitive (depending on the domestic context), this suggests the need for the EU to adjust the substance of its policies in each target country accordingly in order to ensure a greater success of its instruments. In the context of Central Asia, this would mean a departure from the EU's regional approach and reformulation of the current democratization agenda with the view to accommodate the existing differences among the Central Asian states.

Third, the study revealed some positive outcomes of EU efforts in terms of achieving certain micro-level changes and it confirmed the relevance of the substance of the promoted norms. Yet, there appeared to be a discrepancy between the EU's intent to democratize target states and what was actually possible within those states (especially apparent in the case of Uzbekistan). Given the conclusion that the EU is more likely to succeed in fostering less politically sensitive changes, the EU would be advised to adapt its policies accordingly. In the context of consolidated authoritarian regimes with a high concentration of power, this means shifting the focus from promoting the core principles of liberal democracy to enhancing social welfare and economic growth as supporting conditions for a democratic development (cf. Wetzel and Orbie 2011a). Yet, in this case the EU may end up providing support to the social and economic sectors of authoritarian states and thus help maintain their legitimacy and stability without significantly contributing to liberalization of the established political regimes. In authoritarian environments, the urge for success at the micro-level may thus contradict the EU's macro-level political objectives.

Drawing on the rationalist-constructivist framework, this study supports the assumption by Warkotsch (2008b and 2009) that contextual adjustment of EU policies may be useful for opening up certain niches and achieving greater results at the micro-level. Yet, empirical evidence does not suggest that such an adjustment would lead to liberalization of an authoritarian political regime in the long run. Hence, further research is needed to specify the interrelation of the micro-level changes and the long-term processes of democratic development.

While the case studies limited in their geographic scope to two Central Asian states allow only conditional generalizations, the presented conclusions are applicable to EU democracy and human rights promotion in the broader region and may allow certain inferences about EU engagement beyond Central Asia. This particularly concerns the relevance of the substance of what is promoted for the success of EU efforts at the micro-level and the context-dependence of what constitutes politically sensitive norms and changes. The case studies suggest that countries that are more open to a democratic change see the potential for greater results at the micro-level. It may be further hypothesised that a policy adjustment by the EU with the view to attain success at the micro-level in such countries would be more likely to be in concord with the EU's stated objectives to contribute to the countries' democratization processes. Yet, in stable authoritarian states such an adjustment may hinder the EU in implementing what it initially intended to achieve at the macro-level. Further research on a wider range of states is needed to confirm or refute these assumptions.

Finally, the research strategy suggested in this work may be useful for evaluating effects of the other external actors' engagements in Central Asia and beyond the region. The existing scholarly assessments often concentrate on the broader effects of democracy and human rights promotions at the level of polity (cf. Heller 2013) and only occasionally include an analysis of specific democratization tools (e.g. Richter 2009). The research approach used in this study complements these assessments by enabling a micro-level analysis that links the study of democratization instruments and their effects to the examination of the substance.

References

Abdusalyamova, L. and Warren, H. (2007). Organisational Capacity Building in Central Asia: Reflections from Kyrgyzstan and Kazakhstan. *INTRAC Praxis Paper No. 15*, at: http://www.intrac.org/data/files/resources/412/Praxis-Paper-15-Organisational-Capacity-Building-in-Central-Asia.pdf (accessed 16 March 2012).

Aeschlimann, A. and Roggo, N. (2007). *Visits to Persons Deprived of Their Freedom: The Experience of the ICRC*, at: http://www.icrc.org/eng/resources/documents/article/other/detention-visits-article-300906.htm (accessed 20 September 2011).

Akiner, S. (2005). Violence in Andijan, 13 May 2005: An Independent Assessment. *Silk Road Paper, July 2005*. Central Asia-Caucasus Institute, Silk Road Studies Program, at: http://www.silkroadstudies.org/new/inside/publications/0507Akiner.pdf (accessed 25 May 2010).

Alderson, K. (2001). Making Sense of State Socialization. *Review of International Studies, 27 (3)*, pp. 415-433.

Amnesty International (2010). *Uzbekistan—Amnesty International Report 2010*, at: http://www.amnesty.org/en/region/uzbekistan/report-2010 (accessed 27 July 2011).

Amnesty International (2008, 11 January). *Uzbekistan Abolishes the Death Penalty*, at: http://www.amnesty.org/en/news-and-updates/good-news/uzbekistan-abolishes-death-penalty-20080111 (23 March 2012).

Anderson, J. (1999). *Kyrgyzstan: Central Asia's Island of Democracy?* Amsterdam: Harwood Academic Publishers.

Axyonova, V. (2012). EU Human Rights and Democratisation Assistance to Central Asia: In Need of Further Reform. *EUCAM Policy Brief No. 22*, at: http://www.eucentralasia.eu/fileadmin/user_upload/PDF/Policy_Briefs/PB_EUCAM-22.pdf (accessed 17 July 2012).

Axyonova, V. (2011). The EU-Central Asia Human Rights Dialogues: Making a Difference? *EUCAM Policy Brief No. 16*, at: http://www.eucentralasia.eu/fileadmin/user_upload/PDF/Policy_Briefs/Vera.Axyonova.PB16.April11.pdf (accessed 12 February 2012).

Babadjanov, K. (2008). Uzbekistan Hosts Media Freedom Seminar, But Bars Journalists from Covering It. *Radio Free Europe/Radio Liberty, 02 October 2008*, at: http://www.rferl.org/content/Uzbekistan_Hosts_Media_Freedom_Seminar_But_Bars_Journalists_From_Covering_It/1293346.html (accessed 12 March 2012).

Babajanian, B., Freizer, S. and Stevens, D. (2005). Introduction: Civil Society in Central Asia and the Caucasus. *Central Asian Survey, 24 (3)*, pp. 209-224.

Barnes, J. F., Skidmore, M. J. and Tripp, M. C. (1980). *The World of Politics: A Concise Introduction*. New York: St. Martins Press.

Bick, M. (2010, September). *EU—Central Asia Civil Society Seminar on Women's Rights, Brussels 21-24 June 2010. Final Report*, at: http://eeas.europa.eu/human_rights/dialogues/civil_society/docs/2010_ca_final_report_en.pdf (accessed 22 November 2010).

Blagov, S. (2005). Uzbekistan and Russia Sign Mutual Defense Pact. *Eurasianet.org, 14 November 2005*, at: http://www.eurasianet.org/departments/insight/articles/eav111505.shtml (accessed 21 May 2011).

Bogaards, M. (2009). How to Classify Hybrid Regimes? Defective Democracy and Electoral Authoritarianism. *Democratization, 16 (2),* pp. 399-423.

Bogner, A. and Menz, W. (2009). The Theory-Generating Expert Interview: Epistemological Interest, Forms of Knowledge, Interaction. In A. Bogner, B. Littig and W. Menz (eds.), *Interviewing Experts.* Houndmills: Palgrave Macmillan, pp. 43-80.

Boonstra, J. (2012). Democracy in Central Asia: Sowing in Unfertile Fields? *EUCAM Policy Brief No. 23*, at: http://www.eucentralasia.eu/fileadmin/user_upload/PDF/Policy_Briefs/PB-EUCAM-23.pdf (accessed 22 July 2012).

Boonstra, J. and Hale, J. (2010). EU Assistance to Central Asia: Back to the Drawing Board? *EUCAM Working Paper No. 8*, at: http://www.fride.org/download/EUCAM_WP8_UE_Central_Asia_ENG_Ene10.pdf (accessed 14 April 2012).

Börzel, T. A. and Risse, T. (2004). One Size Fits All! EU Policies for the Promotion of Human Rights, Democracy and the Rule of Law. *Paper Prepared for the Workshop on Democracy Promotion, October 4-5 2004, Center for Development, Democracy and the Rule of Law, Stanford University,* at: http://iis-db.stanford.edu/pubs/20747/Risse-Borzel-stanford_final.pdf (accessed 19 October 2008).

Börzel, T. A. and Risse, T. (2002). Die Wirkung internationaler Institutionen. Von der Normanerkennung zur Normeinhaltung. In M. Jachtenfuchs and M. Knodt (eds.), *Regieren in internationalen Institutionen.* Opladen: Leske und Budrich, pp. 141-181.

Bossuyt, F. and Kubicek, P. (2011). Advancing Democracy on Difficult Terrain: EU Democracy Promotion in Central Asia. *European Foreign Affairs Review, 16,* pp. 639-658.

Brzoska, M. (2013). Research on the Effectiveness of International Sanctions. In H. Hegemann, R. Heller and M. Kahl (eds.), *Studying 'Effectiveness' in International Relations: A Guide for Students and Scholars.* Opladen (among others): Barbara Budrich Publishers, pp. 143-160.

Bureau of Human Rights and Rule of Law Uzbekistan (2009). *Uzbekistan: NGO Report on the Implementation of the ICCPR (Prior to the Adoption of the List of Issues),* at: http://www2.ohchr.org/english/bodies/hrc/docs/ngos/BHRRL_Uzbekistan96.pdf (accessed 20 June 2011).

Burnashev, R. and Chernykh, I. (2007). Changes in Uzbekistan's Military Policy after the Andijan Events. *China and Eurasia Forum Quarterly, 5 (1),* pp. 67-73.

Burnell, P. (2008). Promoting Democracy. In D. Caramani (ed.), *Comparative Politics.* Oxford: Oxford University Press, pp. 625-651.

Burnell. P. (2007). Does International Democracy Promotion Work? *DIE Discussion Paper 17/2007*, Bonn.

Burnell, P. (2000). Democracy Assistance: The State of the Discourse. In P. Burnell (ed.), *Democracy Assistance. International Cooperation for Democratization*. London: Frank Cass, pp. 3-33.

Buxton, C. (2009). NGO Networks in Central Asia and Global Civil Society: Potentials and Limitations. *Central Asian Survey, 28 (1)*, pp. 43-58.

Carothers, T. (2009). Democracy Assistance: Political vs. Developmental? *Journal of Democracy, 20 (1)*, pp. 5-19.

Carothers, T. (1999). *Aiding Democracy Abroad: The Learning Curve*. Washington, DC: Carnegie Endowment for International Peace.

Checkel, J. T. (2005). International Socialization and Socialization in Europe. Introduction and Framework. *International Organization, 59 (4)*, pp. 801-826.

Checkel, J. T. (2001). Why Comply? Social Learning and European Identity Change. *International Organization, 55 (3)*, pp. 553-588.

Child Rights International Network (2010). *Kyrgyzstan: Children's Rights References in the Universal Periodic Review*, at: http://www.crin.org/resources/infodetail.asp?ID=22295 (accessed 12 November 2012).

Cooley, A. (2008). Principles in the Pipeline: Managing Transatlantic Values and Interests in Central Asia. *International Affairs, 84 (6)*, pp. 1173-1188.

Coppieters, B., Emerson, M., Kovziridze, T., Noutcheva, G., Tocci, N., and Vahl, M. (2004). *Europeanisation and Conflict Resolution: Case Studies from the European Periphery*. Ghent: Academia Press.

Cortell, A. P. and Davis, J. W. (2000). Understanding the Domestic Impact of International Norms: A Research Agenda. *International Studies Review, 2 (1)*, pp. 65-97.

Cotton Campaign (n/a). *Reports on Forced Labour of Adults and Children in the Cotton Sector of Uzbekistan*, at: http://www.cottoncampaign.org/reports/ (accessed 16 November 2012).

Council of Europe (2010). *Final Narrative Report. European Rule of Law Initiative for Central Asia: Voluntary Contribution of the Ministry of Foreign Affairs of Germany*, at: http://www.venice.coe.int/site/main/Central_Asia/resources/Report_German%20VC.pdf (accessed 16 July 2012).

Council of the European Communities (1991). Resolution of the Council and the Member States Meeting in the Council on Human Rights, Democracy and Development, 28 November 1991. *Bulletin of the European Communities, 11/1991*, at: http://aei.pitt.edu/1802/01/democracy_declaration_1991.pdf (accessed 18 October 2008).

Council of the European Union (2012). *EU Strategic Framework and Action Plan on Human Rights and Democracy, Luxembourg, 25 June 2012, 11855/12*, at: http://www.consilium.europa.eu/uedocs/cms_data/docs/pressdata/EN/foraff/131181.pdf (accessed 12 September 2012).

Council of the European Union (2010a). *Press Release, 24 June 2010. 3rd EU—Turkmenistan Human Rights Dialogue*, at: http://www.consilium.europa.eu/uedocs/cmsUpload/100621-PRESS_RELEASE-3rdEU-TurkmenistanHumanRightsDialogue_EN.pdf (accessed 8 July 2010).

Council of the European Union (2010b). *Press Release, 21 June 2010. Women's Rights Seminar Seeks Real Change in Central Asia*, at: http://www.consilium.europa.eu/uedocs/cmsUpload/100621-PRESS_RELEASE_EU-Central_Asia_Civil_Society_Seminar-finalEN.pdf (accessed 8 July 2010).

Council of the European Union (2010c). *The European Union—Uzbekistan Human Rights Dialogue, Brussels, 7 May 2010, 9540/10 (Presse 103)*, at: http://www.consilium.europa.eu/uedocs/cms_Data/docs/pressdata/en/er/114260.pdf (accessed 12 June 2010).

Council of the European Union (2009a, 17 November). *Council Conclusions on Democracy Support in the EU's External Relations*, at: http://www.consilium.europa.eu/uedocs/cms_data/docs/pressdata/en/gena/111250.pdf (accessed 12 April 2010).

Council of the European Union (2009b, March). *EU Guidelines: Human Rights and International Humanitarian Law*. Luxembourg: Office for Official Publications of the European Communities.

Council of the European Union (2009c). Human Rights Dialogues with Third Countries. In Council of the European Union (2009b), *EU Guidelines: Human Rights and International Humanitarian Law*. Luxembourg: Office for Official Publications of the European Communities, pp. 21-29.

Council of the European Union (2008a, 11 November). Council Common Position 2008/843/CFSP of 10 November 2008 Amending and Extending Common Position 2007/734/CFSP Concerning Restrictive Measures against Uzbekistan. *Official Journal of the European Union, L300*, at: http://eur-lex.europa.eu/LexUriServ/LexUriServ.do?uri=OJ:L:2008:300:0055:0055:EN:PDF (accessed 14 May 2010).

Council of the European Union (2008b, 30 April). Council Common Position 2008/348/CFSP of 29 April 2008 Concerning Restrictive Measures against Uzbekistan. *Official Journal of the European Union, L116*, at: http://eur-lex.europa.eu/LexUriServ/LexUriServ.do?uri=OJ:L:2008:116:0056:0056:EN:PDF (accessed 14 May 2010).

Council of the European Union (2007a, 14 November). Council Common Position 2007/734/CFSP of 13 November 2007 Concerning Restrictive Measures against Uzbekistan. *Official Journal of the European Union, L295*, at: http://eur-lex.europa.eu/LexUriServ/LexUriServ.do?uri=OJ:L:2007:295:0034:0039:EN:PDF (accessed 14 May 2010).

Council of the European Union (2007b, 16 May). Council Common Position 2007/338/CFSP of 14 May 2007 Renewing Certain Restrictive Measures against Uzbekistan. *Official Journal of the European Union, L128*, at: http://eur-lex.europa.eu/ LexUriServ/site/en/oj/2007/l_128/l_12820070516en00500052.pdf (accessed 14 May 2010).

Council of the European Union (2007c). *European Union and Central Asia: Strategy for a New Partnership*. Brussels, at: http://consilium.europa.eu/uedocs/cms_data/ librairie/PDF/EU_CtrlAsia_EN-RU.pdf (accessed 10 October 2009).

Council of the European Union (2006, 17 November). Council Common Position 2006/787/CFSP of 13 November 2006 Renewing Certain Restrictive Measures against Uzbekistan. *Official Journal of the European Union, L318*, at: http://eur-lex.europa.eu/LexUriServ/LexUriServ.do?uri=OJ:L:2006:318:0043:0043:EN:PDF (accessed 14 May 2010).

Council of the European Union (2005a, 16 November). Council Common Position 2005/792/CFSP of 14 November 2005 Concerning Restrictive Measures against Uzbekistan. *Official Journal of the European Union, L299*, at: http://www.sipri.org/data bases/embargoes/eu_arms_embargoes/uzbekistan/792 (accessed 14 May 2010).

Council of the European Union (2005b). Council Joint Action 2005/588/CFSP of 28 July 2005, Appointing a Special Representative of the European Union for Central Asia. *Official Journal of the European Union, L199*, at: http://eur-lex.europa.eu/ LexUriServ/site/en/oj/2005/l_199/l_19920050729en01000102.pdf (accessed 10 October 2009).

Council of the European Union (2005c, November). *Joint Statement by the Council and the Representatives of the Governments of the Member States Meeting within the Council, the European Parliament and the Commission: 'The European Consensus on Development'*, at: http://ec.europa.eu/development/icenter/repository/DPS_2005 _en.pdf (accessed 18 October 2008).

Council of the European Union (2004, 31 December). Council Regulation (EC) No 2242/2004 of 22 December 2004 Amending Regulation (EC) No 976/1999 Laying Down the Requirements for the Implementation of Community Operations, Other Than Those of Development Cooperation, Which, Within the Framework of Community Cooperation Policy, Contribute to the General Objective of Developing and Consolidating Democracy and the Rule of Law and to That of Respecting Human Rights and Fundamental Freedoms in Third Countries. *Official Journal of the European Union, L 390*, at: http://ec.europa.eu/europeaid/what/human-rights/documents/976_99-modif_en.pdf (accessed 12 April 2010).

Council of the European Union (2003). *EU Annual Report on Human Rights 2003*, at: http://www.consilium.europa.eu/uedocs/cmsUpload/HR2003EN.pdf (accessed 12 October 2009).

Council of the European Union (2002). *Council Regulation (EC, Euratom) No 1605/2002 of 25 June 2002 on the Financial Regulation Applicable to the General Budget of the European Communities. Official Journal of the European Communities, L 248*, at: http://www.bsrinterreg.net/programm/_downloads/EC_No_2002_1605_en_Budgetary_principles.pdf (accessed 16 February 2010).

Council of the European Union (2000, 18 January). *Council Regulation (Euratom, EC) No 99/2000 of 29 December 1999 Concerning the Provision of Assistance to the Partner States in Eastern Europe and Central Asia. Official Journal of the European Communities, L 12*, at: http://www.interreg.gov.pl/NR/rdonlyres/CAF22E20-27B5-4A1B-86AD-4200CF30BB50/0/interreg3_euratom99.pdf (accessed 12 April 2010).

Council of the European Union (1999a, 8 May). *Council Regulation (EC) No 975/1999 of 29 April 1999 Laying Down the Requirements for the Implementation of Development Co-operation Operations Which Contribute to the General Objective of Developing and Consolidating Democracy and the Rule of Law and to That of Respecting Human Rights and Fundamental Freedoms. Official Journal of the European Communities, L 120*, at: http://eur-lex.europa.eu/LexUriServ/LexUriServ.do?uri=OJ:L:1999:120:0001:0007:EN:PDF (accessed 12 April 2010).

Council of the European Union (1999b, 8 May). *Council Regulation (EC) No 976/1999 of 29 April 1999 Laying Down the Requirements for the Implementation of Community Operations, Other Than Those of Development Cooperation, Which, Within the Framework of Community Cooperation Policy, Contribute to the General Objective of Developing and Consolidating Democracy and the Rule of Law and to That of Respecting Human Rights and Fundamental Freedoms in Third Countries. Official Journal of the European Communities, L 120*, at: http://ec.europa.eu/europeaid/what/human-rights/documents/976_99_en.pdf (accessed 12 April 2010).

Council of the European Union (n/a). *The Human Rights Dialogues with Central Asia*, at: http://www.consilium.europa.eu/showPage.aspx?id=1716&lang=SV (accessed 2 April 2010).

Council of the European Union, External Relations Council (2009). *Council Conclusions on Uzbekistan, 27 October 2009*, at: http://www.consilium.europa.eu/uedocs/cms_Data/docs/pressdata/en/gena/110783.pdf (accessed 21 May 2010).

Council of the European Union, External Relations Council (2008a). *Council Conclusions on Uzbekistan, 13 October 2008*, at: http://www.consilium.europa.eu/uedocs/cmsUpload/103295.pdf (accessed 21 May 2010).

Council of the European Union, External Relations Council (2008b). *Council Conclusions on Uzbekistan, 29 April 2008*, at: http://www.eu2008.si/en/News_and_Documents/Council_Conclusions/April/0428_GAERC4.pdf (accessed 21 May 2010).

Council of the European Union, External Relations Council (2007a). *Council Conclusions on Uzbekistan, 16 October 2007*, at: http://www.consilium.europa.eu/ueDocs/cms_Data/docs/pressData/en/gena/96513.pdf (accessed 21 May 2010).

Council of the European Union, External Relations Council (2007b). *Council Conclusions on Uzbekistan, 14 May 2007*, at: http://www.europa-eu-un.org/articles/en/article_7025_en.htm (accessed 21 May 2010).

Council of the European Union, External Relations Council (2005a). *Council Conclusions Concerning the Situation of Eastern Uzbekistan, 23 May 2005*, at: http://www.europa-eu-un.org/articles/fr/article_4736_fr.htm#top (accessed 21 May 2010).

Council of the European Union, External Relations Council (2005b). *Council Conclusions Concerning Uzbekistan, 13 June 2005*, at: http://www.europa-eu-un.org/articles/fr/article_4802_fr.htm (accessed 21 May 2010).

Council of the European Union, External Relations Council (2005c). *Council Conclusions on Uzbekistan, 03 October 2005*, at: http://www.europa-eu-un.org/articles/fr/article_5082_fr.htm (accessed 21 May 2010).

Cracknell, B. E. (2000). *Evaluating Development Aid: Issues, Problems and Solutions*. London: Sage Publications.

Crawford, G. (2008). EU Human Rights and Democracy Promotion in Central Asia: From Lofty Principles to Lowly Self-interests. *Perspectives on European Politics and Society, 9 (2)*, pp. 172-191.

Crawford, G. (2003a). Promoting Democracy from Without—Learning from Within (Part I). *Democratization, 10 (1)*, pp. 77-98.

Crawford, G. (2003b). Promoting Democracy from Without—Learning from Within (Part II). *Democratization, 10 (2)*, pp. 1-20.

Crawford, G. (2002). Evaluating European Union Promotion of Human Rights, Democracy and Good Governance: Towards a Participatory Approach. *Journal of International Development, 14 (6)*, pp. 911-926.

Crawford, G. (2001). *Foreign Aid and Political Reform. A Comparative Analysis of Democracy Assistance and Political Conditionality*. Houndmills: Palgrave.

Crawford G. (2000). Promoting Democratic Governance in the South. *The European Journal of Development Research, 12 (1)*, pp. 23-57.

Crawford, G. and Kearton, I. (2001, December). Evaluating Democracy and Governance Assistance. *ESCOR Research Report No. 7894*, at: http://www.research4development.info/PDF/Outputs/Mis_SPC/R7894-FinRep.pdf (accessed 16 March 2010).

Delegation of the European Union to the Kyrgyz Republic (n/a). *List of Projects*, at: http://eeas.europa.eu/delegations/kyrgyzstan/projects/list_of_projects/projects_en.htm (accessed 26 February 2011).

Deutsche Botschaft Taschkent (2010). *Europe-Asia Dialogue in a Conversation with Germany's Ambassador*, at: http://www.taschkent.diplo.de/Vertretung/taschkent/ru/07/Archiv__Interviews/Interview__2010__01__DPUz__en.html (accessed 21 May 2011).

Diamond, L. (2002). Thinking about Hybrid Regimes. *Journal of Democracy, 13 (2),* pp. 21-34.

Diamond, L. (1999). *Developing Democracy: Toward Consolidation.* Baltimore: John Hopkins University Press.

Eckert, J. M. (1996). *Das unabhängige Usbekistan: Auf dem Weg von Marx zu Timur. Politische Strategien der Konfliktregelung in einem Vielvölkerstaat.* Münster: Lit.

Embassy of Uzbekistan to the United States, Press Office (2005a, 16 May). *Press-Conference by the President of the Republic of Uzbekistan Islam Karimov on Events in Andijan, Tashkent, 14 May 2005,* at: http://www.uzbekistan.org/press/archive/189/ (accessed 12 May 2011).

Embassy of Uzbekistan to the United States, Press Office (2005b, 10 June). *Press-Release of the Ministry of Foreign Affairs of the Republic of Uzbekistan, 10 June 2005,* at: http://www.uzbekistan.org/press/archive/220/ (accessed 12 May 2011).

Embassy of Uzbekistan to the United States, Press Office (2005c, 20 November). *Statement of the Supreme Court of the Republic of Uzbekistan, 20 November 2005,* at: http://www.uzbekistan.org/press/archive/301/ (accessed 12 May 2011).

Emerson, M. (2004). *The Wider Europe Matrix.* Brussels: Centre for European Policy Studies.

Emerson, M., Boonstra, J., Hasanova, N., Laruelle, M. and Peyrouse, S. (2010). *Into EurAsia: Monitoring the EU's Central Asia Strategy. Report of the EUCAM Project.* Centre for European Policy Studies and Fundacion para Relaciones Internationales y el Dialogo Exterior, at: http://www.eucentralasia.eu/fileadmin/user_upload/PDF/Final_Report/EUCAM-Final-Report.pdf (accessed 12 April 2010).

Erdmann, G. and Kneuer, M. (Eds.) (2009). *Externe Faktoren der Demokratisierung.* Baden-Baden: Nomos.

Eschment, B. (2000). Autoritäre Präsidialregime statt Parteiendemokratien in Zentralasien. *Aus Politik und Zeitgeschichte, B21,* at: http://www.bpb.de/publikationen/Y40OEM.html (accessed 12 November 2009).

Ethier, D. (2003). Is Democracy Promotion Effective? Comparing Conditionality and Incentives. *Democratization, 10 (1),* pp. 99-120.

EU-Central Asia Monitoring (n/a). *Factsheet on EU Assistance to Central Asia,* unpublished.

Europa House in Uzbekistan (n/a). *TACIS in Uzbekistan,* at: http://www.europahouse.uz/en/eu-uzb/stat/projects (accessed 14 January 2011).

European Center for Constitutional and Human Rights (n/a). *Criminal Complaint Against Zakir Almatov,* at: http://www.ecchr.eu/index.php/almatov_case.html (accessed 24 May 2011).

European Commission (2011, January). *Institution Building and Partnership Programme (IBPP): Civil Society Projects in Uzbekistan*, at: http://ec.europa.eu/europeaid/where/asia/country-cooperation/uzbekistan/documents/11.02.03_ibpp_brochure_final_2011.pdf (accessed 06 March 2011).

European Commission (2010a). *Commission Decision of 14/07/2010 on the Annual Action Programme 2010 (Part 1) in Favour of Uzbekistan to Be Financed under Article 19.10 02 of the General Budget of the European Union, C(2010)4850–PE/2010/4327. Action Fiche No. 2 for Uzbekistan*, Brussels, at: http://ec.europa.eu/europeaid/documents/aap/2010/af_aap_2010_uzb.pdf (accessed 28 November 2010).

European Commission (2010b). *The European Instrument for Democracy and Human Rights (EIDHR) Compendium 2007-2009. Promoting Democracy and Human Rights in Asia*, at: http://ec.europa.eu/europeaid/what/human-rights/documents/compendium_asia_2007-2009_en.pdf (accessed 10 December 2010).

European Commission (2009a). *EU—Kyrgyz Republic Civil Society Seminar. Cooperation in Protection and Promotion of Children's and Prisoner's Rights, 5-6 March 2009, Bishkek. Final Report*, at: http://ec.europa.eu/external_relations/human_rights/dialogues/civil_society/docs/2009_kyrgyzstan_final_report_en.pdf (accessed 10 February 2010).

European Commission (2009b). *European Union and Central Asia. EU Human Rights Dialogues in Central Asia*, at: http://ec.europa.eu/external_relations/central_asia/docs/factsheet_hr_dialogue_en.pdf (accessed 10 February 2010).

European Commission (2009c). *The European Union and Central Asia: The New Partnership in Action*. Brussels, at: http://www.eeas.europa.eu/central_asia/docs/2010_strategy_eu_centralasia_en.pdf (accessed 14 October 2010).

European Commission (2008, December). *Programming Guide for Strategy Papers: Democracy and Human Rights*, at: http://ec.europa.eu/development/icenter/repository/F20_human_rights_en.pdf (accessed 18 October 2009).

European Commission (2007a). *Central Asia Indicative Programme 2007–2010*, at: http://eeas.europa.eu/central_asia/rsp/nip_07_10_en.pdf (accessed 13 March 2012).

European Commission (2007b). *European Community Regional Strategy Paper for Assistance to Central Asia for the period 2007–2013*, at: http://www.eeas.europa.eu/central_asia/rsp/07_13_en.pdf (accessed 10 August 2010).

European Commission (2007c). *European Instrument for Democracy and Human Rights Strategy Paper 2007–2010*, at: http://ec.europa.eu/europeaid/where/worldwide/eidhr/documents/eidhr-strategy-paper-2007_en.pdf (accessed 15 October 2008).

European Commission (2007d). *European Instrument for Democracy and Human Rights Projects 2003-2006*, at: http://ec.europa.eu/europeaid/where/worldwide/eidhr/documents/070515_eidhr_contracts_signed_2003-2006.xls (accessed 18 October 2008).

European Commission (2007e). *The European Union: Furthering Human Rights and Democracy Across the Globe*, at: http://ec.europa.eu/external_relations/human_rights/doc/brochure07_en.pdf (accessed 15 October 2008).

European Commission (2007f). *Thematic Programme Non-State Actors and Local Authorities in Development. Annual Action Programme for 2007,* Brussels at: http://ec.europa.eu/europeaid/documents/aap/2007/af_aap_2007_dci-nsa.pdf (accessed 28 February 2011).

European Commission (2006a). *Communication from the Commission to the Council and the European Parliament of 25 January 2006—Thematic Programme for the Promotion of Democracy and Human Rights Worldwide Under the Future Financial Perspectives (2007-2013).* COM(2006) 23 final, at: http://eur-lex.europa.eu/LexUriServ/LexUriServ.do?uri=COM:2006:0023:FIN:EN:PDF (accessed 14 May 2009).

European Commission (2006b, January). *Communication from the Commission to the Council, the European Parliament, the European Economic and Social Committee and the Committee of the Regions of 25 January 2006—The Thematic Programme 'Non-State Actors and Local Authorities in Development'.* COM(2006) 19 final, at: http://ec.europa.eu/europeaid/how/finance/documents/non-state-actors/communicatio n_nsa_en.pdf (accessed 10 June 2010).

European Commission (2006c). *Thematic Programme Non-State Actors and Local Authorities in Development. Strategy Paper 2007-2010,* at: http://ec.europa.eu/europeaid/what/civil-society/documents/nsa_la_strategy_paper_2007_2010_en.pdf (accessed 12 February 2011).

European Commission (2004a). *European Initiative for Democracy and Human Rights (EIDHR) Programming for 2005 and 2006,* at: http://ec.europa.eu/europeaid/what/human-rights/documents/eidhr-programming-2005-2006_en.pdf (accessed 14 May 2009).

European Commission (2004b). *Tacis Central Asia Indicative Programme, 2005-2006.* Brussels, at: http://ec.europa.eu/external_relations/asia/rsp/tcaip_04-08_en.pdf (accessed 05 September 2008).

European Commission (2002). *Strategy Paper 2002–2006 and Indicative Programme 2002–2004 for Central Asia.* Brussels, at: http://www.eeas.europa.eu/central_asia/rsp/02_06_en.pdf (accessed 12 May 2010).

European Commission (2001a). *Communication from the Commission to the Council and the European Parliament of 8 May 2001 - The European Union's Role in Promoting Human Rights and Democratisation in Third Countries.* COM(2001) 252 final, at: http://eur-lex.europa.eu/LexUriServ/LexUriServ.do?uri=COM:2001:0252:FIN:EN:PDF (accessed 14 May 2009).

European Commission (2001b). *European Governance. A White Paper.* COM(2001) 428 final, at: http://eur-lex.europa.eu/LexUriServ/site/en/com/2001/com2001_0428en01.pdf (accessed 14 May 2009).

European Commission (2001c). *Commission Staff Working Document. European Initiative for Democracy and Human Rights Programming Document 2002-2004,* at: http://ec.europa.eu/europeaid/what/human-rights/documents/programming_2002_20 04_document_eidhr_en.pdf (accessed 14 August 2013).

European Commission (1999, April). *Final Report. Evaluation of the MEDA Democracy Programme 1996-1998.* Brussels, at: http://ec.europa.eu/europeaid/how/evaluation/evaluation_reports/reports/med/951460_en.pdf (accessed 17 March 2010).

European Commission (1998). *Communication from the Commission to the Council and the European Parliament of 12 March 1998—Democratization, the Rule of Law, Respect for Human Rights and Good Governance: The Challenges of the Partnership between the European Union and the ACP States.* COM(1998) 146 final, at: http://eur-lex.europa.eu/LexUriServ/LexUriServ.do?uri=COM:1998:0146:FIN:EN:PDF (accessed 14 May 2009).

European Commission (1997, November). *Final Report. Evaluation of the PHARE and TACIS Democracy Programme 1992-1997,* at: http://ec.europa.eu/europeaid/how/evaluation/evaluation_reports/reports/cards/951432_en.pdf (accessed 17 March 2010).

European Commission (1995). *Communication from the Commission to the Council and the European Parliament of 22 November 1995 - The European Union and the External Dimension of Human Rights Policy: From Rome to Maastricht and Beyond.* COM(95) 567, at: http://aei.pitt.edu/5140/01/001621_1.pdf (accessed 25 October 2009).

European Commission (n/a). *Compendium by Location. EIDHR Activities 2000-2006,* at: http://ec.europa.eu/europeaid/what/human-rights/projects_en.htm (accessed 10 December 2009).

European Commission and High Representative of the European Union for Foreign Affairs and Security Policy (2011). *Joint Communication to the European Parliament and the Council of 12 December 2011 - Human Rights and Democracy at the Heart of EU External Action—Towards a More effective Approach.* COM(2011) 886 final, at: http://eur-lex.europa.eu/LexUriServ/LexUriServ.do?uri=COM:2011:0886:FIN:EN:PDF (accessed 12 September 2012).

European Commission, EuropeAid (2011). *Action Fiche Kyrgyz Republic / Central Asia: Sector Policy Support Programme, Social Protection and Public Finance Management—Kyrgyzstan 2011,* at: http://ec.europa.eu/europeaid/documents/aap/2011/af_aap_2011_kgz.pdf (accessed 25 March 2013).

European Commission, EuropeAid (2010). Uzbekistan—TACIS / Uzbekistan—DCI. *EuropeAid Database* (restricted access).

European Commission, EuropeAid (2008). *Action Fiche No. 1 for the Kyrgyz Republic 2008: Sector Policy Support Programme, Social Protection and PFM—Kyrgyzstan 2007-2009—Second Allocation,* at: http://ec.europa.eu/europeaid/documents/aap/2008/af_aap_2008_kgz.pdf (accessed 25 March 2013).

European Commission, EuropeAid (2007). *TACIS Institution Building and Partnership Programme (IBPP)—Support to Civil Society and Local Initiatives. Open Call for Proposals. Guidelines for Grant Applicants Funded from the 2006 Action Programme for Uzbekistan,* at: http://ec.europa.eu/europeaid/tender/data/d18/AOF87218.pdf (accessed 14 December 2010).

European Commission, EuropeAid (n/a). *Institution Building and Partnership Programme in Uzbekistan*, at: http://ec.europa.eu/europeaid/where/asia/country-cooperation/uzbekistan/ibpp_en.htm (accessed 12 February 2011).

European Commission, External Relations (2008). *Joint Progress Report by the Council and the European Commission to the European Council on the Implementation of the EU Central Asia Strategy, 24 June 2008*, at: http://www.eeas.europa.eu/central_asia/docs/progress_report_0608_en.pdf (accessed 23 April 2011).

European Communities (1987). The Single European Act. *Official Journal of the European Communities, L 169/1*, at: http://www.unizar.es/euroconstitucion/library/historic%20documents/SEA/Single%20European%20Act.pdf (accessed 30 October 2009).

European Communities (1973). Document on the European Identity Published by the Nine Foreign Ministers, Copenhagen, 14 December 1973. *Bulletin of the European Communities, 12,* pp. 118-122.

European Communities (1972). *Declaration of the Heads of State and Government of the EC Member States at the First Summit Conference of the Enlarged Community in Paris, 21 October 1972*, at: http://aei.pitt.edu/1919/02/paris_1972_communique.pdf (accessed 23 October 2009).

European Communities, their Member States and Kyrgyz Republic (1999). Partnership and Cooperation Agreement. *Official Journal of the European Communities, L 196/48, 28 July 1999*, Brussels.

European Communities, their Member States and Republic of Uzbekistan (1999). Partnership and Cooperation Agreement. *Official Journal of the European Communities, L 229/3, 31 August 1999*, Brussels.

European Council (2003, December). *European Security Strategy: A Secure Europe in a Better World*, at http://ue.eu.int/uedocs/cmsUpload/78367.pdf (accessed 15 October 2008).

European Council, Political and Security Committee (2006, June). *The EU Approach to Democracy Promotion in External Relations. Food for Thought*, at: http://www.democracyteam.org (accessed 14 June 2009).

European External Action Service (2010). *Human Rights and Democracy in the World. Report on EU Action—July 2008 to December 2009*, at: http://ec.europa.eu/external_relations/human_rights/docs/hr_report_2010_en.pdf (accessed 29 July 2010).

European Forum for Democracy and Solidarity (n/a). *Uzbekistan*, at: http://www.europeanforum.net/country/uzbekistan (accessed 20 July 2011).

European Parliament (2010). *Getting Acquainted: Setting the Stage for Democracy Assistance. Democracy Support in EU External Relations*. Brussels: Office for Promotion of Parliamentary Democracy.

European Parliament and Council of the European Union (2006a, 29 December). Regulation (EC) No 1889/2006 of the European Parliament and of the Council of 20 December 2006 on Establishing a Financial Instrument for the Promotion of Democracy and Human Rights Worldwide. *Official Journal of the European Union, L 386*, at: http://eur-lex.europa.eu/LexUriServ/LexUriServ.do?uri=OJ:L:2006:386:0001:0011:en:PDF (accessed 21 October 2010).

European Parliament and Council of the European Union (2006b, 27 December). Regulation (EC) No 1905/2006 of the European Parliament and of the Council of 18 December 2006 Establishing a Financing Instrument for Development Cooperation. *Official Journal of the European Union, L 378*, at: http://eur-lex.europa.eu/lex/LexUriServ/LexUriServ.do?uri=OJ:L:2006:378:0041:0071:EN:PDF (accessed 21 October 2010).

European Union (2010). Consolidated Version of the Treaty on European Union. *Official Journal of the European Union, C 83/13*, at: http://eur-lex.europa.eu/LexUriServ/LexUriServ.do?uri=OJ:C:2010:083:0013:0046:EN:PDF (accessed 30 June 2010).

European Union (2008). *EU Annual Report on Human Rights 2008*, at: http://eeas.europa.eu/human_rights/docs/report08_en.pdf (accessed 20 January 2012).

European Union (2007). *EU Annual Report on Human Rights 2007*, at: http://eeas.europa.eu/human_rights/docs/report07_en.pdf (accessed 20 January 2012).

European Union (2006). Consolidated Versions of the Treaty on European Union and of the Treaty Establishing the European Community. *Official Journal of the European Union, C321 E/1*, at: http://eur-lex.europa.eu/LexUriServ/LexUriServ.do?uri=OJ:C:2006:321E:0001:0331:EN:PDF (accessed 30 October 2009).

European Union (2000, December). Charter of Fundamental Rights of the European Union. *Official Journal of the European Communities, C364*, at: http://www.europarl.europa.eu/charter/pdf/text_en.pdf (accessed 15 October 2009).

European Union (1992). Treaty on European Union. *Official Journal of the European Union, C 191*, at: http://eur-lex.europa.eu/en/treaties/dat/11992M/htm/11992M.html#0001000001 (accessed 30 October 2009).

European Union, External Action (2010). *Human Rights and Democracy in the World. Report on EU Action - July 2008 to December 2009*, at: http://eeas.europa.eu/human_rights/docs/2010_hr_report_en.pdf (accessed 20 January 2012).

Fearon, J. D. (1991). Counterfactuals and Hypothesis Testing in Political Science. *World Politics, 43 (2)*, pp. 169-195.

Featherstone, K. and Radaelli, C. M. (Eds.) (2003). *The Politics of Europeanization*. Oxford: Oxford University Press.

Fergana News Information Agency (2006, October). *Uzbekistan Parliamentary Commission Completed Investigation of the Events in Andijan*, at: http://enews.ferganaNews.com/article.php?id=1673 (accessed 21 May 2010).

Fierro, E. (2003). *The EU's Approach to Human Rights Conditionality in Practice*. The Hague: Kluwer Law International.

Fish, M. S. (2001). When More Is Less: Superexecutive Power and Political Underdevelopment in Russia. In V. E. Bonnell and G. W. Breslauer (eds.), *Russia in the New Century: Stability or Disorder?* Boulder: Westview Press, pp. 15-34.

Fitzpatrick, C. A. (2010, 28 October). *Outgoing UN Special Rapporteur on Torture Calls for Visit to Uzbekistan*, at: http://www.eurasianet.org/node/62260 (accessed 25 June 2011).

Flockhart, T. (Ed.) (2005). *Socializing Democratic Norms: The Role of International Organizations for the Construction of Europe*. Basingstoke: Palgrave Macmillan.

Freedom House (2010). Uzbekistan. *Nations in Transit 2010*, pp. 569-583, at: http://www.freedomhouse.org/images/File/nit/2010/NIT2010Uzbekistanfinal2.pdf (accessed 12 June 2011).

Freedom House (2009). Uzbekistan. *Nations in Transit 2009*, pp. 575-592, at: http://www.freedomhouse.org/uploads/nit/2009/Uzbekistan-WEB-full-report.pdf (accessed 12 June 2011).

Freedom House (2008). Uzbekistan. *Nations in Transit 2008*, at: http://www.freedomhouse.org/template.cfm?page=47&nit=473&year=2008 (accessed 12 June 2011).

Freedom House (n/a). *Nations in Transit,* at: http://www.freedomhouse.org/report-types/nations-transit (accessed 22 November 2012).

Freyburg, T., Lavenex, S., Schimmelfennig, F., Skripka, T. and Wetzel, A. (2009). EU Promotion of Democratic Governance in the Neighbourhood. *Journal of European Public Policy, 16*, pp. 916-934.

Freyburg, T. and Richter, S. (2010). National Identity Matters: The Limited Impact of EU Political Conditionality in the Western Balkans. *Journal of European Public Policy, 17 (2)*, pp. 263-281.

Freyburg, T. and Richter, S. (2009). Antizipierte EU-Mitgliedschaft: Zur Wirkung politischer Konditionalität auf Demokratisierungsprozesse in der Europäischen Nachbarschaft. In *Das Ende des postsozialistischen Raums? (Ent-)Regionalisierung in Osteuropa. Beiträge für die 17. Tagung junger Osteuropa-Experten, No. 104, September 2009*. Bremen: Forschungsstelle Osteuropa, pp. 43-46.

Front Line (2007, October). *Uzbekistan: EU's Easing of Uzbek Sanctions "Absurd"*, at: http://www.frontlinedefenders.org/node/1198 (accessed 19 May 2011).

Gawrich, A. and Lapins, W. (2006). *Demokratieförderung als europäische Herausforderung: Perspektiven für die östlichen Nachbarländer der EU*. Berlin: Friedrich-Ebert-Stiftung.

George, A. L. and Bennett, A. (2005). *Case Studies and Theory Development in the Social Sciences*. Cambridge, Mass. (among others): MIT Press.

Gheciu, A. (2005). Security Institutions as Agents of Socialization? NATO and the 'New Europe'. *International Organization, 59 (4)*, pp. 973-1012.

Giffen, J. M., Buxton C. H., Naumann, M. L., and Hinchliff, S. P. (2007). *The European Union's TACIS Programme for Central Asia. Evaluation of the Institution Building and Partnership Programme in Central Asia. Final Report*. IBF International Consulting and INTRAC—International NGO Training and Research Centre.

Gillespie, R. and Youngs, R. (Eds.) (2002). *The European Union and Democracy Promotion: The Case of North Africa*. London: Frank Cass Publishers.

Gläser J. and Laudel, G. (2004). *Experteninterviews und qualitative Inhaltsanalyse*. Wiesbaden. VS-Verlag.

Gleason, G. (2001). Asian Values and the Democratic Transition in Central Asia. *Harvard Asia Quarterly, 5 (1)*, at: http://www.asiaquarterly.com/content/view/91/40/ (accessed 15 September 2008).

Golovko, L. (2010). The Space for Legal Reform in Central Asia: Between Political Limits and Theoretical Deformations. *OSCE Yearbook 2010*, pp. 105-115.

Government of the Kyrgyz Republic and UNICEF (2012). *Country Programme Action Plan Between the Government of the Kyrgyz Republic and United Nations Children's Fund: Programme of Cooperation for 2012-2016*, at: http://www.unicef.org/kyrgyzstan/CPAP_2012_2016_English.pdf (accessed 12 November 2012).

Gowan, R., Youngs, R., Emerson, M., Smith, K. E., and Whitman, R. (2005). *Global Europe: New Terms of Engagement*. London: Foreign Policy Centre.

Grabbe, H. (2006). *The EU's Transformative Power: Europeanization through Conditionality in Central and Eastern Europe*. Basingstoke: Palgrave Macmillan.

Gratius, S. (2003). *Kuba unter Castro—Das Dilemma der dreifachen Blockade. Die kontraproduktive Politik der "Demokratieförderung" seitens der USA und der EU*. Opladen: Leske und Budrich.

Grugel, J. (2002). *Democratization: A Critical Introduction*. Houndmills: Palgrave Macmillan.

Gumppenberg, M. C. von and Steinbach, U. (Eds.) (2004). *Zentralasien. Geschichte, Politik, Wirtschaft. Ein Lexikon*. Munich: Verlag C.H. Beck.

Hall, P. A. (2003). Aligning Ontology and Methodology in Comparative Research. In J. Mahoney and D. Rueschemeyer (eds.), *Comparative Historical Analysis in the Social Sciences*. Cambridge: Cambridge University Press, pp. 373-404.

Hazelzet, H. (2001). *Carrots or Sticks? EU and US Reactions to Human Rights Violations (1989-2000)*. Florence: European University Institute.

Hegemann, H., Heller, R. and Kahl, M. (Eds.) (2013). *Studying 'Effectiveness' in International Relations: A Guide for Students and Scholars*. Opladen (among others): Barbara Budrich Publishers.

Heller, R. (2013). Assessing the Effectiveness of International Human Rights and External Democracy Promotion. In H. Hegemann, R. Heller and M. Kahl (eds.), *Studying 'Effectiveness' in International Relations: A Guide for Students and Scholars*. Opladen (among others): Barbara Budrich Publishers, pp. 197-216.

Helm, C. and Sprinz D. (2000). Measuring the Effectiveness of International Environmental Regimes. *The Journal of Conflict Resolution, 44 (5)*, pp. 630-652.

Herrero, S. (2009). A Decade of Democracy Promotion through the European Initiative for Democracy and Human Rights. *The EPD Working Papers Series on Democracy Support 1/2009*, at: http://www.epd.eu/uploads/ce702c4b2eafbc10b5a4e94c37387ccf.pdf (accessed 12 October 2010).

Hoffmann, K. (2010). The EU in Central Asia: Successful Good Governance Promotion? *Third World Quarterly, 31 (1)*, pp. 87-103.

Huber, D. (2008). Democracy Assistance in the Middle East and North Africa: A Comparison of US and EU Policies. *Mediterranean Politics, 13 (1)*, pp. 43-62.

Human Rights Watch (2010, 05 February). *Imprisoned Human Rights Defenders in Uzbekistan*, at: http://www.hrw.org/node/87341 (accessed 21 June 2011).

Human Rights Watch (2006, 05 April). *Germany: Prosecutor Denies Uzbek Victims Justice*, at: http://www.hrw.org/en/node/71357 (accessed 12 April 2009).

Human Rights Watch (2005, June). *"Bullets Were Falling Like Rain". The Andijan Massacre, May 13, 2005*, at: http://www.hrw.org/reports/2005/Uzbekistan0605/ (accessed 12 April 2009).

Human Rights Watch (n/a). *Uzbekistan: Andijan Crisis Aftermath*, at: http://www.hrw.org/campaigns/uzbekistan/andijan (accessed 18 May 2009).

Ilkhamov, A. (2005). The Thorny Path of Civil Society in Uzbekistan. *Central Asian Survey, 24 (3)*, pp. 297-317.

Institute of War and Peace Reporting (2008, 22 February). *Uzbek Amnesty Designed to Please West*, at: http://iwpr.net/report-news/uzbek-amnesty-designed-please-west (accessed 25 June 2011).

International Center for Non-for-Profit Law (n/a). *NGO Law Monitor: Uzbekistan*, at: http://www.icnl.org/research/monitor/uzbekistan.html (accessed 22 July 2012).

International Crisis Group (2006a, April). *Central Asia: What Role for the European Union? Asia Report No. 113*, at: http://www.crisisgroup.org/library/documents/asia/central_asia/113_central_asia_what_role_for_the_eu.pdf (accessed 15 October 2008).

International Crisis Group (2006b, November). *Uzbekistan: Europe's Sanctions Matter. Asia Briefing No. 54*, at: http://www.crisisgroup.org/~/media/Files/asia/central-asia/uzbekistan/b54_uzbekistan___europes_sanctions_matte.pdf (accessed 15 October 2008).

International Crisis Group (2001). Kyrgyzstan at Ten: Trouble in the "Island of Democracy". *Asia Report No. 22*, at: http://www.crisisgroup.org/~/media/Files/asia/central-asia/kyrgyzstan/Kyrgyzstan%20at%20Ten%20Trouble%20in%20the%20Island%20of%20Democracy.pdf (accessed 15 October 2008).

International Crisis Group (n/a). *Crisis Watch Database*, at: http://www.crisisgroup.org (accessed 16 June 2011).

International Labour Organization (2001). *Child Labour in Kyrgyzstan: An Initial Study*. Bishkek: International Programme on the Elimination of Child Labour.

International Labour Organization (n/a). Ratifications for Kyrgyzstan. *NORMLEX Information System on International Labour Standards*, at: http://www.ilo.org/dyn/normlex/en/f?p=1000:11200:432028672935489::NO:11200:P11200_COUNTRY_ID:103529 (accessed 22 March 2012).

Jackson, N. J. (2010). The Role of External Factors in Advancing Non-Liberal Democratic Forms of Political Rule: A Case Study of Russia's Influence on Central Asian Regimes. *Contemporary Politics, 16*, pp. 101-118.

Joffé, G. (2008). The European Union, Democracy and Counter-Terrorism in the Maghreb. *Journal of Common Market Studies, 46*, pp. 147-171.

Johnston, A. I. (2001). Treating International Institutions as Social Environments. *International Studies Quarterly, 45 (4)*, pp. 487-515.

Jünemann, A. and Knodt, M. (Eds.) (2007). *European External Democracy Promotion*. Baden-Baden: Nomos.

Kassenova, N. (2011). EU-Central Asian Bilateral Cooperation. In A. Warkotsch (ed.), *The European Union and Central Asia*. London and New York: Routledge, pp. 48-52.

Kassenova, N. (2009). China as an Emerging Donor in Tajikistan and Kyrgyzstan. *Russie.Nei.Visions No. 36*, IFRI Russia/NIS Center, at: http://www.ifri.org/?page=contribution-detail&id=5257&id_provenance=97 (accessed 16 June 2012).

Kelley, J. G. (2006). New Wine in Old Wineskins: Promoting Political Reforms through the New European Neighborhood Policy. *Journal of Common Market Studies, 44 (1)*, pp. 29-55.

Kelley, J. G. (2004). International Actors on the Domestic Scene: Membership Conditionality and Socialization by International Institutions. *International Organization, 58*, pp. 425-457.

Klingebiel, S. (2006). Mehr Geld—mehr Wirkung? Neue Risiken durch vermehrte Entwicklungshilfe. *GIGA Focus, 11*, at: http://www.giga-hamburg.de/dl/download.php?d=/content/publikationen/pdf/gf_afrika_0611.pdf (accessed 12 March 2012).

Kneuer, M. (2007). *Demokratisierung durch die EU. Süd- und Ostmitteleuropa im Vergleich*. Wiesbaden: Verlag für Sozialwissenschaften.

Knill, C. and Becker, F. (2003). Divergenz trotz Diffusion? Rechtsvergleichende Aspekte des Verhältnismäßigkeitsprinzips in Deutschland, Großbritannien und in der Europäischen Union. *Die Verwaltung, 36 (4)*, pp. 447-481.

Knill, C. and Lehmkuhl, D. (1999). How Europe Matters: Mechanisms of Europeanization. *European Integration Online Papers, 3 (7)*, at: http://eiop.or.at/eiop/texte/1998-007a.htm (accessed 20 October 2008).

Kohler-Koch, B. (2012). Post-Maastricht Civil Society and Participatory Democracy. *Journal of European Integration, 34 (7)*, pp. 809-824.

Kopstein, J. and Reilly, D. A. (2000). Geographic Diffusion and the Transformation of the Postcommunist World. *World Politics, 53 (1)*, pp. 1-37.

Krasner S. D. (1982). Structural Causes and Regime Consequences: Regimes as Intervening Variables. *International Organization, 36 (2)*, pp. 185-205.

Kubicek, P. J. (Ed.). (2003). *The European Union and Democratization*. London: Routledge.

Kurki, M. (2012). How the EU Can Adopt a New Type of Democracy Support. *FRIDE Working Paper No. 112*, at: http://www.fride.org/publication/998/how-the-eu-can-adopt-a-new-type-of-democracy-support (accessed 14 May 2013).

Kyrgyz Republic (2000). *Report of the Kyrgyz Republic on the Review of the Progress in Implementing Decisions of the World Summit for Children* [in Russian: Отчет Кыргызской Республики по анализу результатов выполнения решений Всемирной встречи в верхах в интересах детей], at: http://www.unicef.org/specialsession/how_country/index.html (accessed 12 November 2012).

Kyrgyzstan Inquiry Commission (n/a). *About KIC. Cooperation with the Government*, at: http://www.k-ic.org/en/about-kic.html (accessed 23 November 2011).

Lauth, H. J. and Pickel, G. (2009). Diffusion der Demokratie—Transfer eines erfolgreichen Modells? In G. Erdmann and M. Kneuer (eds.), *Externe Faktoren der Demokratisierung*. Baden-Baden: Nomos, pp. 37-74.

Lavin, F. (1996). Asphyxiation or Oxygen? The Sanctions Dilemma. *Foreign Policy, 104*, pp. 139-153.

Legislative Chamber of the Olyi Majlis of Republic of Uzbekistan (n/a). *Laws Approved*, at: http://www.parliament.gov.uz/en (accessed 26 June 2011).

Levitsky, S. and Way, L. A. (2010). *Competitive Authoritarianism: Hybrid Regimes after the Cold War*. Cambridge: Cambridge University Press.

Levitsky, S. and Way, L. A. (2005). International Linkage and Democratization. *Journal of Democracy, 16 (3)*, pp. 20-34.

Levy, M., Young, O. and Zürn, M. (1995). The Study of International Regimes. *European Journal of Interantional Relations, 1 (3)*, pp. 267-330.

Linz, J. and Stepan, A. (1996). *Problems of Democratic Transition and Consolidation: Southern Europe, South America and Post-Communist Europe*. Baltimore: The Johns Hopkins University Press.

Lister, M. (1999). *The European Union and the South. Relations with Developing Countries.* London: Routledge.

Mabry, L. (2008). Case Study in Social Research. In P. Alasuutari, L. Bickman and J. Brannen (eds.), *The SAGE Handbook of Social Research Methods.* London (among others): SAGE Publications, pp. 214-227.

Mair, P. (2004). The Europeanization Dimension. *Journal of European Public Policy, 11,* pp. 337–348.

Manners, I. (2002). Normative Power Europe: A Contradiction in Terms? *Journal of Common Market Studies, 40 (2),* pp. 235-258.

McDermott, R. (2006, 07 November). Germany Offers Uzbekistan Hope on Lifting EU Sanctions. *Eurasia Daily Monitor, 3 (206),* at: http://www.jamestown.org/single/?no_cache=1&tx_ttnews[tt_news]=32209 (accessed 23 May 2011).

Melvin, N. J. (Ed.) (2008). *Engaging Central Asia. The European Union's New Strategy in the Heart of Eurasia.* Brussels: Centre for European Policy Studies.

Melvin, N. J. (2000). *Uzbekistan: Transition to Authoritarianism on the Silk Road.* Amsterdam: Harwood Academic Publishers.

Melvin, N. J. and Boonstra, J. (2008). The EU Strategy for Central Asia at One Year. *EUCAM Policy Brief No.1.* Brussels: Centre for European Policy Studies, at: http://shop.ceps.eu/BooksList.php?category_id=29& (accessed 15 September 2009).

Merkel, W. (1999). *Systemtransformation. Eine Einführung in die Theorie und Empirie der Transformationsforschung.* Opladen: Leske und Budrich.

Meuser, M. and Nagel, U. (2009). The Expert Interview and Changes in Knowledge Production. In A. Bogner, B. Littig and W. Menz (eds.), *Interviewing Experts.* Houndmills: Palgrave Macmillan, pp. 17-42.

Meuser, M. and Nagel, U. (1991). ExpertInneninterviews—vielfach erprobt, wenig bedacht. Ein Beitrag zur qualitativen Methodendiskussion. In D. Garz and K. Kraimer (eds.), *Qualitativ-empirische Sozialforschung. Konzepte, Methoden, Analysen.* Opladen: Westdeutscher Verlag, pp. 441-471.

Morlino, L. and Magen, A. (2009). Methods of Influence, Layers of Impact, Cycles of Change: A Framework for Analysis. In A. Magen and L. Morlino (eds.), *International Actors, Democratization and the Rule of Law: Anchoring Democracy?* New York and London: Routledge, pp. 26-52.

Najimova, A. and Kimmage, D. (2006). Uzbekistan: Karimov Reappraises Andijon. *Radio Free Europe/Radio Liberty, 19 October 2006,* at: http://www.rferl.org/content/article/1072151.html (accessed 25 June 2011).

Nichol, J. (2012, August). *Uzbekistan: Recent Developments and U.S. Interests. CRS Report for Congress, RS21238.* Washington, DC: Congressional Research Service, at: http://www.fas.org/sgp/crs/row/RS21238.pdf (accessed 16 October 2012).

Nichol, J. (2010, March). *Central Asia's Security: Issues and Implications for U.S. Interests. CRS Report for Congress, RL30294.* Washington, DC: Congressional Research Service, at: http://fpc.state.gov/documents/organization/139241.pdf (accessed 14 July 2010).

Nye, J. S. (2004). *Soft Power: The Means to Success in World Politics.* New York: Public Affairs.

Office of the United Nations High Commissioner for Human Rights (n/a). *List of Human Rights Issues,* at: http://www.ohchr.org/EN/Issues/Pages/ListOfIssues.aspx (accessed 25 June 2011).

Olcott, M. B. (2005). *Central Asia's Second Chance.* Washington, DC: Carnegie Endowment for Peace.

Olsen, J. P. (2002). The Many Faces of Europeanization, *ARENA Working Papers, WP 01/2,* at: http://www.arena.uio.no/publications/wp02_2.htm (accessed 15 March 2009).

Omelicheva, M. Y. (2011). Western and Central Asian Perspectives on Democracy and Democratization: Comparing the Models of Democracy Promoted by the EU, US, and Kazakhstan. *Paper presented at the workshop "Comparative Perspectives on the Substance of EU Democracy Promotion",* Ghent University, Belgium, 24 June 2011.

Organization for Economic Co-operation and Development (2010). *Conflict and Fragility. The State's Legitimacy in Fragile Situations: Unpacking Complexity,* at: http://www.oecd.org/dataoecd/45/6/44794487.pdf (accessed 11 November 2011).

OSCE Office for Democratic Institutions and Human Rights (2006). *Annual Report 2005,* at: http://www.osce.org/files/documents/3/b/18937.pdf (accessed 12 January 2011).

OSCE Office for Democratic Institutions and Human Rights (2005, June). *Preliminary Findings on the Events in Andijan, Uzbekistan, 13 May 2005.* Warsaw, at: http://www.osce.org/odihr/15653 (accessed 21 May 2010).

Payne, R. A. (2001). Persuasion, Frames and Norm Construction. *European Journal of International Relations, 7 (1),* pp. 37-61.

Pevehouse, J. C. (2005). *Democracy from Above: Regional Organizations and Democratization.* Cambridge: Cambridge University Press.

Polat, A. (2007). Reassessing Andijan: The Road to Restoring U.S.-Uzbek Relations. *The Jamestown Foundation Occasional Paper, June 2007,* at: http://www.jamestown.org/uploads/media/Jamestown-Andijan.pdf (accessed 12 May 2011).

Popescu, N. (2006). The EU and South Caucasus: Learning from Moldova and Ukraine. *Eurojournal.org,* at: http://eurojournal.org/more.php?id=212_0_1_0_M14 (accessed 15 March 2009).

Pravda, A. (2001). Introduction. In J. Zielonka and A. Pravda (eds.), *Democratic Consolidation in Eastern Europe: International and Transnational Factors* (Volume 2). Oxford: Oxford University Press, pp. 1-28.

Presidency of the Council of the European Union (2006). *Press Release, General Affairs and External Relations, 14 December 2006. EU-Uzbek Experts Discussed Andijan Events in Tashkent,* at: http://www.eu2006.fi/NEWS_AND_DOCUMENTS/PRESS_ RELEASES/VKO50/EN_GB/1166085153941/INDEX.HTM (accessed 12 July 2011).

Pridham, G. (2005). *Designing Democracy: EU Enlargement and Regime Change in Post-Communist Europe.* Basingstoke: Palgrave Macmillan.

Radio Free Europe/Radio Liberty (2007, 27 June). *Kyrgyzstan Abolishes Death Penalty,* at: http://www.rferl.org/content/article/1077353.html (accessed 22 November 2010).

Radio Free Europe/Radio Liberty (2006, 22 December). *Controversial Uzbek Interior Minister Resigns,* at: http://www.rferl.org/content/article/1064076.html (accessed 12 July 2011).

Radio Free Europe/Radio Liberty (2005, 20 September). *Andijon Uprising Trial Opens in Uzbekistan,* at: http://www.rferl.org/content/article/1061533.html (accessed 12 July 2011).

Reiber, T. (2009). Instrumente der Demokratieförderung: Wer, wann, wie? Eine Strukturierung von Erfolgsbedingungen. In G. Erdmann and M. Kneuer (eds.), *Externe Faktoren der Demokratisierung.* Baden-Baden: Nomos, pp. 213-234.

Richter, S. (2009). *Zur Effektivität externer Demokratisierung: Die OSZE in Südosteuropa als Partner, Mahner, Besserwisser?* Baden-Baden: Nomos.

Risse, T., Ropp, S. C. and Sikkink, K. (Eds.) (1999). *The Power of Human Rights: International Norms and Domestic Change.* Cambridge: Cambridge University Press.

Risse, T. and Sikkink, K. (1999). The Socialization of International Human Rights Norms into Domestic Practices. In T. Risse, S. C. Ropp and K. Sikkink (eds.), *The Power of Human Rights: International Norms and Domestic Change.* Cambridge: Cambridge University Press, pp. 6-11.

Roy, O. (2000). *The New Central Asia: The Creation of Nations.* London and New York: I.B.Tauris Publishers.

Ruffin, M. H. (1999). Introduction. In M. H. Ruffin and D. C. Waugh (eds.), *Civil Society in Central Asia.* Seattle: Center for Civil Society International, pp. 3-26.

Rumer, B. Z. (Ed.) (2003). *Central Asia in Transition: Dilemmas of Political and Economic Development.* Delhi: Aakar Books.

Ryan, R. (2006). Germany Aims at Improved EU Relations with Uzbekistan. *Deutsche Welle, 02 November 2006,* at: http://www.dw-world.de/dw/article/0,,2223509,00.html (accessed 12 July 2011).

Saidazimova, G. (2005). Uzbekistan: Andijon Defendants Sentenced after Being Convicted. *Radio Free Europe/Radio Liberty, 14 November 2005,* at: http://www.rferl.org/content/article/1062921.html (accessed 12 July 2011).

Schatz, E. (2006). Legitimacy Claims and Democracy Promotion in Authoritarian Central Asia. *International Political Science Review, 27 (3),* pp. 263-284.

Schimmelfennig, F. (2011). How Substantial Is Substance? Concluding Reflections on the Study of Substance in EU Democracy Promotion. *European Foreign Affairs Review, 16 (5),* pp. 727-734.

Schimmelfennig, F. (2009a). EU Political Accession Conditionality after the 2004 Enlargement: Consistency and Effectiveness. In R. A. Epstein and U. Sedelmeier (eds.), *International Influence Beyond Conditionality: Postcommunist Europe after EU Enlargement.* London and New York: Routledge, pp. 123-142.

Schimmelfennig, F. (2009b). Europeanization beyond Europe. *Living Reviews in European Governance, 4 (3),* at: http://www.livingreviews.org/lreg-2009-3 (accessed 10 January 2010).

Schimmelfennig, F. (2005). Strategic Calculation and International Socialization: Membership Incentives, Party Constellations, and Sustained Compliance in Central and Eastern Europe. *International Organization, 59 (4),* pp. 827-860.

Schimmelfennig, F. (2003). Internationale Sozialisation: Von einem "erschöpften" zu einem produktiven Forschungsprogramm? In G. Hellmann, K. D. Wolf and M. Zürn (eds.), *Die neuen Internationalen Beziehungen. Forschungsstand und Perspektiven in Deutschland.* Baden-Baden: Nomos, pp. 401-427.

Schimmelfennig, F., Engert, S. and Knobel, H. (2006). *International Socialization in Europe: European Organizations, Political Conditionality and Democratic Change.* Basingstoke: Palgrave Macmillan.

Schimmelfennig, F., Engert, S. and Knobel, H. (2002). Costs, Commitment, and Compliance. The Impact of EU Democratic Conditionality on European Non-Member States. *EUI Working Paper RSC 2002, 29.*

Schimmelfennig, F. and Scholtz, H. (2008). EU Democracy Promotion in the European Neighbourhood. Political Conditionality, Economic Development and Transnational Exchange. *European Union Politics, 9 (2),* pp. 187-215.

Schimmelfennig, F. and Sedelmeier U. (Eds.) (2005). *The Europeanization of Central and Eastern Europe.* London: Cornell University Press.

Schmidt, S. (1999). Die Demokratie- und Menschenrechtsförderung der Europäischen Union unter besonderer Berücksichtigung Afrikas. *Arbeitspapiere zu Problemen der Internationalen Politik und der Entwicklungsländerforschung, Nr. 28,* Forschungsstelle Dritte Welt, Ludwig-Maximilianus-Universität, München, at: http://www.gsi.uni-muenchen.de/forschung/forsch_zentr/publikationen/arbeitspapier/ap28.pdf (accessed 12 December 2009).

Schmitter, P. C. (1996). The Influence of the International Context upon the Choice of National Institutions and Policies in Neo-Democracies. In L. Whitehead (ed.), *The International Dimension of Democratization—Europe and the Americas.* Oxford: Oxford University Press, pp. 26-54.

Schmitter, P. C. and Brouwer, I. (1999). Conceptualizing Research and Evaluating Democracy Promotion and Protection. *EUI Working Paper SPS No. 99/9*, at: http://cadmus.eui.eu/bitstream/handle/1814/309/sps99_9.pdf?sequence=1 (accessed 17 March 2010).

Schmitz, A. (2009). Whose Conditionality? The Failure of EU Sanctions on Uzbekistan. *Central Asia-Caucasus Institute Analyst, 11/11/2009*, at: http://www.cacianalyst.org/?q=node/5216 (accessed 12 February 2012).

Schuster, M. (2011). The EU's Rule of Law Initiative for Central Asia: From Initiative to More Substance? *EUCAM Policy Brief No. 18*, at: http://www.eucentralasia.eu/fileadmin/user_upload/PDF/Policy_Briefs/EUCAM-Brief.18.pdf (accessed 10 October 2012).

Smith, K. E. (2005). Engagement and Conditionality: Incompatible or Mutually Reinforcing? In R. Youngs (ed.), *Global Europe: New Terms of Engagement*. London: Foreign Policy Centre, pp. 23-29.

Smith, K. E. (1997). The Use of Political Conditionality in the EU's Relations with Third Countries: How Effective? *European University Institute SPS Working Papers 1997/07*.

Stokke, O. (1995). Aid and Political Conditionality: Core Issues and State of the Art. In O. Stokke (ed.), *Aid and Political Conditionality*. London: Frank Cass, pp. 1-87.

Stroehlein, A. (2008, 18 July). *Uzbekistan: "The Ghost of Sanctions (Not Quite) Past"*, at: http://www.crisisgroup.org/en/regions/asia/central-asia/uzbekistan/stroehlein-uzbekistan-the-ghost-of-sanctions-not-quite-past.aspx (accessed 12 June 2011).

Stroehlein, A. (2006, 22 November). *Uzbekistan: Beyond Sanctions*, at: http://www.crisisgroup.org/en/regions/asia/central-asia/uzbekistan/uzbekistan-beyond-sanctions.aspx (accessed 12 June 2011).

Swedish Presidency of the European Union (2009, 14 October). *EU-Kyrgyzstan Human Rights Dialogue*, at: http://www.se2009.eu/en/meetings_news/2009/10/14/eu-kyrgyzstan_human_rights_dialogue (accessed 16 February 2010).

Tilly, C. (2007). *Democracy*. Cambridge: Cambridge University Press.

Tynan, D. (2011a). Kyrgyzstan: Is Bishkek Tripping Over Its Own Red Tape? *Eurasianet.org, 16 May 2011*, at: http://www.eurasianet.org/node/63494 (accessed 22 September 2012).

Tynan, D. (2011b). Uzbekistan: Germany Sharply Boosts Payments for Air Base. *Eurasianet.org, 21 April 2011*, at: http://www.eurasianet.org/node/63344 (accessed 20 May 2011).

UNCTAD (n/a). *Market Information in the Commodities Area: Cotton*, at: http://r0.unctad.org/infocomm/anglais/cotton/market.htm (accessed 12 February 2012).

Underdal, A. (2004). Methodological Challenges in the Study of Regime Effectiveness. In A. Underdal and O. R. Young (eds.), *Regime Consequences: Methodological Challenges and Research Strategies.* Dordrecht: Kluwer Academic Publishers, pp. 27-48.

Underdal, A. (1992). The Concept of Regime 'Effectiveness'. *Cooperation and Conflict, 27 (3),* pp. 227-240.

Underdal, A. and Young, O. R. (Eds.) (2004). *Regime Consequences: Methodological Challenges and Research Strategies.* Dordrecht: Kluwer Academic Publishers.

UNHCR Refworld (n/a). *UN Committee on the Rights of the Child (CRC),* at: http://www.unhcr.org/refworld/publisher,CRC,STATEPARTIESREP,KGZ,,0.html (accessed 16 November 2012).

UNICEF (n/a). *Kyrgyzstan: Overview,* at: http://www.unicef.org/kyrgyzstan/overview.html (accessed 14 November 2012).

United Nations Committee on the Rights of the Child (2007). *Consideration of Reports Submitted by States Parties under Article 12 (1) of the Optional Protocol to the Convention on the Rights of the Child on the Sale of Children, Child Prostitution and Child Pornography. Concluding Observations: Kyrgyzstan,* at: http://www.unhchr.ch/tbs/doc.nsf/898586b1dc7b4043c1256a450044f331/5ce0f99c4ced72cbc12572ed00388945/$FILE/G0741604.pdf (accessed 12 November 2012).

United Nations Special Rapporteur on Torture and Other Cruel, Inhuman or Degrading Treatment or Punishment (2003). *Civil and Political Rights, Including the Questions of Torture and Detention. Torture and Other Cruel, Inhuman or Degrading Treatment. Report of the Special Rapporteur on the Question of Torture, Theo van Boven, Submitted in Accordance with Commission Resolution 2002/38. Mission to Uzbekistan,* at: http://daccess-dds-ny.un.org/doc/UNDOC/GEN/G03/107/66/PDF/G0310766.pdf?OpenElement (accessed 21 May 2011).

University of Minnesota, Human Rights Library (n/a). *Ratification of International Human Rights Treaties—Kyrgyzstan,* at: http://www1.umn.edu/humanrts/research/ratification-kyrgyzstan.html (accessed 22 March 2012).

Urdze, S. (2010). *Die Externe Demokratieförderung der EU in den zentralasiatischen Staaten.* Baden-Baden: Nomos.

U.S. Department of State (2011a). 2010 Human Rights Report: Kyrgyz Republic. *2010 Country Reports on Human Rights Practices,* at: http://www.state.gov/j/drl/rls/hrrpt/2010/sca/154482.htm (accessed 22 March 2012).

U.S. Department of State (2011b). 2010 Human Rights Report: Uzbekistan. *2010 Country Reports on Human Rights Practices,* at: http://www.state.gov/j/drl/rls/hrrpt/2010/sca/154489.htm (accessed 22 March 2012).

U.S. Department of State (2010a). 2009 Human Rights Report: Kyrgyz Republic. *2009 Country Reports on Human Rights Practices,* at: http://www.state.gov/j/drl/rls/hrrpt/2009/sca/136089.htm (accessed 28 June 2011).

U.S. Department of State (2010b). 2009 Human Rights Report: Uzbekistan. *2009 Country Reports on Human Rights Practices*, at: http://uzbekistan.usembassy.gov/hrr_2009.html (accessed 28 June 2011).

U.S. Energy Information Administration (n/a). *Country Analysis: Uzbekistan*, at: http://205.254.135.7/countries/cab.cfm?fips=UZ (accessed 12 February 2012).

Uzbek-German Forum for Human Rights (2012). *Cotton—It's Not a Plant, It's Politics: The System of Forced Labour in Uzbekistan's Cotton Sector*, at: http://www.cottoncampaign.org/wp-content/uploads/2012/12/Cotton-its-not-a-plant-its-politics.pdf (accessed 16 November 2012).

Uznews.net (2010, 01 April). *Germany Trains Uzbek Military Despite EU Sanctions*, at: http://www.uznews.net/article_single.php?lng=en&cid=22&aid=719 (accessed 21 May 2011).

Vachudova, M. A. (2005). *Europe Undivided: Democracy, Leverage, and Integration after Communism*. Oxford: Oxford University Press.

Vogel, B. (1995). 'Wenn der Eisberg zu schmelzen beginnt...'—Einige Reflexionen über den Stellenwert und die Probleme des Experteninterviews in der Praxis der empirischen Sozialforschung. In C. Brinkmann, A. Deeke and B. Völkel (eds.), *Experteninterviews in der Arbeitsmarktforschung. Beiträge zur Arbeitsmarkt- und Berufsforschung Nr. 191*. Nürnberg: Bundesanstalt für Arbeit, pp. 73-84.

Warkotsch, A. (2011). Human Rights, Democratization and Good Governance. In A. Warkotsch (ed.), *The European Union and Central Asia*. London and New York: Routledge, pp. 102-114.

Warkotsch, A. (2009). The European Union's Democracy Promotion Approach in Central Asia: On the Right Track? *European Foreign Affairs Review, 14*, pp. 249-269.

Warkotsch, A. (2008a). Non-Compliance and Instrumental Variation in EU Democracy Promotion. *Journal of European Public Policy, 15 (2)*, pp. 227-245.

Warkotsch, A. (2008b). Normative Suasion and Political Change in Central Asia. *Caucasian Review of International Affairs, 2 (4)*, pp. 62-71.

Warkotsch, A. (2008c). Preis der Partnerschaft. Die Zentralasienstrategie der EU: Eine Bilanz. *Osteuropa, 58 (12)*, pp. 81-91.

Warkotsch, A. (2007). Die Demokratisierungspolitik der EU in Zentralasien. In A. Jünemann and M. Knodt (eds.), *European External Democracy Promotion*. Baden-Baden: Nomos, pp. 185-203.

Warkotsch, A. (2006a). *Die Zentralasienpolitik der Europäischen Union. Interessen, Strukturen und Reformoptionen*. Frankfurt a.M.: Peter Lang.

Warkotsch, A. (2006b). The European Union and Democracy Promotion in Bad Neighbourhoods: The Case of Central Asia. *European Foreign Affairs Review, 11 (4)*, pp. 509-525.

Warkotsch, A. (2004). Zentralasiens Regime und der Islam. *Osteuropa, 11*, pp. 3-14.

Weber, M. (2009). *The Theory of Social and Economic Organization.* New York: The Free Press.

Werthes, S. and Bosold, D. (2005). Human Security and Smart Sanctions—Two Means to a Common End? *International Affairs Review, 14 (2),* pp. 111-136.

Wetzel, A. (2013). International Socialization: From Studying Effectiveness to More Effective Studies? In H. Hegemann, R. Heller and M. Kahl (eds.), *Studying 'Effectiveness' in International Relations: A Guide for Students and Scholars.* Opladen (among others): Barbara Budrich Publishers, pp. 177-194.

Wetzel, A. and Orbie, J. (2012). The EU's Promotion of External Democracy: In Search of the Plot. *CEPS Policy Brief No. 281, 13 September 2012,* at: http://www.ceps.eu/book/eu%E2%80%99s-promotion-external-democracy-search-plot (30 September 2012).

Wetzel, A. and Orbie, J. (2011a). Promoting Embedded Democracy? Researching the Substance of EU Democracy Promotion. *European Foreign Affairs Review, 16,* pp. 565-588.

Wetzel, A. and Orbie, J. (2011b). With Map and Compass on Narrow Paths and through Shallow Waters: Discovering the Substance of EU Democracy Promotion. *European Foreign Affairs Review, 16,* pp. 705-725.

Whitehead, L. (Ed.) (2001). *The International Dimensions of Democratization: Europe and the Americas.* Oxford: Oxford University Press.

Wichmann, N. (2007). *Democratisation Without Societal Participation? The European Union as an External Actor in the Democratization Processes of Serbia and Croatia.* Berlin: Lit Verlag.

World Bank (1992). *Diagnostic Study for the Development of an Action Plan for the Aral Sea.* Washington, D.C.

Wouters J., Basu, S., Lemmens, P., Marx, A. and Schunz, S. (2007, July). EU Human Rights Dialogues: Current Situation, Outstanding Issues and Resources. *Leuven Centre for Global Governance Studies Policy Brief No. 1,* at: http://www.ggs.kuleuven.be/nieuw/publications/policy%20briefs/pb01.pdf (accessed 22 June 2010).

Wroblewski, A. and Leitner, A. (2009). Between Scientific Standards and Claims to Efficiency: Expert Interviews in Programme Evaluation. In A. Bogner, B. Littig and W. Menz (eds.), *Interviewing Experts.* Houndmills: Palgrave Macmillan, pp. 235-251.

Young, O. R. (2001). Inferences and Indices: Evaluating the Effectiveness of International Environmental Regimes. *Global Environmental Politics, 1 (1),* pp. 99-121.

Youngs, R. (2010, September). The End of Democratic Conditionality: Good Riddance? *FRIDE Working Paper No. 102,* at: http://www.fride.org/download/WP102_The_end_democratic_conditionality_ENG_set10.pdf (accessed 17 July 2012).

Youngs, R. (2008). Trends in Democracy Assistance: What Has Europe Been Doing? *Journal of Democracy, 19 (2),* pp. 160-169.

Youngs, R. (2001). *The European Union and the Promotion of Democracy*. Oxford: Oxford University Press.

Zhovtis, E. (2008). Democratization and Human Rights in Central Asia: Problems, Development Prospects and the Role of the International Community. In N. J. Melvin (ed.), *Engaging Central Asia. The European Union's New Strategy in the Heart of Eurasia*. Brussels: Centre for European Policy Studies, pp. 20-42.

Zielonka, J. and Pravda, A. (Eds.) (2001). *Democratic Consolidation in Eastern Europe: International and Transnational Factors* (Volume 2). Oxford: Oxford University Press.

Annex I: List of Expert Interviews

Interview 1
22 June 2009, Berlin
German Foreign Office

Interview 2
23 June 2009, Berlin
Uzbek Embassy in Berlin

Interview 3
24 June 2009, Berlin
German CSO representative

Interview 4
24 June 2009, Berlin
German Foreign Office

Interview 5
20 July 2009, Almaty
Central Asian CSO representative

Interview 6
21 July 2009, Almaty
European Commission's Delegation
to Kazakhstan, Kyrgyzstan and Tajikistan

Interview 7
22 July 2009, Almaty
Central Asian CSO representative

Interview 8
23 July 2009, Almaty
Central Asian CSO representatives

Interview 9
27 August 2009, Almaty
Central Asian human rights activist

Interview 10
27 August 2009, Almaty
European Commission's Delegation
to Kazakhstan, Kyrgyzstan and Tajikistan

Interview 11
20 April 2010, Brussels
Council Secretariat of the EU, Human Rights Unit

Interview 12
21 April 2010, Brussels
European Commission, DG RELEX

Interview 13
21 April 2010, Brussels
European Commission, DG RELEX

Interview 14
21 April 2010, Brussels
Brussels-based CSO representative

Interview 15
23 April 2010, Brussels
European Commission, DG RELEX

Interview 16
20 July 2010, Almaty
European Commission's Delegation
to Kazakhstan, Kyrgyzstan and Tajikistan

Interview 17
20 July 2010, Almaty
European Commission's Delegation
to Kazakhstan, Kyrgyzstan and Tajikistan

Interview 18
10 October 2010, Brussels
Brussels-based CSO representative

Interview 19
4 November 2010, Brussels
Brussels-based CSO representative

Interview 20
17 November 2010, Brussels
Council Secretariat of the EU, Human Rights Unit

Interview 21
10 December 2010, Brussels
European Commission, DG DEVCO (AIDCO)

Interview 22
10 December 2010, Brussels
Member of the European Parliament

Interview 23
16 December 2010, Brussels
European External Action Service
(former European Commission's DG RELEX official)

Interview 24
16 December 2010, Brussels
European Commission, DG DEVCO (AIDCO)

Interview 25
17 December 2010, Brussels
Council Secretariat of the EU

Interview 26
17 December 2010, Brussels
European Commission, DG DEVCO (AIDCO)

Interview 27
24 March 2011 (telephone interview)
European External Action Service

Interview 28
03 November 2011, Brussels
European CSO representative

Interview 29
03 November 2011, Brussels
European External Action Service

Interview 30
03 November 2011, Brussels
European External Action Service

Interview 31
04 November 2011, Brussels
European External Action Service

Interview 32
04 November 2011, Brussels
European Commission, DG DEVCO

Interview 33
15 November 2011 (telephone interview)
Central Asian CSO representative

Annex II: IBPP Projects implemented in Kyrgyzstan in 2002–2009

No	Area	Project title and focus	Grant amount	Kyrgyz partners	EU partners	Starting year
1	Social services Women	Social Rehabilitation Centre for vulnerable women	€100,606	Red Crescent Society Kyrgyzstan	The Netherlands Red Cross	Not identified
2	Local economic development	Promoting entrepreneurship at grass roots level	€192,967	Counterpart Consortium Kyrgyzstan	Counterpart Deutschland	Not identified
3	Social reforms Elderly people	Building capacity to improve sit of vulnerable old people	€149,000	Foundation of Tolerance	Help Age International (UK)	Not identified
4	Social services Vocational education	Social partnership in vocational education and training	€184,963	Adult Training Centre	Institute for International Cooperation of the German Adult Education Association (IIZ/DVV)	Not identified
5	Social services Women	Social Rehabilitation Centre for vulnerable women	€165,200	Red Crescent Society Kyrgyzstan	The Netherlands Red Cross	2005
6	Improving capacity of civil society	Strong social partnership—strong community development: Supporting local NGOs to improve their relationships with the state	€180,000	Network of 10 NGOs from Chui, Naryn and Issyk-Kul regions	EU Vest TIC, and Esbjerg Municipality (Denmark)	2005

7	Improving capacity of local authorities Environ-mental sustainability	Green agenda in Kyrgyzstan: Helping local authorities develop environmental action plans	€198,916	Institute for Humanitarian Projects	Stichting Milieukontakt Oost-Europa (the Netherlands)	2005
8	Social services Children	Complex social help for street children	€133,963	Associations Alnas, Putnik, and Aitana	Jugendhilfe Luneburg (Germany)	2007
9	Social reforms	Saving lives through first aid and road safety campaigns	€174,000	National Red Crescent Society	The Netherlands Red Cross	2007
10	Administrative reforms/ Capacity building Governance	Development of participation in public policy and social cohesion in Kyrgyzstan	€150,000	Centre for Innovative Education	Euro-Net (Italy)	2007
11	Administrative reforms/ Capacity building Governance	Improvement of quality of services of local self-government bodies	€182,600	Foundation for Tolerance	European Perspective (Greece)	2007
12	Social reforms Elderly people	Increasing the involvement of elder people in decision-making processes at local and national levels	€187,975	Babushka Adoption	Help Age (UK)	2007
13	Social services Unemployment	Enhancing employment and income-earning opportunities for unemployed poor adults in rural areas	€151,183	Kyrgyz Adult Education Association	Institute for International Cooperation of the German Adult Education Association (IIZ/DVV)	2007

| 14 | Social reforms Women | Strengthening the role and socio-economic conditions of vulnerable women in Kyrgyz society | €143,558 | Red Crescent Society Kyrgyzstan | British Red Cross | 2007 |

Source: Giffen et al. 2007

Annex III: IBPP Projects implemented in Uzbekistan in 2003–2010

No	Area	Project title and focus	Grant amount	Uzbek partners	EU partners	Starting year
1	Social services Persons with disabilities	Disability information resources network	€200,000	Associations Business Women's Centre of Kokhand, Umidvorlik, and Status	Handicap International (France)	2003
2	Improving capacity of civil society Women	Strengthening the Uzbek Network of women's NGOs	€199,808	Crisis Centre Sabr	Women's Aid Federation (UK)	2003
3	Improving capacity of civil society	Capacity building and networking of NGOs in Uzbekistan	€182,978	LAS Legal Aid Society	Organisation Mondiale contre la Torture (Belgium)	2003
4	Local economic development Women	Women economic empowerment	€196,242	Women's Business Association of Uzbekistan Tadbirkor Ayol	Liaise with Europe (France)	2003
5	Social services Health education	Environmental education - learning for life: HIV/AIDS prevention	€173,417	Public Centre for Healthy Life	Field Studies Council (UK)	2003
6	Administrative reforms Improving capacity of local authorities	Support of municipality (re-) management of power grid	€183,580	City of Tashkent, TTCOA	City of Mannheim (European Office, Germany)	2003
7	Local economic development Tourism	Regional training and support for SME tourism	€181,120	Support Centre for Small Tourism Business	Institute for International Cooperation of German Adult Education Association (IIZ/DVV), and European Institute for Cultural Tourism Albena (Bulgaria)	2003

8	Social services Persons with disabilities	Assistance to disabled women, institution and network building	€188,000	Kibrai District Society of Disabled Women Opa Singilar	Hungarian Interchurch Aid	2005
9	Improving capacity of civil society	Regional integration, governance and headway training: Capacity-building for NGOs working with refugees and displaced persons	€194,423	Hamroh-Consulting	Christian Outreach Relief and Development (UK)	2005
10	Community development Education	Schools partnership to improve conservation of energy	€144,475	Hokhimyat of Bukhara City	City of Bonn (Germany)	2005
11	Community development Education	Strengthening infrastructure and capacity of Uzbek colleges for unemployed	€200,000	BT&C	Institute for International Cooperation of German Adult Education Association (IIZ/DVV)	2006
12	Social services Persons with disabilities	Disability information resources and employment centre network	€200,000	Millennium, and Women's Business Association	Handicap International (France)	2006
13	Social services Persons with disabilities	Training system for young people with learning disorders	€172,422	ATLAS	Foederband gGmbH (Germany)	2006
14	Community development Environmental education	Youth empowerment leading to improved local environment	€140,629	Environment for Healthy Life, and Oydin Hayot (Pure Life)	Field studies Council (UK)	2006
15	Social services Health education	Choices for youth: Preventing HIV/AIDS	€181,000	World Vision Uzbekistan	World Vision Germany	2007

16	Social services Adult education Poverty reduction	Financial education programme (FEP) for low-income households	€49,550	Association of Microfinance Organizations and Credit Unions of Uzbekistan—NAMOCU	Microfinance Centre for CEE and NIS (Poland)	2009
17	Improving capacity of civil society	Promotion of youth participation: Improving capacity of youth NGOs	€198,900	Youth NGO FAOL	European Perspective (Greece)	2009
18	Social services Improving capacity of civil society Women	Promoting a culture of Women's rights—An integrated project to reduce social marginality and empower vulnerable women	€199,364	The Civic Initiatives Support Centre	FORMAPER—Agency of the Milan Chamber of Commerce, Industry, Craft, and Agriculture (Italy), Lef-Italia (Italy), and The Resource Centre for Women—Marta (Latvia)	2009
19	Social services Persons with disabilities	Improving inclusion for disabled young people through environmental education	€154,998	Republican Education-Methodological Centre for Youth—BIOECOSAN, and Republican Centre for Children's Social Adaptation	Field Studies Council (UK)	2009
20	Community development Renewable energy Improving capacity of civil society	New jobs through the establishment of a rural cooperative and the supply of renewable energy	€199,407	Association of Farmers of Uzbekistan	Athens Network of Collaborating Experts Greece)	2009

| 21 | Local economic development Poverty reduction | Support of women and youth entrepreneurship in remote districts | €199,985 | Uzbek association of consulting Engineers | Centre for Business and Technological Development of Attica—KETA ATTIKIS, Hellenic Management Consulting Association—ELESMA, and Athens Network of Collaborating Experts (Greece) | 2009 |

Sources: Giffen et al. 2007, European Commission 2011, Europa House in Uzbekistan n/a

Annex IV: EIDHR Regional Projects implemented in Central Asia in 2003-2010

No	Theme (as defined by the EU)	Area (as defined by the EU)	Project title	Targeted states	Implementing organizations	Starting year
1	International criminal justice	Managed by CSOs	Information and ratification campaign on the ICC in CA countries and Mongolia	KZ,KG,UZ, TJ, Moldova, Mongolia	Gustav Stresemann Institut e.V.	2003
2	International criminal justice Governance	Managed by ICC and the ad hoc tribunals and special chambers HR Education, Training, and Awareness-Raising. Abolition of the death penalty. Measures of supporting electoral processes	Promoting legislation reform and criminal justice in Central Asia Advancing Human Rights and Democratization in Central Asia and Developing Guidelines for Media Monitoring in Elections	KZ, KG, UZ, TM, TJ	OSCE ODIHR	2005
3	Death Penalty	Abolition of the death penalty	A coordinated civil society campaign to abolish the death penalty in CA states	KZ, KG, TJ, UZ	International Helsinki Federation for Human Rights	2005
4	Torture	Torture prevention	Combating torture in CA	KZ, KG, TJ	Freedom House Public Service and Democracy Development Public Benefit Company	2007

5	Women	Law enforcement and legal reforms for equal treatment and opportunities incl. implementation of international legal standards	Strengthening Human Rights in CA	KZ, KG, TJ	OSCE ODIHR	2007
6	Women	Media development	Mobilizing the media in support of women's and children's rights in CA	KZ, KG, TJ	BBC World Service Trust	2007
7	HR defenders	Media and public outreach	Building CA human rights protection & education through media	KZ, KG, UZ, TM, TJ	Institute for War and Peace Reporting	2008

Sources: European Commission 2007d, European Commission 2010b, European Commission n/a

Annex V: EIDHR Macro- and Micro-Projects (CBSS) implemented in Kyrgyzstan in 2004-2010

No	Theme (as defined by the EU)	Area (as defined by the EU)	Project title	Grant amount	Implementing organizations	Starting year
1	Governance	Independence of Media and Freedom of Press	Media Ombudsperson Institute	€24,152	Internews	2004
2	Governance	Political participation by citizens and democratic political representation	Human Rights and Social Participation	€17,000	Adult Training Centre	2004
3	Governance	Political participation by citizens and democratic political representation	Institute for War and Peace Reporting: Voter education Activities for Youth	€25,335	Institute for War and Peace Reporting	2004
4	Governance	Political participation by citizens and democratic political representation	United Youth Union Golden Goal	€12,829	Youth Publication Union Golden Goal	2004
5	Persons with Disabilities	Social integration of vulnerable groups	External Socio-Psychological Integration of Invalids and Their Families	€23,493	Lenin District Association of Invalids	2004

6	Promotion and Protection of HR and Fundamental Freedoms	HR Education, Training, and Awareness-Raising	Strengthening of NGO Capacity to Protect and promote the HR of the Vulnerable Population in Kyrgyzstan	€49,478	Centre on Sociological, Political and Socio-Economic Researches	2004
7	Promotion and Protection of HR and Fundamental Freedoms	HR Education, Training, and Awareness-Raising	Promotion of a Democratic Society in the Kyrgyz Republic	€43,845	Centre on Sociological, Political and Socio-Economic Researches	2004
8	Promotion and Protection of HR and Fundamental Freedoms	HR Education, Training, and Awareness-Raising	Development and support of a remedial network in Nooken region	€16,000	Public Association Fingbeks	2004
9	Promotion and Protection of HR and Fundamental Freedoms	Monitoring of HR	Civilian control over observing HR among the Military Men of the Kyrgyz Republic	€23,580	Public Association of Soldiers Mothers	2004
10	Rule of Law and Justice incl. the Penal System	Human Prison System	Ray of Light in the Kingdom of Darkness: Human Rights awareness raising in places of detention	€18,062	Nurjolber	2004
11	Women	Gender equality promotion	Promoting gender equality and women rights in Kyrgyzstan	€49,185	Association Gender Information Center	2004
12	Women	Domestic violence	Mobilization of Community in Protection of Women Rights	€49,050	Association of Crisis Centers	2004

13	Women	Domestic violence	Kyrgyz Women: Using Television to Raise HR Awareness	€43,409	Internews	2004
14	Governance	Political participation by citizens and democratic political representation	Youth for Democratic Presidential Elections	€22,409	Adult Training Center	2005
15	Governance	Political participation by citizens and democratic political representation	Participation of Rural Women in the Election	€47,475	Association of Crisis Centers	2005
16	Governance	Political participation by citizens and democratic political representation	Youth Electorate Mobilization and Empowerment Project	€73,296	Centre of Innovative Education Peremena Public Foundation	2005
17	Governance	Political participation by citizens and democratic political representation	Youth and Elections	€50,000	Educational Complex Ilim	2005
18	Governance	Political participation by citizens and democratic political representation	Elections and school teachers	€24,300	Institute for War and Peace Reporting	2005

19	Governance	Political participation by citizens and democratic political representation	From keeping HR among the military personnel and their active participation in elections to the stable state	€42,921	Public Association of Soldiers Mothers	2005
20	Governance	Political participation by citizens and democratic political representation	Your Voice Is the Voice of the History of Kyrgyzstan—the Year 2005	€53,290	Public Fund Rampa	2005
21	Governance	Political participation by citizens and democratic political representation	Golden Goal: Raising awareness about electoral rights and the right of consciousness	€21,243	Youth Publication Union Golden Goal	2005
22	Promotion and Protection of HR and Fundamental Freedoms	Monitoring of HR	Elections without bribery and pressure on voters	€10,566	Public Union Young Lawyers of South Association	2005
23	Children	Children's Rights	CAM 2 2005: Project for Strengthening Child's Rights Protection in Kyrgyzstan	€58,500	Centre of Innovative Education Peremena Public Foundation	2006

24	Governance	Political participation by citizens and democratic political representation	CAM 3 2005: Creation of enabling environment for the inclusion of youth of the Kyrgyz Republic in the democratic process	€99,999	Center Interbilim Association	2006
25	Governance	Political participation by citizens and democratic political representation	CAM 3 2005: Community Conversations: Community-Based Radio Stations in Kyrgyzstan	€85,738	Internews	2006
26	Promotion and Protection of HR and Fundamental Freedoms	HR Education, Training, and Awareness-Raising	CAM 3 2005: The Centre of Civil and Legal Education	€39,004	Youth Publication Union Golden Goal	2006
27	Promotion and Protection of HR and Fundamental Freedoms	Monitoring of HR	Project for building the capacity of HR actors in Kyrgyzstan	€60,000	Centre of Innovative Education Peremena Public Foundation	2006
28	Promotion and Protection of HR and Fundamental Freedoms	Monitoring of HR	CAM 2 2005: Forming the culture of observing the HR in the disciplinary military unit and the guardhouses of the national army of the Kyrgyz Republic	€52,432	Public Association of Soldiers' Mothers	2006
29	Strengthening of Civil Society	Capacity Building of Organizations	Support of Civil Initiatives in a Transition Period	€305,914	Soros Foundation Kyrgyzstan	2006

30	Torture	Torture Prevention	CAM 2 2005: Regional HR Network. Struggle against Tortures in Law Enforcement Bodies	€45,264	Nurjolber	2006
31	Women	HR Education, Training, and Awareness-Raising	Increase of Rural Women's Awareness on HR and Gender Equality	€30,004	Nongovernmental Public Movement Crisis-Psychological and Rehabilitation Centre Altynai Association	2006
32	Governance	Strengthening of the democratic public institutions. Measures of supporting electoral processes	Democratization of the electoral process through the network of trade union leaders and activist members	€35,764	Kyrgyz Adult Education	2007
33	Promotion and Protection of HR and Fundamental Freedoms	Torture Prevention. HR education, training and awareness-raising. Human prison system	Actions against torture and fostering a culture of HR in correctional institution no. 10 (Jalal-Abad)	€36,496	Egalitee Foundation	2007
34	Strengthening Civil Society	Capacity building of organizations	Establishment of the Educational and Legal Centres in Chui and Jalal-Abad Oblasts of the Kyrgyz Republic	€51,517	Counterpart-Sheriktesh Association	2007

35	Strengthening Civil Society	Networking between CSOs. Independence of media and freedom of the press	What is Your News? Introduction of a Citizen Journalism Network for Radio and Online Community in Talas	€34,802	Public Foundation Mediamost	2007
36	Trafficking of Human Beings	HR education, training and awareness-raising	Trafficking Prevention through Awareness Raising Programmes	€27,062	Kyrgyz Adult Education	2007
37	Women	Domestic Violence (incl. young girls under 18)	Development of Mechanisms and Implementation of Social and Legal Protection from Violence against Women	€200,000	Soros Foundation Kyrgyzstan	2007
38	Governance	Measures of supporting electoral processes	Women Initiatives in Action	€73,693	Development and Cooperation Central Asia Foundation	2008
39	Governance	Political Participation by citizens and democratic political representation. Measures of supporting electoral processes	Promoting the Exercise of Fundamental Democratic Rights	€85,040	Eurasia Foundation of Central Asia	2008

40	Promotion and Protection of HR and Fundamental Freedoms	HR education, training and awareness-raising	Project for Inclusion of HR in the Kyrgyz Police	€68,000	Centre of Innovative Education Peremena Public Foundation	2008
41	Strengthening Civil Society	Capacity building of organizations	Improving the Lives of People with Disabilities	€107,517	Eurasia Foundation of Central Asia	2008
42	Strengthening Civil Society	Capacity building of organizations	National Video Dialogue Network	€149,994	Coalition for Democracy and Civil Society Association	2008
43	The Rights of Persons Belonging to Minorities and Ethnic Groups	Political Participation by citizens and democratic political representation	Support Centre of National Minority Rights	€63,889	Youth Publication Union Golden Goal	2008
44	Women	Equal participation of women and men in civil society, social, economic and political life	Increase Efficiency of National Mechanisms on Gender Equality Achievement	€53,820	Altynai Association	2008
45	Children	Constitutional and Legislative Reform. Children	Empowerment of NGOs Working in the Field of Children's Rights in the Kyrgyz Republic	€281,250	Folkekirkens Nodhjaelp Danchurchaid	2009
46	Promotion and Protection of HR and Fundamental Freedoms	HR education, training and awareness-raising. Capacity building of organizations	Bir-Duyno—One World Kyrgyzstan 2009	€50,000	Human Rights Center Citizens Against Corruption	2009

47	Promotion and Protection of HR and Fundamental Freedoms	Strengthening of the democratic public institutions Managed by CSOs	Cooperation of Civil Society and Military Institution as a Guarantee of Human Rights Observance of the Military Team	€113,536	Public Association of Soldiers' Mothers	2009
48	Torture	Torture Prevention	Torture Prevention and Support to Victims of Torture in Kyrgyzstan	€95,000	Golos Svobody Foundation	2009
49	Promotion and Protection of HR and Fundamental Freedoms	Strengthening of the democratic public institutions. Political Participation by citizens and democratic political representation	Youth Rights Inclusion and Political Engagement in Southern Kyrgyzstan	€187,305	Eurasia Foundation of Central Asia	2010
50	Strengthening Civil Society	Networking between CSOs. Capacity building of organizations	Strengthening of Dialogue between NGO and Public Sectors on Social Protection of Vulnerable People in Kyrgyzstan	€209,452	Pro NGO	2010

Sources: European Commission 2007d, European Commission 2010b, European Commission n/a, Delegation of the European Union to the Kyrgyz Republic n/a

AN INTERDISCIPLINARY SERIES
OF THE CENTRE FOR INTERCULTURAL AND EUROPEAN STUDIES

INTERDISZIPLINÄRE SCHRIFTENREIHE
DES CENTRUMS FÜR INTERKULTURELLE UND EUROPÄISCHE STUDIEN

CINTEUS • Fulda University of Applied Sciences • Hochschule Fulda

ISSN 1865-2255

1 *Julia Neumeyer*
  Malta and the European Union
  A small island state and its way into a powerful community
  ISBN 978-3-89821-814-6

2 *Beste İşleyen*
  The European Union in the Middle East Peace Process
  A Civilian Power?
  ISBN 978-3-89821-896-2

3 *Pia Tamke*
  Die Europäisierung des deutschen Apothekenrechts
  Europarechtliche Notwendigkeit und nationalrechtliche Vertretbarkeit einer Liberalisierung
  ISBN 978-3-89821-964-8

4 *Stamatia Devetzi und Hans-Wolfgang Platzer (Hrsg.)*
  Offene Methode der Koordinierung und Europäisches Sozialmodell
  Interdisziplinäre Perspektiven
  ISBN 978-3-89821-994-5

5 *Andrea Rudolf*
  Biokraftstoffpolitik und Ernährungssicherheit
  Die Auswirkungen der EU-Politik auf die Nahrungsmittelproduktion am Beispiel Brasilien
  ISBN 978-3-8382-0099-6

6 *Gudrun Hentges / Justyna Staszczak*
  Geduldet, nicht erwünscht
  Auswirkungen der Bleiberechtsregelung auf die Lebenssituation geduldeter Flüchtlinge in Deutschland
  ISBN 978-3-8382-0080-4

7   *Barbara Lewandowska-Tomaszczyk / Hanna Pułaczewska (Eds. / Hrsg.)*
    Intercultural Europe
    Arenas of Difference, Communication and Mediation
    ISBN 978-3-8382-0198-6

8   *Janina Henning*
    In Dubio Pro Europa?
    An Analysis of the European External Action Structures
    after the Treaty of Lisbon
    ISBN 978-3-8382-0298-1

9   *Claas Oehlmann*
    Europa auf dem Weg zur Recycling-Gesellschaft?
    Die EU-Rohstoffinitiative im Kontext der Strategie Europa 2020
    ISBN 978-3-8382-0401-7

10 *Volker Hinnenkamp / Hans-Wolfgang Platzer (Eds. / Hrsg.)*
    Interkulturalität und Europäische Integration
    ISBN 978-3-8382-0573-1

11 *Vera Axyonova*
    The European Union's Democratization Policy for Central Asia
    Failed in Success or Succeeded in Failure?
    ISBN 978-3-8382-0614-1

12 *Lisa Moessing*
    Lobbying Uncovered?
    Lobbying Registration in the European Union and the United States
    ISBN 978-3-8382-0616-5

Sie haben die Wahl:

Bestellen Sie die
Interdisziplinäre Schriftenreihe des Centrums für interkulturelle und europäische Studien
einzeln oder im **Abonnement**

per E-Mail: vertrieb@ibidem-verlag.de | per Fax (0511/262 2201)
als Brief (*ibidem*-Verlag | Leuschnerstr. 40 | 30457 Hannover)

Bestellformular

☐ Ich abonniere die *Interdisziplinäre Schriftenreihe des Centrums für interkulturelle und europäische Studien* ab Band # ____

☐ Ich bestelle die folgenden Bände der *Interdisziplinären Schriftenreihe des Centrums für interkulturelle und europäische Studien*
____ ; ____ ; ____ ; ____ ; ____ ; ____ ; ____ ; ____ ; ____ ; ____

Lieferanschrift:

Vorname, Name ....

Anschrift ....

E-Mail.. | Tel.: ....

Datum .... | Unterschrift ....

Ihre Abonnement-Vorteile im Überblick:

- Sie erhalten jedes Buch der Schriftenreihe pünktlich zum Erscheinungstermin – immer aktuell, ohne weitere Bestellung durch Sie.
- Das Abonnement ist jederzeit kündbar.
- Die Lieferung ist innerhalb Deutschlands versandkostenfrei.
- Bei Nichtgefallen können Sie jedes Buch innerhalb von 14 Tagen an uns zurücksenden.

ibidem-Verlag

Melchiorstr. 15

D-70439 Stuttgart

info@ibidem-verlag.de

www.ibidem-verlag.de
www.ibidem.eu
www.edition-noema.de
www.autorenbetreuung.de